Oracle ERP Essentials

Unlocking Business Potential

Kiet Huynh

Table of Contents

CHAPTER I
Introduction to Oracle ERP

1.1 What is Oracle ERP?

1.1.1 Definition and Overview

Oracle ERP (Enterprise Resource Planning) is a suite of integrated applications developed by Oracle Corporation that helps organizations manage and automate core business processes. These processes can range from financial management, supply chain operations, human resources, to customer relationship management. Oracle ERP provides a unified platform that ensures data consistency, operational efficiency, and informed decision-making across an enterprise.

Overview of Oracle ERP:

At its core, Oracle ERP is designed to streamline business processes, improve collaboration, and enhance productivity by providing a comprehensive set of tools and applications that are interconnected. The system allows for real-time data access, ensuring that users can make informed decisions quickly and efficiently. Oracle ERP is scalable and can be customized to meet the specific needs of any organization, regardless of size or industry.

Key Features of Oracle ERP:

1. Integration: Oracle ERP integrates various business functions into a single system, eliminating data silos and ensuring seamless information flow across departments. This integration improves coordination, reduces redundancy, and enhances overall operational efficiency.

2. Real-Time Data Access: With Oracle ERP, users have access to real-time data and analytics, enabling them to make informed decisions promptly. This feature is crucial for maintaining competitiveness in fast-paced business environments.

3. Scalability: Oracle ERP is highly scalable, making it suitable for businesses of all sizes. It can grow and adapt to the changing needs of an organization, whether it's expanding into new markets or scaling operations.

4. Customization: The system can be customized to fit the unique requirements of an organization. This customization includes tailoring workflows, reports, and interfaces to align with specific business processes.

5. Security: Oracle ERP provides robust security features to protect sensitive business data. It includes role-based access control, encryption, and compliance with various industry standards and regulations.

6. Cloud-Based Deployment: Oracle ERP can be deployed on the cloud, on-premises, or in a hybrid model. Cloud-based deployment offers benefits such as reduced IT infrastructure costs, automatic updates, and remote access capabilities.

Benefits of Oracle ERP:

1. Improved Efficiency: By automating and streamlining business processes, Oracle ERP helps organizations achieve higher levels of efficiency. Tasks that were once manual and time-consuming can be completed more quickly and with fewer errors.

2. Enhanced Collaboration: With all departments using a single system, collaboration between teams improves. Employees can access the information they need when they need it, fostering better communication and teamwork.

3. Better Decision-Making: The real-time data and analytics provided by Oracle ERP enable managers to make informed decisions based on accurate and up-to-date information. This capability is critical for strategic planning and operational management.

4. Cost Savings: By improving efficiency and reducing redundancies, Oracle ERP helps organizations lower operational costs. Additionally, the cloud-based deployment option can further reduce IT expenses.

5. Scalability and Flexibility: Oracle ERP's scalability ensures that the system can grow with the organization. Its flexibility allows businesses to adapt the system to their unique needs and changing market conditions.

Components of Oracle ERP:

Oracle ERP is composed of several modules, each designed to manage specific business functions. The primary modules include:

1. Financial Management: This module handles financial transactions, general ledger, accounts payable and receivable, fixed assets, and financial reporting. It ensures accurate financial records and compliance with accounting standards.

2. Supply Chain Management: This module covers procurement, inventory management, order management, and logistics. It optimizes the supply chain processes, ensuring efficient procurement, production, and delivery.

3. Human Capital Management: This module manages employee data, payroll, benefits, recruitment, and performance management. It helps organizations effectively manage their workforce and HR processes.

4. Customer Relationship Management: This module focuses on managing customer interactions, sales, and marketing. It helps organizations improve customer service, increase sales, and enhance customer satisfaction.

5. Project Management: This module assists in planning, executing, and monitoring projects. It provides tools for project scheduling, resource allocation, budgeting, and performance tracking.

6. Enterprise Performance Management: This module supports strategic planning, budgeting, forecasting, and financial consolidation. It helps organizations align their strategic goals with their operational activities.

Implementation of Oracle ERP:

Implementing Oracle ERP involves several phases, including planning, configuration, testing, and deployment. The process begins with a thorough analysis of the organization's business processes and requirements. Based on this analysis, the system is configured to meet the specific needs of the organization.

During the testing phase, the configured system is tested to ensure that it functions correctly and meets the business requirements. Any issues identified during testing are addressed before the system goes live. Once the system is deployed, users are trained to use the new system effectively.

Post-implementation support is crucial to address any issues that arise and to ensure that the system continues to meet the organization's needs. Regular updates and maintenance are also necessary to keep the system running smoothly and to incorporate new features and improvements.

Conclusion:

Oracle ERP is a powerful and versatile tool that can transform the way organizations manage their business processes. By providing a unified platform for various business functions, Oracle ERP enhances efficiency, collaboration, and decision-making. Its scalability, customization options, and robust security features make it a suitable solution for organizations of all sizes and industries.

Understanding the definition and overview of Oracle ERP is the first step in leveraging its capabilities to unlock business potential. As we delve deeper into the various modules and features of Oracle ERP, you will gain a comprehensive understanding of how this system can drive your organization's success.

1.1.2 History and Evolution

Origins of ERP Systems

The concept of Enterprise Resource Planning (ERP) systems traces its roots back to the 1960s, during the advent of computer technologies in business environments. Initially, companies utilized simple inventory management and control systems. These early systems were primarily developed to manage the manufacturing processes and were known as Material Requirements Planning (MRP) systems. The focus of MRP systems was on ensuring that materials were available for production and products were available for delivery to customers.

As businesses grew more complex, there was a need for integrated systems that could handle not just manufacturing, but also other business processes. By the 1970s, MRP evolved into MRP II (Manufacturing Resource Planning). MRP II systems included additional features such as shop floor control, distribution planning, and capacity requirements planning. These systems allowed companies to manage a wider range of manufacturing processes and provided better integration across different functions.

Emergence of ERP

The 1990s marked a significant shift in the evolution of these systems, with the introduction of the term ERP. ERP systems extended beyond the scope of MRP II by integrating core business processes across various functional areas such as finance, human resources, supply chain, and customer relationship management. This integration was aimed at creating a unified system that could provide a single source of truth for all business operations, thus improving data consistency, reducing redundancies, and streamlining processes.

Oracle Corporation, founded in 1977 by Larry Ellison, Bob Miner, and Ed Oates, emerged as one of the pioneers in the development of integrated software systems. Initially known for its database management systems, Oracle expanded its offerings to include comprehensive ERP solutions. The company's commitment to innovation and strategic acquisitions helped it to become a leader in the ERP market.

Oracle's Entry into ERP

Oracle entered the ERP market in the late 1980s and early 1990s, leveraging its expertise in database technologies to offer integrated business applications. Oracle's ERP solutions were built on the foundation of its robust database systems, providing reliable and scalable platforms for managing enterprise data.

In 1987, Oracle released its first set of business applications, which included financial software and database management tools. These applications laid the groundwork for Oracle's ERP offerings, combining database technology with business process management.

Evolution of Oracle ERP Solutions

Throughout the 1990s and 2000s, Oracle continued to expand its ERP capabilities through both internal development and strategic acquisitions. Key milestones in the evolution of Oracle ERP solutions include:

- Acquisition of PeopleSoft (2005): Oracle acquired PeopleSoft, a leading provider of human resource management systems (HRMS) and customer relationship management (CRM) software. This acquisition significantly enhanced Oracle's ERP portfolio by integrating PeopleSoft's robust HR and CRM functionalities.

- Acquisition of JD Edwards (2005): Oracle's acquisition of JD Edwards brought advanced supply chain management (SCM) and manufacturing capabilities into its ERP suite. JD Edwards was known for its comprehensive solutions tailored for midsize companies, which complemented Oracle's existing offerings.

- Oracle E-Business Suite (EBS): Oracle EBS, introduced in the early 2000s, was a comprehensive suite of integrated business applications that included modules for financial management, supply chain management, human resources, and more. EBS provided a flexible and scalable platform for organizations to manage their business processes.

- Acquisition of Siebel Systems (2006): Oracle's acquisition of Siebel Systems, a leading provider of CRM software, further strengthened its ERP capabilities. Siebel's CRM solutions were integrated into Oracle's ERP suite, providing customers with advanced tools for managing customer relationships and sales processes.

- Oracle Fusion Applications (2011): Oracle Fusion Applications represented a significant leap forward in the evolution of Oracle ERP solutions. Built on Oracle's modern technology stack, Fusion Applications integrated the best features from Oracle's existing ERP products, including EBS, PeopleSoft, and JD Edwards. Fusion Applications offered a unified user experience, advanced analytics, and a modular architecture that allowed for flexible deployment options.

Transition to Cloud-Based ERP

The advent of cloud computing in the late 2000s and early 2010s revolutionized the ERP landscape. Cloud-based ERP solutions offered numerous advantages over traditional on-premises systems, including lower upfront costs, faster deployment times, and greater scalability. Recognizing the potential of cloud technology, Oracle began to transition its ERP offerings to the cloud.

- Oracle Cloud ERP: Oracle Cloud ERP, part of Oracle Cloud Applications, is a comprehensive suite of cloud-based business applications that includes modules for financial management, procurement, project management, supply chain management, and more. Oracle Cloud ERP leverages the power of cloud computing to provide organizations with a flexible, scalable, and secure platform for managing their business processes.

- Oracle Autonomous Database: Oracle introduced the Oracle Autonomous Database, an innovative cloud-based database management system that leverages machine learning and artificial intelligence to automate routine database management tasks. The Autonomous Database enhances the performance and reliability of Oracle Cloud ERP by ensuring optimal database operations with minimal human intervention.

Key Features and Innovations

Oracle ERP solutions have continuously evolved to incorporate advanced technologies and address the changing needs of businesses. Some key features and innovations in Oracle ERP include:

- Integrated Suite of Applications: Oracle ERP offers a comprehensive suite of integrated applications that cover various business functions, including finance, human resources, supply chain, and customer relationship management. This integration ensures data consistency and streamlines business processes.

- Advanced Analytics and Reporting: Oracle ERP provides advanced analytics and reporting capabilities, enabling organizations to gain valuable insights from their data. Features such as real-time dashboards, data visualization, and predictive analytics help businesses make informed decisions.

- Scalability and Flexibility: Oracle ERP solutions are designed to scale with the growth of an organization. Whether deployed on-premises or in the cloud, Oracle ERP can handle the needs of small, midsize, and large enterprises, providing flexibility in deployment options.

- User Experience: Oracle places a strong emphasis on user experience, offering intuitive and user-friendly interfaces across its ERP applications. The modern user interface of Oracle Cloud ERP enhances productivity and user satisfaction.

- Security and Compliance: Oracle ERP includes robust security features to protect sensitive business data. Compliance with industry standards and regulations is ensured through comprehensive security controls and regular updates.

- Artificial Intelligence and Machine Learning: Oracle ERP incorporates AI and machine learning technologies to automate routine tasks, improve decision-making, and enhance overall efficiency. Features such as intelligent process automation and predictive maintenance leverage AI to optimize business operations.

Future Trends and Directions

The evolution of Oracle ERP is ongoing, with continuous advancements in technology driving the future of ERP systems. Some key trends and directions for the future of Oracle ERP include:

- Increased Adoption of AI and Machine Learning: The integration of AI and machine learning into Oracle ERP will continue to grow, enabling more intelligent and automated processes. AI-driven insights and recommendations will enhance decision-making and operational efficiency.

- Expansion of Cloud-Based Solutions: Cloud-based ERP solutions will remain a significant focus for Oracle. The shift towards cloud computing will continue, with more organizations adopting Oracle Cloud ERP for its flexibility, scalability, and cost-efficiency.

- Enhanced User Experience: Oracle will continue to invest in improving the user experience across its ERP applications. User-centric design, intuitive interfaces, and mobile accessibility will be key areas of focus.

- Focus on Industry-Specific Solutions: Oracle will develop industry-specific ERP solutions tailored to the unique needs of various sectors, such as manufacturing, healthcare, retail, and financial services. These solutions will provide industry-specific functionalities and best practices.

- Emphasis on Data Security and Privacy: As data security and privacy concerns grow, Oracle will continue to enhance the security features of its ERP solutions. Advanced encryption, access controls, and compliance with data protection regulations will be prioritized.

- Integration with Emerging Technologies: Oracle ERP will integrate with emerging technologies such as the Internet of Things (IoT), blockchain, and augmented reality (AR) to provide innovative solutions for businesses. These technologies will enable new use cases and enhance the capabilities of ERP systems.

Conclusion

The history and evolution of Oracle ERP reflect the dynamic nature of business technology and the continuous drive for innovation. From its origins in inventory management systems to the modern cloud-based ERP solutions, Oracle has played a pivotal role in shaping the ERP landscape. With a commitment to leveraging advanced technologies and addressing the evolving needs of businesses, Oracle ERP continues to unlock business potential and drive organizational success.

1.2 Importance of ERP Systems

Enterprise Resource Planning (ERP) systems have revolutionized the way businesses operate, offering an integrated approach to managing a company's resources. ERP systems are crucial in ensuring that all departments and functions within an organization are integrated into a single system. This integration allows for seamless communication and data sharing across the entire organization, resulting in increased efficiency and productivity.

1.2.1 Benefits of ERP

Implementing an ERP system can bring numerous benefits to an organization. These advantages span across various areas such as efficiency, decision-making, data management, and customer satisfaction. Let's explore these benefits in detail:

1. Improved Efficiency and Productivity

One of the primary benefits of ERP systems is the significant improvement in operational efficiency and productivity. By integrating various business processes into a single unified system, ERP eliminates the need for disparate systems and manual processes. This integration ensures that data is entered only once and is accessible across all departments, reducing redundancy and minimizing errors.

ERP systems automate routine tasks such as order processing, inventory management, and financial reporting, allowing employees to focus on more strategic activities. Automation also speeds up business processes, leading to faster turnaround times and improved overall productivity.

2. Enhanced Decision-Making

ERP systems provide real-time access to accurate and consistent data, which is crucial for informed decision-making. Managers and executives can rely on comprehensive reports and analytics generated by the ERP system to gain insights into various aspects of the business. These insights help in identifying trends, spotting potential issues, and making data-driven decisions.

With ERP, organizations can perform detailed financial analysis, sales forecasting, and demand planning. The ability to analyze data from different departments and functions in one place allows for more strategic and proactive decision-making.

3. Better Data Management and Security

ERP systems centralize data storage, making it easier to manage and secure information. Instead of having data scattered across multiple systems or departments, all information is stored in a single database. This centralization ensures data consistency and accuracy, as any updates or changes are reflected across the entire system.

ERP systems also come with robust security features to protect sensitive business information. Role-based access controls ensure that only authorized personnel can access specific data. Additionally, ERP systems often include audit trails, which track changes made to the data, providing a layer of accountability and security.

4. Streamlined Business Processes

ERP systems standardize and streamline business processes by providing best practices and predefined workflows. These standardized processes ensure that all employees follow the same procedures, leading to consistency and efficiency. For example, the procurement process in an ERP system might include predefined steps for requisition, approval, and purchase order creation, ensuring that all purchases go through a consistent and efficient process.

Standardized processes also make it easier to onboard new employees, as they can quickly learn and adhere to the established workflows. This consistency improves overall operational efficiency and reduces the risk of errors or miscommunication.

5. Improved Collaboration and Communication

ERP systems facilitate better collaboration and communication within an organization. By providing a single source of truth, ERP ensures that all employees have access to the same information. This transparency eliminates silos and fosters collaboration between departments.

For example, the sales team can access inventory levels in real-time to provide accurate delivery estimates to customers. Similarly, the finance department can view the status of sales orders and payments, ensuring accurate financial reporting. This interconnectedness enhances teamwork and improves overall organizational efficiency.

6. Enhanced Customer Satisfaction

ERP systems play a significant role in improving customer satisfaction. With access to real-time data, organizations can respond to customer inquiries and requests more quickly and accurately. For example, customer service representatives can access a customer's order history, track shipments, and resolve issues promptly.

ERP systems also enable better demand forecasting and inventory management, ensuring that products are available when customers need them. By streamlining order processing and reducing lead times, organizations can deliver products and services more efficiently, leading to higher customer satisfaction.

7. Scalability and Flexibility

ERP systems are designed to be scalable and flexible, allowing organizations to adapt to changing business needs. As a company grows, its ERP system can be easily expanded to accommodate additional users, processes, and functionalities. This scalability ensures that the ERP system can support the organization's growth without requiring a complete overhaul.

ERP systems also offer flexibility in terms of customization and configuration. Organizations can tailor the system to meet their specific business requirements, whether it's adding new modules, integrating with other software, or customizing workflows. This flexibility ensures that the ERP system aligns with the organization's unique needs and processes.

8. Regulatory Compliance

Compliance with industry regulations and standards is critical for many organizations. ERP systems help ensure regulatory compliance by providing built-in features and functionalities that adhere to industry-specific requirements. For example, ERP systems can automate compliance reporting, track and manage quality control processes, and ensure adherence to financial regulations.

By maintaining accurate records and providing audit trails, ERP systems also facilitate internal and external audits. This capability reduces the risk of non-compliance and helps organizations avoid penalties and legal issues.

9. Cost Savings

Although the initial investment in an ERP system can be significant, the long-term cost savings can outweigh the initial expenditure. ERP systems streamline operations, reduce manual processes, and improve efficiency, leading to cost savings in various areas.

For example, by automating inventory management, organizations can reduce excess stock and minimize carrying costs. Streamlined procurement processes can lead to better supplier negotiations and cost savings. Additionally, improved financial management and accurate reporting help organizations identify cost-saving opportunities and optimize resource allocation.

10. Competitive Advantage

Implementing an ERP system can provide organizations with a competitive advantage. By improving efficiency, decision-making, and customer satisfaction, ERP systems help organizations stay ahead of their competitors. The ability to respond quickly to market changes, optimize business processes, and deliver high-quality products and services gives organizations a significant edge in the market.

ERP systems also enable organizations to innovate and adapt to new business models. For example, organizations can leverage ERP data to identify new revenue streams, explore new markets, or introduce new products and services. This agility and innovation drive business growth and success.

11. Integration with Other Systems

ERP systems often integrate with other business systems and applications, providing a comprehensive view of the organization's operations. Integration with Customer Relationship Management (CRM) systems, Human Resources (HR) systems, and other specialized software ensures that all critical business functions are connected and can communicate seamlessly.

This integration eliminates data silos and ensures that information flows smoothly across the organization. For example, integration with a CRM system allows the sales team to access customer information and history directly within the ERP system, improving customer interactions and sales processes.

12. Real-Time Reporting and Monitoring

ERP systems provide real-time reporting and monitoring capabilities, allowing organizations to track key performance indicators (KPIs) and monitor business processes continuously. Real-time dashboards and reports provide up-to-date information on sales, inventory levels, financial performance, and other critical metrics.

This real-time visibility enables organizations to identify issues and opportunities as they arise and make timely decisions. For example, if inventory levels fall below a certain threshold, the ERP system can trigger an alert, allowing the procurement team to reorder stock and avoid disruptions in production.

13. Improved Supplier and Vendor Management

ERP systems enhance supplier and vendor management by providing tools for supplier evaluation, performance tracking, and relationship management. Organizations can track supplier performance metrics such as delivery times, quality, and pricing, enabling better supplier selection and negotiation.

By maintaining a centralized database of supplier information, ERP systems also streamline the procurement process. Purchase orders, contracts, and communication with suppliers are managed within the system, ensuring consistency and transparency in supplier interactions.

14. Better Financial Management

ERP systems provide comprehensive financial management capabilities, including accounting, budgeting, and financial reporting. By automating financial processes and ensuring data accuracy, ERP systems help organizations maintain accurate financial records and produce reliable financial statements.

ERP systems also support budgeting and forecasting, allowing organizations to plan and allocate resources effectively. Financial managers can create detailed budgets, monitor actual performance against budgets, and adjust forecasts as needed. This capability improves financial planning and control, ensuring that organizations stay on track to achieve their financial goals.

15. Environmental and Sustainability Initiatives

ERP systems can support environmental and sustainability initiatives by providing tools for tracking and managing sustainability metrics. Organizations can monitor energy consumption, waste generation, and resource utilization, enabling them to identify areas for improvement and implement sustainable practices.

By optimizing supply chain processes and reducing waste, ERP systems help organizations minimize their environmental impact. For example, better inventory management reduces excess stock and associated waste, while streamlined production processes minimize resource consumption.

Conclusion

The benefits of ERP systems are vast and far-reaching. From improving efficiency and productivity to enhancing decision-making and customer satisfaction, ERP systems provide a comprehensive solution for managing and optimizing business processes. By integrating various functions into a single system, ERP systems enable organizations to operate more effectively, adapt to changing business needs, and achieve their strategic goals.

Implementing an ERP system is a significant investment, but the long-term advantages make it a worthwhile endeavor for organizations of all sizes and industries. As businesses continue to evolve and face new challenges, ERP systems will remain a critical tool for driving success and maintaining a competitive edge in the market.

1.2.2 Key Features of Oracle ERP

Oracle ERP (Enterprise Resource Planning) stands out as one of the leading solutions for managing complex business operations. It provides a unified platform that integrates various business processes, enhancing efficiency and data visibility. Below, we delve into the key features that make Oracle ERP an essential tool for modern enterprises.

Comprehensive Financial Management

Oracle ERP's financial management suite provides robust tools for managing a company's finances. It covers general ledger, accounts payable, accounts receivable, fixed assets, and cash management. This suite ensures accurate financial reporting, compliance with global accounting standards, and streamlined financial operations.

- General Ledger: Oracle ERP's general ledger module supports multiple ledgers and currencies, allowing businesses to consolidate financial data from various entities and operations. It provides real-time financial insights, flexible reporting, and comprehensive drill-down capabilities.

- Accounts Payable and Receivable: The accounts payable and receivable modules automate invoice processing, payment execution, and collections. These modules reduce manual entry errors, accelerate payment cycles, and improve cash flow management.

- Fixed Assets Management: This module manages the lifecycle of fixed assets, from acquisition to disposal. It supports various depreciation methods and provides detailed tracking and reporting on asset performance and value.

Advanced Supply Chain Management

Oracle ERP offers a suite of supply chain management tools designed to optimize the end-to-end supply chain processes, from procurement to production and distribution.

- Procurement Management: Oracle ERP streamlines the procurement process by automating purchase requisitions, orders, and supplier management. It enhances procurement efficiency, reduces costs, and ensures compliance with procurement policies.

- Inventory Management: The inventory management module provides real-time visibility into inventory levels, locations, and movements. It supports multiple inventory valuation methods, automated replenishment, and detailed inventory reporting.

- Order Management: This module facilitates the order-to-cash process, ensuring efficient order entry, fulfillment, and billing. It integrates with other modules to provide a seamless flow of information and enhance customer satisfaction.

Human Capital Management (HCM)

Oracle ERP's HCM suite helps organizations manage their workforce effectively. It covers recruitment, onboarding, payroll, performance management, and employee development.

- Recruitment and Onboarding: The recruitment module automates job postings, candidate tracking, and hiring processes. The onboarding tools ensure a smooth transition for new hires, providing them with necessary resources and training.

- Payroll Management: Oracle ERP's payroll module ensures accurate and timely payroll processing. It handles complex payroll calculations, tax compliance, and benefits administration.

- Performance Management: This module supports employee performance evaluations, goal setting, and career development. It helps organizations align employee objectives with business goals and enhance overall performance.

Robust Reporting and Analytics

Oracle ERP provides powerful reporting and analytics tools that enable businesses to gain actionable insights from their data. These tools support data-driven decision-making and strategic planning.

- Standard Reports: Oracle ERP comes with a wide range of pre-built reports covering various business functions. These reports provide real-time insights into financial performance, operational efficiency, and workforce management.

- Custom Reports: The custom report builder allows users to create tailored reports to meet specific business needs. Users can design reports with various data sources, filters, and visualizations.

- Data Analysis Tools: Oracle ERP includes advanced data analysis tools such as Oracle BI Publisher and Oracle Analytics Cloud. These tools support complex data modeling, predictive analytics, and interactive dashboards.

Integration and Customization Capabilities

Oracle ERP is designed to integrate seamlessly with other enterprise systems and third-party applications. It offers extensive customization options to meet unique business requirements.

- Integration: Oracle ERP supports integration with various business applications, including CRM, SCM, and HCM systems. It uses APIs and middleware to ensure smooth data flow and process synchronization across different systems.

- Customization: The platform offers extensive customization options, allowing businesses to tailor workflows, forms, and reports to their specific needs. Users can leverage Oracle's development tools to create custom extensions and applications.

Enhanced Security and Compliance

Security and compliance are critical aspects of Oracle ERP. The platform includes robust security features and compliance tools to protect sensitive data and ensure regulatory compliance.

- Data Security: Oracle ERP provides multi-layered security controls, including user authentication, role-based access control, and data encryption. It ensures that only authorized users can access sensitive information.

- Compliance: The compliance tools in Oracle ERP help businesses adhere to industry regulations and standards. These tools support audit trails, financial reporting standards (e.g., GAAP, IFRS), and regulatory requirements (e.g., GDPR, SOX).

Workflow Automation and Process Management

Oracle ERP includes powerful workflow automation tools that streamline business processes and enhance efficiency. These tools automate repetitive tasks, reduce manual errors, and ensure consistent process execution.

- Workflow Automation: Oracle ERP's workflow engine allows users to design and automate complex business processes. Users can define rules, conditions, and actions to automate tasks such as approvals, notifications, and data updates.

- Process Management: The process management tools provide visibility into process performance and bottlenecks. Users can monitor process metrics, identify areas for improvement, and optimize workflows for better efficiency.

Scalability and Flexibility

Oracle ERP is built to support businesses of all sizes, from small enterprises to large corporations. Its scalable architecture ensures that it can grow with the business and adapt to changing needs.

- Scalability: Oracle ERP can handle large volumes of transactions and data, making it suitable for growing businesses. Its modular design allows organizations to add new modules and features as needed.

- Flexibility: The platform supports various deployment options, including on-premises, cloud, and hybrid environments. This flexibility allows businesses to choose the deployment model that best fits their needs and resources.

User-Friendly Interface

Oracle ERP provides a user-friendly interface that enhances user experience and productivity. The intuitive design and navigation make it easy for users to access information and perform tasks.

- Intuitive Navigation: The user interface is designed for easy navigation, with a logical layout and clear menu structure. Users can quickly find the information and tools they need.

- Customization: Users can customize their dashboards and workspaces to suit their preferences and workflows. This personalization enhances user experience and efficiency.

Mobile Access and Collaboration

In today's mobile-driven world, Oracle ERP provides mobile access and collaboration tools to support remote work and teamwork.

- Mobile Access: Oracle ERP offers mobile applications that allow users to access the system from anywhere, at any time. These apps provide real-time data and functionality on mobile devices, ensuring that users can stay connected and productive on the go.

- Collaboration Tools: The collaboration tools in Oracle ERP facilitate communication and teamwork. Features such as shared workspaces, document sharing, and real-time messaging enhance collaboration among team members.

Continuous Innovation

Oracle ERP is continuously evolving, with regular updates and new features to meet the changing needs of businesses. Oracle invests heavily in research and development to ensure that its ERP solution remains at the forefront of technology and innovation.

- Regular Updates: Oracle releases regular updates that include new features, enhancements, and security patches. These updates ensure that businesses always have access to the latest tools and technologies.

- Innovation: Oracle ERP incorporates cutting-edge technologies such as artificial intelligence (AI), machine learning (ML), and blockchain. These technologies enable advanced capabilities such as predictive analytics, intelligent automation, and secure transactions.

Conclusion

Oracle ERP is a comprehensive and versatile solution that provides a wide range of features to support business operations. Its robust financial management, advanced supply chain management, effective human capital management, and powerful reporting and analytics make it an essential tool for modern enterprises. The platform's integration capabilities, customization options, security features, and user-friendly interface further enhance its value. With continuous innovation and support for mobile access and collaboration, Oracle ERP ensures that businesses can stay competitive and agile in a rapidly changing environment.

By leveraging the key features of Oracle ERP, businesses can streamline their operations, improve efficiency, and gain valuable insights into their performance. This enables them to make informed decisions, optimize resources, and achieve their strategic goals. As businesses continue to evolve and face new challenges, Oracle ERP provides the flexibility and scalability needed to adapt and thrive. Whether you are a small business looking to grow or a large corporation seeking to enhance your operations, Oracle ERP offers the tools and capabilities to unlock your business potential.

1.3 Overview of Oracle ERP Modules

1.3.1 Financial Management

Oracle ERP Financial Management is a robust and comprehensive suite of applications that supports a wide range of business activities and ensures accurate financial reporting, efficient financial operations, and improved decision-making. This module is designed to handle all aspects of financial operations within an organization, from managing day-to-day financial transactions to consolidating financial data for strategic planning and analysis. Here's an in-depth look into the various components and functionalities of Oracle ERP Financial Management:

1.3.1.1 General Ledger

The General Ledger (GL) is the central component of Oracle ERP Financial Management. It provides a comprehensive view of an organization's financial health by recording all financial transactions in a structured manner. Key features of the General Ledger include:

- Chart of Accounts: The Chart of Accounts is a framework for categorizing financial transactions. It allows organizations to define a flexible and hierarchical structure that aligns with their reporting needs. Accounts can be segmented to capture detailed information for various business units, departments, or projects.

- Journal Entries: Journal entries are used to record financial transactions in the General Ledger. Oracle ERP provides tools for creating, editing, and posting journal entries, ensuring that all financial data is accurately captured. Users can create recurring journal entries for regular transactions, simplifying the process and reducing manual effort.

- Multi-Currency Support: The General Ledger supports multiple currencies, allowing organizations to manage financial transactions in different currencies and perform currency conversions as needed. This is particularly useful for multinational companies that operate in various countries with different currencies.

- Financial Consolidation: Oracle ERP enables the consolidation of financial data from multiple subsidiaries or business units into a single set of financial statements. This ensures that organizations can present a unified view of their financial performance to stakeholders.

- Real-Time Reporting and Analytics: The General Ledger provides real-time access to financial data, enabling organizations to generate up-to-date financial reports and perform detailed analyses. This helps in identifying trends, making informed decisions, and ensuring regulatory compliance.

1.3.1.2 Accounts Payable

The Accounts Payable (AP) module automates the process of managing an organization's liabilities and payments to suppliers. It streamlines the entire payables process, from invoice receipt to payment processing. Key features include:

- Invoice Processing: Oracle ERP allows for the efficient capture and processing of supplier invoices. Invoices can be entered manually or imported electronically, and the system supports various invoice types, including standard, prepayment, and recurring invoices. The module also provides tools for matching invoices to purchase orders and receipts, ensuring accuracy and preventing duplicate payments.

- Payment Processing: The AP module automates the payment process, enabling organizations to manage payments to suppliers effectively. Users can schedule payments, generate payment batches, and process electronic payments through various methods such as checks, wire transfers, and electronic funds transfers (EFT). The system also provides tools for managing payment terms and discounts.

- Supplier Management: Oracle ERP helps organizations maintain comprehensive records of their suppliers, including contact information, payment terms, and transaction history. This enables better supplier relationship management and ensures that all supplier-related information is easily accessible.

- Expense Management: The AP module includes functionality for managing employee expenses. Employees can submit expense reports for approval, and the system automates the reimbursement process, ensuring timely and accurate payments.

1.3.1.3 Accounts Receivable

The Accounts Receivable (AR) module manages the organization's receivables and ensures timely collection of payments from customers. It helps organizations improve cash flow, reduce outstanding receivables, and maintain accurate customer records. Key features include:

- Customer Invoicing: Oracle ERP automates the creation and distribution of customer invoices. Invoices can be generated based on sales orders, contracts, or manual entries. The system supports various invoice formats and delivery methods, including email and electronic data interchange (EDI).

- Cash Receipts: The AR module streamlines the process of recording and applying customer payments. Payments can be received through various methods, such as checks, credit cards, and electronic payments. The system automatically applies payments to open invoices, ensuring accurate and timely updates to customer accounts.

- Credit Management: Oracle ERP provides tools for managing customer credit limits and assessing credit risk. Organizations can define credit policies and perform credit checks on new and existing customers, helping to mitigate the risk of bad debts.

- Collections Management: The AR module includes functionality for managing the collections process. Users can create and track collection strategies, send reminders to customers with overdue balances, and generate aging reports to monitor outstanding receivables.

1.3.1.4 Fixed Assets

The Fixed Assets module helps organizations manage their fixed assets throughout their lifecycle, from acquisition to disposal. It provides tools for tracking asset information, calculating depreciation, and generating financial reports. Key features include:

- Asset Management: Oracle ERP enables organizations to maintain detailed records of their fixed assets, including acquisition cost, location, and maintenance history. Users can categorize assets, assign asset numbers, and track asset movements within the organization.

- Depreciation Methods: The Fixed Assets module supports various depreciation methods, including straight-line, declining balance, and units of production. Organizations can define depreciation policies and calculate depreciation expense automatically, ensuring compliance with accounting standards.

- Asset Transfers and Retirements: The system provides tools for managing asset transfers between locations or departments and for retiring assets that are no longer in use. Users can record asset disposals, calculate gain or loss on disposal, and update the asset register accordingly.

- Financial Reporting: Oracle ERP generates comprehensive reports on fixed assets, including asset registers, depreciation schedules, and asset reconciliation reports. These reports provide valuable insights into asset utilization and financial performance.

1.3.1.5 Cost Management

The Cost Management module is essential for organizations that need to track and control their production costs and ensure accurate costing of their products or services. It provides tools for managing various costing methods and analyzing cost data. Key features include:

- Standard Costing: Oracle ERP supports the standard costing method, where costs are predefined for each product or service. This helps organizations establish benchmarks and monitor variances between actual and standard costs. The system automatically updates cost records based on production activities and generates variance reports.

- Actual Costing: The Cost Management module also supports actual costing, where costs are recorded based on actual expenses incurred during production. This provides a more accurate reflection of production costs and helps organizations analyze cost trends and make informed pricing decisions.

- Cost Allocation Methods: Oracle ERP allows organizations to allocate costs to different cost centers, departments, or projects. Various cost allocation methods, such as direct, step-down, and activity-based costing, are supported. This ensures that costs are accurately distributed and provides insights into the cost structure of different business units.

- Cost Analysis and Reporting: The Cost Management module includes tools for analyzing cost data and generating detailed reports. Users can create cost summaries, variance reports, and profitability analyses, helping them understand the financial impact of their production activities and make strategic decisions.

Conclusion

Oracle ERP Financial Management provides a comprehensive suite of tools to manage an organization's financial operations effectively. From the General Ledger to Cost Management, each component is designed to streamline processes, ensure accurate financial reporting, and support strategic decision-making. By leveraging the capabilities of Oracle ERP, organizations can enhance their financial performance, improve operational efficiency, and achieve their business goals.

1.3.2 Supply Chain Management

The Supply Chain Management (SCM) module within Oracle ERP is a comprehensive suite of applications designed to optimize and streamline the entire supply chain process, from procurement to production, and from inventory management to order fulfillment. SCM is critical for organizations aiming to improve efficiency, reduce costs, and ensure customer satisfaction. This module integrates various functions and provides real-time visibility across the supply chain, enabling businesses to make informed decisions and respond swiftly to market changes.

1.3.2.1 Procurement Management

Procurement Management is a crucial component of the SCM module, focusing on acquiring goods and services necessary for business operations. Oracle ERP's Procurement Management system supports various procurement activities, including:

- Purchase Requisitions: This function allows employees to request the purchase of goods or services. The system automates the requisition process, from creating and submitting requests to approval workflows. This ensures that all procurement activities are documented and can be tracked easily.

- Supplier Management: Oracle ERP provides tools to manage supplier relationships effectively. This includes maintaining supplier information, evaluating supplier performance, and negotiating contracts. A robust supplier management system helps businesses build strong relationships with suppliers, ensuring timely delivery of quality goods and services.

- Purchase Orders: Once requisitions are approved, they can be converted into purchase orders (POs). The system streamlines the creation, approval, and dispatch of POs. This ensures accuracy in ordering and helps in maintaining a clear record of all purchases.

- Invoice Matching: This feature matches invoices from suppliers with the corresponding purchase orders and goods receipts. It helps in verifying the accuracy of invoices and ensures that payments are made only for received goods and services. This reduces the risk of overpayments and discrepancies.

- Contract Management: Oracle ERP's Procurement Management module also includes contract management capabilities. This involves creating, managing, and monitoring contracts with suppliers to ensure compliance with agreed terms and conditions. Effective contract management helps in mitigating risks and securing favorable terms.

1.3.2.2 Inventory Management

Inventory Management is another vital component of the SCM module. It ensures that the right amount of inventory is available at the right time to meet customer demand while minimizing holding costs. Key features include:

- Inventory Tracking: Oracle ERP provides real-time tracking of inventory levels across multiple locations. This helps in maintaining optimal inventory levels, reducing the risk of stockouts or overstock situations.

- Stock Replenishment: The system supports automated stock replenishment based on predefined criteria, such as reorder points and safety stock levels. This ensures that inventory is replenished in a timely manner, preventing disruptions in production and sales.

- Inventory Valuation: Accurate inventory valuation is essential for financial reporting and decision-making. Oracle ERP supports various inventory valuation methods, including FIFO (First-In, First-Out), LIFO (Last-In, First-Out), and weighted average cost.

- Cycle Counting: This is a method of periodic inventory auditing that involves counting a subset of inventory items on a regular basis. It helps in maintaining inventory accuracy and identifying discrepancies between physical inventory and system records.

- Warehouse Management: Oracle ERP's Inventory Management module includes advanced warehouse management capabilities. This involves optimizing warehouse operations, including receiving, putaway, picking, packing, and shipping. Efficient warehouse management helps in reducing operational costs and improving order fulfillment times.

1.3.2.3 Order Management

Order Management is central to the SCM module, focusing on managing customer orders from order placement to fulfillment. Key features include:

- Sales Order Processing: Oracle ERP streamlines the sales order process, from order entry to delivery. This includes capturing order details, verifying product availability, and generating order acknowledgments. Efficient sales order processing helps in reducing order cycle times and improving customer satisfaction.

- Order Fulfillment: The system supports various fulfillment strategies, including make-to-order, make-to-stock, and drop shipping. It ensures that orders are fulfilled accurately and on time, coordinating activities across the supply chain.

- Pricing and Discounts: Oracle ERP allows businesses to manage pricing and discounts effectively. This includes setting up pricing rules, applying discounts, and managing promotions. Accurate pricing ensures competitiveness and profitability.

- Order Tracking: Customers and internal stakeholders can track the status of orders in real-time. This visibility helps in managing customer expectations and addressing any issues that may arise during the order fulfillment process.

- Returns Management: The system also supports returns management, allowing customers to return products and process refunds or exchanges efficiently. This helps in maintaining customer satisfaction and managing reverse logistics.

1.3.2.4 Manufacturing and Production

Manufacturing and Production are critical aspects of the SCM module, focusing on transforming raw materials into finished goods. Key features include:

- Production Planning: Oracle ERP supports detailed production planning, including demand forecasting, capacity planning, and scheduling. This ensures that production resources are utilized efficiently and that production schedules are met.

- Shop Floor Management: The system provides tools to manage shop floor activities, including work order creation, resource allocation, and production tracking. Real-time visibility into shop floor operations helps in identifying and addressing issues promptly.

- Bill of Materials (BOM): The BOM is a comprehensive list of materials, components, and assemblies required to manufacture a product. Oracle ERP allows businesses to create and manage BOMs, ensuring accuracy and consistency in production.

- Quality Management: Ensuring product quality is essential for customer satisfaction and regulatory compliance. Oracle ERP includes quality management features, such as quality inspections, non-conformance reporting, and corrective actions. This helps in maintaining high-quality standards throughout the production process.

- Cost Management: The system tracks production costs, including material, labor, and overhead costs. This helps in understanding the cost structure of products and making informed pricing and production decisions.

1.3.2.5 Logistics and Transportation

Logistics and Transportation are integral to the SCM module, focusing on the movement of goods from suppliers to customers. Key features include:

- Shipping and Delivery: Oracle ERP streamlines shipping and delivery processes, including carrier selection, shipment tracking, and delivery confirmation. This ensures timely and accurate delivery of goods to customers.

- Transportation Management: The system supports transportation planning and execution, optimizing routes and managing transportation costs. Efficient transportation management helps in reducing shipping costs and improving delivery times.

- Warehouse Operations: As part of logistics management, Oracle ERP includes advanced warehouse operations capabilities. This involves managing warehouse space, optimizing picking and packing processes, and ensuring efficient loading and unloading of goods.

- Freight Management: The system helps in managing freight contracts, tracking freight costs, and optimizing freight utilization. Effective freight management reduces transportation costs and improves profitability.

1.3.2.6 Demand Planning and Forecasting

Demand Planning and Forecasting are crucial for aligning supply chain activities with market demand. Key features include:

- Demand Forecasting: Oracle ERP uses advanced algorithms and historical data to generate accurate demand forecasts. This helps businesses anticipate market demand and plan their supply chain activities accordingly.

- Sales and Operations Planning (S&OP): The system supports the S&OP process, aligning sales plans with production and inventory plans. This ensures that business operations are synchronized with market demand, reducing the risk of overproduction or stockouts.

- Inventory Optimization: Based on demand forecasts, the system helps in optimizing inventory levels, balancing the cost of holding inventory with the need to meet customer demand. This improves inventory turnover and reduces carrying costs.

- Collaborative Planning: Oracle ERP facilitates collaboration between various stakeholders, including suppliers, manufacturers, and customers. This ensures that all parties are aligned and can respond to changes in demand effectively.

1.3.2.7 Supplier Collaboration and Relationship Management

Effective supplier collaboration and relationship management are essential for a resilient and responsive supply chain. Key features include:

- Supplier Portal: Oracle ERP provides a supplier portal, enabling suppliers to access information, submit invoices, and collaborate on procurement activities. This enhances communication and transparency between businesses and their suppliers.

- Supplier Performance Management: The system tracks and evaluates supplier performance based on various criteria, such as delivery time, quality, and cost. This helps in identifying top-performing suppliers and areas for improvement.

- Supplier Risk Management: Oracle ERP includes tools for assessing and managing supplier risks. This involves monitoring supplier stability, compliance with regulations, and potential supply chain disruptions. Effective risk management helps in mitigating risks and ensuring supply chain continuity.

- Collaborative Planning: The system supports collaborative planning with suppliers, enabling joint demand forecasting, inventory planning, and production scheduling. This improves supply chain synchronization and reduces lead times.

1.3.2.8 Analytics and Reporting

Analytics and Reporting are vital for gaining insights into supply chain performance and making data-driven decisions. Key features include:

- Supply Chain Dashboards: Oracle ERP provides interactive dashboards that offer real-time visibility into supply chain metrics, such as inventory levels, order status, and supplier performance. These dashboards help in monitoring supply chain health and identifying issues promptly.

- Advanced Analytics: The system uses advanced analytics tools, such as machine learning and predictive analytics, to uncover patterns and trends in supply chain data. This helps in forecasting demand, optimizing inventory, and improving supply chain efficiency.

- Custom Reports: Oracle ERP allows businesses to create custom reports tailored to their specific needs. This includes generating reports on procurement, inventory, order fulfillment, and production performance. Custom reports provide detailed insights and support decision-making.

- Compliance Reporting: The system supports compliance reporting, ensuring that businesses meet regulatory requirements related to supply chain operations. This includes generating reports on product traceability, quality control, and environmental impact.

In summary, the Supply Chain Management module of Oracle ERP is designed to optimize and integrate all aspects of the supply chain, from procurement to production and from inventory management to order fulfillment. By leveraging the comprehensive features of this module, businesses can enhance their operational efficiency, reduce costs, and deliver superior customer service. The SCM module's capabilities in procurement, inventory management, order

management, manufacturing, logistics, demand planning, supplier collaboration, and analytics make it an indispensable tool for modern enterprises aiming to achieve supply chain excellence.

1.3.3 Human Capital Management

Human Capital Management (HCM) within Oracle ERP is a comprehensive suite of applications designed to help organizations manage their workforce effectively. HCM focuses on maximizing employee performance and aligning human resources (HR) processes with business objectives. This module covers various aspects of HR management, including recruitment, payroll, performance management, and more. Here's an in-depth look at the components and functionalities of Oracle HCM:

Recruitment and Talent Acquisition

One of the critical functions of HCM is to streamline the recruitment process. Oracle HCM provides tools for creating job postings, managing applications, and tracking candidates throughout the hiring process.

- Job Postings and Advertising: Users can create and manage job postings within the system, ensuring that open positions are advertised both internally and externally. The system can integrate with various job boards and social media platforms to extend the reach of job advertisements.

- Applicant Tracking: Oracle HCM includes an applicant tracking system (ATS) that helps HR professionals manage candidate information, schedule interviews, and track the status of each application. This feature ensures that no candidate is overlooked and that the recruitment process is efficient.

- Interview Management: The module supports scheduling interviews, sending automated reminders, and collecting feedback from interviewers. This coordination helps to ensure a smooth interview process and provides a central location for all interview-related activities.

- Onboarding: Once a candidate is hired, Oracle HCM facilitates the onboarding process. New hires can complete necessary documentation, access training materials, and become acquainted with company policies through the system.

Core HR Management

Core HR management forms the backbone of HCM. It encompasses employee data management, organizational structures, and compliance with legal and regulatory requirements.

- Employee Records: Oracle HCM maintains comprehensive employee records, including personal information, employment history, qualifications, and certifications. This centralized database ensures that all employee information is up-to-date and easily accessible.

- Organizational Structure: The module allows for the creation and management of organizational structures, such as departments, teams, and reporting hierarchies. This feature helps in visualizing the organization and managing changes effectively.

- Compliance and Reporting: Oracle HCM ensures compliance with local and international labor laws by maintaining records and generating necessary reports. This functionality is crucial for avoiding legal issues and ensuring that the organization adheres to all relevant regulations.

Payroll Management

Payroll is a critical function of any organization, and Oracle HCM offers robust payroll management capabilities to ensure accurate and timely compensation for employees.

- Payroll Processing: The system automates payroll calculations, taking into account various factors such as salaries, hourly wages, overtime, bonuses, and deductions. This automation reduces the risk of errors and ensures that employees are paid correctly.

- Tax Management: Oracle HCM handles tax calculations and deductions, ensuring compliance with local, state, and federal tax regulations. The system can generate necessary tax forms and reports, simplifying the tax filing process.

- Direct Deposit and Pay Slips: The module supports direct deposit, allowing employees to receive their salaries directly into their bank accounts. Additionally, it generates detailed pay slips that employees can access electronically.

- Garnishments and Benefits: Oracle HCM can manage garnishments, such as child support or tax levies, and process employee benefits like health insurance, retirement plans, and more.

Performance Management

Performance management within Oracle HCM is designed to help organizations evaluate and improve employee performance, ensuring alignment with business goals.

- Goal Setting and Tracking: Managers and employees can set performance goals that align with organizational objectives. The system allows for tracking progress toward these goals and provides a framework for regular performance reviews.

- Performance Appraisals: Oracle HCM supports various types of performance appraisals, including self-assessments, peer reviews, and manager evaluations. This comprehensive approach ensures a holistic view of employee performance.

- Continuous Feedback: The module facilitates continuous feedback between employees and managers, encouraging regular communication and development. This feature helps in identifying areas for improvement and recognizing achievements in real-time.

- Development Plans: Based on performance evaluations, managers can create personalized development plans for employees. These plans may include training programs, mentorship opportunities, and career progression paths.

Learning and Development

Oracle HCM includes tools for managing employee learning and development, ensuring that the workforce is continuously improving and acquiring new skills.

- Learning Management System (LMS): The LMS within Oracle HCM provides a platform for creating, delivering, and tracking training programs. Employees can access training materials, complete courses, and receive certifications through the system.

- Training Programs: Organizations can develop and manage various training programs, ranging from mandatory compliance training to optional professional development courses. The system ensures that employees complete required training and track their progress.

- Skill Assessments: Oracle HCM includes tools for assessing employee skills and identifying gaps. This feature helps in creating targeted development plans and ensuring that employees possess the necessary skills for their roles.

- Career Development: The module supports career development initiatives, such as succession planning and talent mobility. Employees can explore career opportunities within the organization and receive guidance on achieving their career goals.

Time and Labor Management

Time and labor management is a crucial component of HCM, ensuring accurate tracking of employee work hours and efficient management of labor costs.

- Time Tracking: Oracle HCM provides tools for tracking employee work hours, including clock-in/clock-out functionality, time sheets, and mobile time tracking. This ensures accurate recording of work hours and reduces administrative overhead.

- Leave Management: The module manages employee leave requests, including vacation, sick leave, and other types of absences. Employees can submit leave requests, and managers can approve or deny them through the system.

- Overtime Management: Oracle HCM handles overtime calculations and approvals, ensuring compliance with labor laws and company policies. The system can automatically calculate overtime pay based on predefined rules.

- Labor Costing: The module provides insights into labor costs, helping organizations manage their workforce budgets effectively. This includes analyzing labor costs by department, project, or other criteria.

Employee Self-Service

Oracle HCM includes self-service capabilities that empower employees to manage their HR-related tasks, reducing the administrative burden on HR staff.

- Personal Information Management: Employees can update their personal information, such as contact details, emergency contacts, and marital status, directly in the system.

- Benefits Enrollment: The module allows employees to enroll in and manage their benefits, such as health insurance and retirement plans. This self-service capability simplifies the benefits administration process.

- Time and Attendance: Employees can submit time sheets, request leave, and view their attendance records through the self-service portal.

- Performance Reviews: Employees can participate in performance reviews, set goals, and provide feedback through the self-service platform.

Analytics and Reporting

Analytics and reporting are essential components of Oracle HCM, providing insights into workforce data and supporting data-driven decision-making.

- Workforce Analytics: The module includes tools for analyzing workforce data, such as headcount, turnover rates, and employee demographics. These insights help organizations make informed decisions about their HR strategies.

- Custom Reports: Oracle HCM allows users to create custom reports to meet specific business needs. These reports can cover various aspects of HR management, such as recruitment, performance, and payroll.

- Dashboards: The system includes interactive dashboards that provide a visual representation of key HR metrics. These dashboards can be customized to display the most relevant data for different users.- Compliance Reporting: Oracle HCM generates reports required for compliance with labor laws and regulations. This includes equal employment opportunity (EEO) reports, safety reports, and other regulatory filings.

Integration and Customization

Oracle HCM is designed to integrate seamlessly with other Oracle ERP modules and third-party applications, ensuring a cohesive HR management ecosystem.

- Integration with Financials: The module integrates with Oracle Financials to ensure accurate payroll accounting and financial reporting. This integration helps in managing labor costs and budgeting effectively.

- Integration with Supply Chain Management: Oracle HCM can integrate with supply chain management (SCM) modules to align workforce planning with supply chain needs. This ensures that the right resources are available when needed.

- Third-Party Integrations: The system supports integrations with third-party applications, such as job boards, learning platforms, and benefits providers. This flexibility allows organizations to use the best tools for their HR processes.

- Customization: Oracle HCM provides customization options to meet specific business requirements. This includes custom workflows, user interfaces, and reports. Organizations can tailor the system to their unique needs while maintaining the integrity of the core functionalities.

Mobile Access

In today's fast-paced business environment, mobile access to HR systems is crucial. Oracle HCM provides mobile applications that allow employees and managers to access HR functionalities on the go.

- Mobile Self-Service: Employees can use mobile apps to manage their personal information, submit leave requests, and access pay slips. This convenience enhances employee engagement and satisfaction.

- Manager Access: Managers can use mobile applications to approve leave requests, conduct performance reviews, and manage team activities. This flexibility ensures that HR processes are not delayed, even when managers are away from their desks.

- Mobile Learning: The learning management system (LMS) within Oracle HCM supports mobile learning, allowing employees to access training materials and complete courses from their mobile devices.

Conclusion

Oracle Human Capital Management (HCM) is a powerful and comprehensive module within the Oracle ERP suite, designed to help organizations manage their workforce effectively. By leveraging the capabilities of Oracle HCM, organizations can streamline their HR processes, improve employee performance, and align their human resources with business objectives. Whether it's recruitment, payroll, performance management, or learning and development, Oracle HCM provides the tools and functionalities needed to optimize human capital and drive business success.

1.3.4 Other Modules

Oracle ERP is a comprehensive suite designed to streamline and enhance various business processes. While Financial Management, Supply Chain Management, and Human Capital Management are core areas, Oracle ERP also encompasses a range of other modules that cater to specific business needs. These modules include Project Management, Customer Relationship Management (CRM), Manufacturing, Procurement, and more. This section will delve into these additional modules, providing a detailed overview of their functions and benefits.

1.3.4.1 Project Management

Oracle's Project Management module is designed to help businesses effectively plan, execute, and monitor projects. It integrates with other ERP modules to ensure seamless data flow and real-time insights into project performance.

Key Features:

- Project Planning and Scheduling: Allows for detailed project planning, including task assignment, scheduling, and resource allocation. It supports Gantt charts and other project visualization tools.

- Budgeting and Cost Control: Helps in setting project budgets and tracking expenses against those budgets. Provides alerts for budget overruns.

- Resource Management: Facilitates the optimal allocation of resources, ensuring that the right skills are available for the right tasks.

- Risk Management: Identifies potential risks and develops mitigation strategies to ensure project success.

- Reporting and Analytics: Provides comprehensive reporting tools to monitor project progress, performance, and outcomes.

Benefits:

- Enhanced visibility into project performance.

- Improved resource utilization.

- Better control over project costs and timelines.

- Increased project success rates.

1.3.4.2 Customer Relationship Management (CRM)

The CRM module in Oracle ERP focuses on managing and improving interactions with customers, with the goal of enhancing customer satisfaction and loyalty.

Key Features:

- Sales Force Automation: Automates sales processes, including lead management, opportunity tracking, and sales forecasting.

- Customer Service Management: Provides tools for managing customer service requests, tracking issues, and ensuring timely resolution.

- Marketing Automation: Supports campaign management, email marketing, and customer segmentation to target the right audience with the right message.

- Analytics and Reporting: Offers insights into customer behavior, sales performance, and marketing effectiveness through advanced analytics and reporting tools.

Benefits:

- Improved customer satisfaction and retention.

- Streamlined sales and marketing processes.

- Enhanced ability to track and analyze customer interactions.

- Increased sales and revenue.

1.3.4.3 Manufacturing

The Manufacturing module is designed to streamline production processes, ensuring efficiency and quality in manufacturing operations.

Key Features:

- Production Planning: Facilitates detailed production scheduling and planning to optimize manufacturing processes.

- Shop Floor Management: Provides real-time visibility into shop floor activities, including work order management and labor tracking.

- Quality Management: Ensures adherence to quality standards through comprehensive quality control processes and tools.

- Inventory Management: Integrates with inventory management to ensure that raw materials and finished goods are accurately tracked and managed.

- Cost Management: Tracks production costs to help manage and control manufacturing expenses.

Benefits:

- Increased production efficiency.

- Enhanced product quality.

- Better inventory control.

- Reduced manufacturing costs.

1.3.4.4 Procurement

Oracle's Procurement module streamlines the procurement process, from requisition to payment, ensuring that organizations can acquire goods and services efficiently and cost-effectively.

Key Features:

- Requisition Management: Simplifies the creation and approval of purchase requisitions.

- Supplier Management: Provides tools for managing supplier relationships, including performance tracking and communication.

- Purchase Order Management: Automates the creation, approval, and tracking of purchase orders.

- Invoice Matching: Ensures that invoices match purchase orders and receipts to facilitate accurate payment processing.

- Spend Analysis: Analyzes procurement spend to identify cost-saving opportunities and improve supplier negotiations.

Benefits:

- Streamlined procurement processes.

- Improved supplier relationships.

- Enhanced spend visibility and control.

- Reduced procurement costs.

1.3.4.5 Enterprise Asset Management (EAM)

The EAM module helps organizations manage the lifecycle of their physical assets, ensuring optimal performance and minimizing downtime.

Key Features:

- Asset Tracking: Provides comprehensive tools for tracking the location, condition, and maintenance history of assets.

- Maintenance Management: Supports preventive, predictive, and corrective maintenance processes to ensure asset reliability.

- Work Order Management: Facilitates the creation, assignment, and tracking of maintenance work orders.

- Inventory and Spare Parts Management: Integrates with inventory management to ensure the availability of spare parts for maintenance activities.

- Reporting and Analytics: Offers detailed insights into asset performance, maintenance costs, and equipment reliability.

Benefits:

- Improved asset utilization.

- Reduced maintenance costs.

- Enhanced asset reliability and performance.

- Extended asset lifespan.

1.3.4.6 Risk Management

The Risk Management module helps organizations identify, assess, and mitigate risks across various business functions.

Key Features:

- Risk Assessment: Provides tools for identifying and assessing risks, including financial, operational, and compliance risks.

- Risk Mitigation Planning: Helps develop and implement strategies to mitigate identified risks.

- Monitoring and Reporting: Offers real-time monitoring of risk indicators and comprehensive reporting to track risk management activities.

- Compliance Management: Ensures adherence to regulatory requirements and internal policies.

Benefits:

- Enhanced ability to identify and manage risks.

- Improved compliance with regulatory requirements.

- Reduced potential for financial losses.

- Increased organizational resilience.

1.3.4.7 Governance, Risk, and Compliance (GRC)

Oracle's GRC module integrates governance, risk management, and compliance activities into a unified framework, helping organizations ensure that their processes align with regulatory standards and internal policies.

Key Features:

- Policy Management: Centralizes the creation, distribution, and management of corporate policies.

- Risk Management: Identifies, assesses, and mitigates risks across the organization.

- Compliance Management: Monitors compliance with regulatory requirements and internal policies.

- Audit Management: Facilitates internal and external audits, providing tools for audit planning, execution, and reporting.

- Incident Management: Tracks and manages incidents to ensure timely resolution and prevent recurrence.

Benefits:

- Improved governance and oversight.

- Enhanced risk management capabilities.

- Increased compliance with regulations and policies.

- Streamlined audit processes.

1.3.4.8 Service Management

The Service Management module is designed to enhance service delivery and customer satisfaction by providing comprehensive tools for managing service operations.

Key Features:

- Service Request Management: Automates the creation, assignment, and tracking of service requests.

- Service Level Agreement (SLA) Management: Ensures compliance with SLAs by monitoring service performance and triggering alerts for SLA breaches.

- Field Service Management: Provides tools for managing field service operations, including scheduling, dispatching, and tracking field technicians.

- Knowledge Management: Centralizes service-related knowledge to improve issue resolution and reduce service times.

- Customer Feedback: Collects and analyzes customer feedback to identify areas for service improvement.

Benefits:

- Improved service delivery and customer satisfaction.

- Enhanced ability to meet SLAs.

- Better management of field service operations.

- Reduced service costs.

1.3.4.9 Product Lifecycle Management (PLM)

The PLM module helps organizations manage the entire lifecycle of their products, from inception through design, manufacturing, and service.

Key Features:

- Product Data Management: Centralizes product data, including specifications, designs, and documentation.

- Change Management: Manages product changes, ensuring that updates are tracked and communicated effectively.

- Collaboration Tools: Facilitates collaboration among product development teams, suppliers, and other stakeholders.

- Regulatory Compliance: Ensures that products comply with relevant regulations and standards.

- Analytics and Reporting: Provides insights into product performance, development costs, and time-to-market.

Benefits:

- Improved product quality and innovation.

- Enhanced collaboration across product development teams.

- Reduced time-to-market.

- Better compliance with regulations.

1.3.4.10 Environmental Health and Safety (EHS)

The EHS module helps organizations manage environmental, health, and safety risks to ensure a safe and compliant workplace.

Key Features:

- Incident Management: Tracks and manages workplace incidents, including accidents, near misses, and hazardous conditions.

- Risk Assessment: Identifies and assesses EHS risks, providing tools for developing mitigation plans.

- Compliance Management: Ensures compliance with environmental and safety regulations.

- Training Management: Manages employee training programs to ensure compliance with EHS standards.

- Reporting and Analytics: Provides detailed insights into EHS performance, including incident trends and compliance metrics.

Benefits:

- Improved workplace safety and health.

- Enhanced compliance with EHS regulations.

- Reduced risk of incidents and accidents.

- Increased employee awareness and training.

1.3.4.11 Advanced Planning and Scheduling (APS)

The APS module is designed to optimize production and supply chain processes through advanced planning and scheduling tools.

Key Features:

- Demand Planning: Forecasts demand to ensure that production and inventory levels align with market needs.

- Supply Planning: Optimizes supply chain operations, including procurement, production, and distribution planning.

- Production Scheduling: Schedules production activities to maximize efficiency and minimize lead times.

- Inventory Optimization: Balances inventory levels to reduce carrying costs while ensuring product availability.

- Analytics and Reporting: Provides insights into planning and scheduling performance, helping to identify areas for improvement.

Benefits:

- Improved demand forecasting accuracy.

- Enhanced supply chain efficiency.

- Reduced production lead times.

- Optimized inventory levels.

CHAPTER II
Getting Started with Oracle ERP

2.1 System Requirements

2.1.1 Hardware Requirements

When planning to implement Oracle ERP, understanding the hardware requirements is crucial to ensure optimal performance, reliability, and scalability of the system. The hardware requirements can vary depending on the size of your organization, the number of users, the volume of transactions, and the specific Oracle ERP modules you plan to use. This section provides a comprehensive guide to the hardware components necessary for a successful Oracle ERP deployment.

Server Requirements

Processor (CPU)

The processor, or Central Processing Unit (CPU), is the brain of your server. It performs calculations and executes instructions to run applications. For Oracle ERP, a powerful CPU is essential to handle the complex computations and high transaction volumes typical of enterprise resource planning systems.

- Recommended Specifications:

- Number of Cores: At least 8 cores. For larger implementations, consider processors with 16 or more cores.

- Clock Speed: A minimum of 2.5 GHz per core is recommended. Higher clock speeds can improve performance, especially for single-threaded tasks.

- Type: Intel Xeon or AMD EPYC processors are commonly used in enterprise servers due to their reliability and performance.

Memory (RAM)

Memory, or Random Access Memory (RAM), is critical for the smooth operation of Oracle ERP. It temporarily stores data and instructions that the CPU needs to access quickly. Insufficient RAM can lead to slow performance and increased latency.

- Recommended Specifications:

- Minimum Requirement: 16 GB of RAM for small to medium-sized implementations.

- Optimal Configuration: 32 GB or more for larger installations with multiple users and high transaction volumes.

- Memory Type: DDR4 RAM with ECC (Error-Correcting Code) is recommended to ensure data integrity and system stability.

Storage

Storage is where all your data, applications, and system files are stored. Oracle ERP systems require reliable and fast storage solutions to ensure quick access to data and efficient transaction processing.

- Types of Storage:

- Hard Disk Drives (HDD): Traditional storage solution, suitable for storing large volumes of data. However, they are slower compared to SSDs.

- Solid State Drives (SSD): Provide faster read/write speeds, reducing data access times and improving overall system performance.

- NVMe (Non-Volatile Memory Express): An even faster storage option than SSDs, ideal for high-performance requirements.

- Recommended Specifications:

- Capacity: At least 500 GB for small implementations. For larger installations, consider 1 TB or more, depending on your data volume.

- Configuration: RAID 1 or RAID 10 configurations are recommended for redundancy and improved read/write performance.

Network Interface

A robust network interface is crucial for ensuring seamless communication between the server and client machines. High-speed network connectivity can significantly impact the performance of Oracle ERP applications, especially in environments with many concurrent users.

- Recommended Specifications:

- Network Interface Card (NIC): At least 1 Gbps (Gigabit per second) NIC. For larger installations, consider 10 Gbps NICs to handle increased network traffic.

- Redundancy: Dual NICs configured for failover to ensure network reliability.

Client Requirements

Desktop/Laptop

The client machines, which include desktops and laptops used by end-users to access Oracle ERP, should also meet specific hardware requirements to ensure smooth operation and optimal user experience.

- Processor:

  - Minimum Requirement: Dual-core processor (Intel i3 or equivalent).

  - Recommended: Quad-core processor (Intel i5 or i7, AMD Ryzen 5 or 7).

- Memory:

  - Minimum Requirement: 4 GB of RAM.

  - Recommended: 8 GB or more for better performance, especially when running multiple applications concurrently.

- Storage:

  - Type: SSDs are preferred over HDDs for faster boot times and application loading.

  - Capacity: At least 256 GB, depending on user needs and data storage requirements.

- Display:

  - Resolution: Minimum resolution of 1920 x 1080 (Full HD).

  - Size: 21 inches or larger for desktop monitors to provide a better user experience.

Mobile Devices

With the increasing need for mobility, Oracle ERP offers mobile access, enabling users to perform tasks on the go. Mobile devices, including smartphones and tablets, should meet specific hardware requirements.

- Operating System:

  - iOS: Version 12.0 or later.

- Android: Version 8.0 (Oreo) or later.

- Processor:

  - iOS Devices: Apple A10 Fusion chip or later.

  - Android Devices: Qualcomm Snapdragon 625 or equivalent.

- Memory:

  - Minimum Requirement: 2 GB of RAM.

  - Recommended: 4 GB or more for smoother performance.

- Storage:

  - Capacity: At least 32 GB, with a preference for expandable storage options.

Peripherals

Peripheral devices are also essential for the complete functionality of Oracle ERP, especially for specific modules like inventory management, where barcoding and scanning are required.

- Printers:

  - Network printers with support for high-resolution printing.

  - Compatibility with major operating systems (Windows, macOS, Linux).

- Scanners:

  - Barcode scanners with USB or Bluetooth connectivity.

  - High-speed document scanners for digital document management.

- Point of Sale (POS) Systems:

  - POS terminals with touch screens.

  - Integration capability with Oracle ERP for seamless transaction processing.

Virtualization Requirements

In many enterprise environments, virtualization is employed to optimize resource utilization and reduce hardware costs. Virtual machines (VMs) can run multiple instances of Oracle ERP, enabling efficient resource management.

- Hypervisor:

  - Type: VMware ESXi, Microsoft Hyper-V, or Oracle VM.

  - CPU: Sufficient cores and clock speed to support multiple VMs.

  - Memory: Adequate RAM to allocate to each VM (e.g., 4 GB per VM).

- Storage:

  - Type: High-performance shared storage (e.g., SAN or NAS).

  - Capacity: Adequate to support multiple VM images and data storage needs.

- Network:

  - Configuration: Virtual NICs with sufficient bandwidth to support VM traffic.

  - Redundancy: Dual network interfaces for failover and load balancing.

High Availability and Scalability

For organizations where downtime can result in significant financial loss, high availability (HA) configurations are critical. Scalability is also essential to accommodate future growth without extensive hardware changes.

- Clustering:

  - Configuration: Active-active or active-passive clustering for critical services.

  - Software: Oracle Real Application Clusters (RAC) for database high availability.

- Load Balancing:

  - Hardware: Load balancers to distribute traffic evenly across multiple servers.

  - Software: Application-level load balancing to ensure efficient resource utilization.

- Backup and Recovery:

  - Hardware: Dedicated backup servers or appliances.

  - Software: Enterprise-grade backup solutions (e.g., Oracle RMAN, Veeam).

By adhering to these hardware requirements, organizations can ensure that their Oracle ERP system operates efficiently, providing reliable performance and the capacity to scale as needed. Proper planning and investment in the right hardware components will contribute significantly to the successful deployment and long-term sustainability of Oracle ERP within your enterprise.

2.1.2 Software Requirements

When preparing to implement Oracle ERP, understanding the software requirements is crucial for ensuring smooth installation and optimal performance. This section outlines the necessary software components and configurations needed to run Oracle ERP effectively.

Operating Systems

Oracle ERP is compatible with a variety of operating systems. It is essential to choose an operating system that meets the specific needs of your organization while ensuring compatibility with Oracle ERP. The primary operating systems supported by Oracle ERP include:

- Oracle Linux: This is the most recommended operating system for Oracle ERP due to its seamless compatibility and support.

- Red Hat Enterprise Linux: Another widely used Linux distribution that offers robust performance and stability.

- Microsoft Windows Server: Suitable for organizations that prefer a Windows environment. Ensure that the server version is compatible with Oracle ERP.

- IBM AIX: Ideal for enterprises with IBM systems, offering reliable performance.

- HP-UX: Suitable for Hewlett-Packard enterprise environments.

- Solaris: Supported for Oracle's own Solaris operating system on SPARC and x86 platforms.

Database Requirements

The database is a critical component of Oracle ERP, as it stores all the data used by the ERP system. Oracle ERP is designed to work seamlessly with Oracle Database, which offers robust performance, scalability, and security features. Key requirements and configurations for the Oracle Database include:

- Oracle Database Version: Ensure that you use a version of Oracle Database that is certified for use with your specific version of Oracle ERP. Typically, Oracle Database 12c, 18c, and 19c are widely supported.

- Database Size: Plan the database size based on the expected data volume and growth. Consider factors such as the number of transactions, users, and historical data storage.

- Memory and Storage: Allocate sufficient memory and storage resources to the database to ensure high performance and reliability. This includes setting appropriate values for parameters such as SGA (System Global Area) and PGA (Program Global Area).

- High Availability: Implement high availability solutions such as Oracle Real Application Clusters (RAC) and Data Guard to ensure database availability and disaster recovery.

Middleware and Application Server

Oracle ERP relies on middleware and application servers to manage application logic, user sessions, and communication between different system components. The key middleware and application server requirements include:

- Oracle WebLogic Server: This is the primary application server used with Oracle ERP. Ensure you have a compatible version installed and configured. WebLogic Server offers features such as clustering, load balancing, and high availability.

- Java Development Kit (JDK): Oracle ERP requires a specific version of the JDK. Ensure that the correct JDK version is installed and configured on the server running Oracle WebLogic.

- Oracle Fusion Middleware: Depending on the specific Oracle ERP modules you are using, you may need additional Oracle Fusion Middleware components such as Oracle SOA Suite, Oracle BPM Suite, or Oracle Identity Management.

Client Software

End-users interact with Oracle ERP through client software. Ensuring that client machines meet the necessary software requirements is essential for a seamless user experience. Key client software requirements include:

- Web Browsers: Oracle ERP is primarily accessed through web browsers. Supported browsers typically include the latest versions of Google Chrome, Mozilla Firefox, Microsoft Edge, and Safari. Ensure that browser settings are configured to allow necessary scripts and plugins.

- Java Runtime Environment (JRE): Some Oracle ERP modules and features may require the JRE to be installed on client machines. Ensure that the JRE version is compatible with the Oracle ERP system.

Security Software

Security is paramount when dealing with ERP systems. Ensure that the necessary security software is in place to protect the Oracle ERP system and data. Key security software requirements include:

- Antivirus and Antimalware: Install and regularly update antivirus and antimalware software on all servers and client machines.

- Firewalls: Implement firewalls to protect the network and servers hosting the Oracle ERP system. Configure firewall rules to allow necessary traffic and block unauthorized access.

- SSL/TLS Certificates: Use SSL/TLS certificates to encrypt communication between clients, application servers, and databases.

Integration and Middleware Tools

Oracle ERP often needs to integrate with other systems and applications within the organization. Ensuring compatibility and configuring integration tools is essential for seamless data exchange. Key integration and middleware tools include:

- Oracle Integration Cloud: A comprehensive integration platform that facilitates the connection between Oracle ERP and other cloud or on-premises applications.

- Oracle Data Integrator (ODI): Used for data integration and ETL (Extract, Transform, Load) processes. Ensure that ODI is configured correctly to integrate data from various sources into Oracle ERP.

- APIs and Web Services: Oracle ERP provides various APIs and web services for integration. Ensure that your development and integration teams are familiar with these APIs and can effectively utilize them for system integration.

Patch Management

Keeping the Oracle ERP system up to date with the latest patches and updates is crucial for security and performance. Implementing a robust patch management strategy ensures that the system remains secure and performs optimally. Key considerations for patch management include:

- Patch Testing: Before applying patches to the production system, thoroughly test them in a staging or development environment to identify any potential issues.

- Regular Updates: Stay informed about the latest patches and updates released by Oracle. Schedule regular maintenance windows to apply patches and updates.

- Backup and Recovery: Ensure that you have a reliable backup and recovery plan in place before applying any patches. This allows you to restore the system to its previous state in case of any issues during the patching process.

Performance Monitoring and Tuning Tools

Monitoring and tuning the performance of the Oracle ERP system is essential to ensure that it operates efficiently. Key performance monitoring and tuning tools include:

- Oracle Enterprise Manager: Provides comprehensive monitoring and management capabilities for Oracle databases, middleware, and applications. Use Oracle Enterprise

Manager to monitor the performance of your Oracle ERP system and identify potential bottlenecks.

- AWR (Automatic Workload Repository) Reports: Use AWR reports to analyze database performance and identify areas for improvement.

- Performance Tuning Advisors: Oracle provides various performance tuning advisors, such as the SQL Tuning Advisor and the ADDM (Automatic Database Diagnostic Monitor). Utilize these advisors to optimize the performance of your Oracle ERP system.

Backup and Recovery Solutions

Implementing robust backup and recovery solutions is critical for ensuring data protection and business continuity. Key backup and recovery solutions include:

- Oracle Recovery Manager (RMAN): A powerful tool for backing up and recovering Oracle databases. Ensure that RMAN is configured correctly and that regular backups are performed.

- Data Guard: Use Oracle Data Guard to create standby databases and ensure high availability and disaster recovery.

- Cloud Backup Solutions: Consider using Oracle Cloud or other cloud-based backup solutions to store backups offsite and ensure data protection.

Licensing and Compliance

Ensuring compliance with Oracle's licensing requirements is essential to avoid legal and financial penalties. Key considerations for licensing and compliance include:

- License Types: Understand the different types of Oracle licenses available, such as perpetual licenses, subscription licenses, and user-based licenses. Choose the appropriate license type based on your organization's needs.

- Compliance Audits: Regularly conduct compliance audits to ensure that your Oracle ERP system is correctly licensed. Maintain accurate records of software usage and licenses.

- Enterprise Agreements: If applicable, review your enterprise agreement with Oracle to understand the terms and conditions related to software usage and support.

This detailed section on software requirements should provide comprehensive guidance for preparing to implement Oracle ERP, ensuring that all necessary software components are in place for a successful deployment.

2.2 Installation and Setup

2.2.1 Installation Steps

Installing Oracle ERP is a crucial step in setting up a robust system to manage your business operations. This section provides a comprehensive guide on the installation process, ensuring that your system is set up correctly and efficiently. We will cover the pre-installation steps, actual installation process, and post-installation configuration to ensure a smooth setup.

Pre-Installation Steps

1. Planning and Preparation

  - Define Objectives: Clearly define the objectives of implementing Oracle ERP in your organization. Understand the key modules you need and the business processes they will support.

  - Resource Allocation: Allocate necessary resources, including hardware, software, and personnel. Ensure that your team includes skilled IT professionals familiar with Oracle ERP installation.

  - Backup Current Data: Before starting the installation, back up all existing data and systems to prevent any loss during the installation process.

2. System Requirements Check

  - Hardware Requirements: Ensure that your hardware meets the minimum requirements specified by Oracle. This includes servers, storage, memory, and network infrastructure.

  - Software Requirements: Verify that your operating system and database software are compatible with the version of Oracle ERP you are installing. Install any necessary updates or patches.

3. Network Configuration

  - IP Address Allocation: Allocate static IP addresses for the servers that will host the Oracle ERP system.

- Firewall Configuration: Configure firewalls to allow necessary ports for Oracle ERP communication.

- Domain Name System (DNS): Ensure proper DNS setup for resolving hostnames to IP addresses.

4. Download Installation Files

- Oracle Software Delivery Cloud: Access the Oracle Software Delivery Cloud and download the necessary installation files for Oracle ERP. Ensure you have the latest version and all required components.

- Verify Integrity: Check the integrity of the downloaded files using checksums provided by Oracle to ensure they are not corrupted.

Installation Process

1. Setting Up the Database

- Database Software Installation: Install the Oracle Database software. Follow the installation wizard, providing necessary inputs such as the installation location, database edition, and administrative passwords.

- Database Configuration: Create a new database instance for Oracle ERP. Configure memory allocation, storage options, and other parameters as per your requirements.

- Listener Configuration: Configure the Oracle Net Listener to enable communication between the database and Oracle ERP applications. Start the listener service to ensure it is running correctly.

2. Installing Oracle WebLogic Server

- Download WebLogic Installer: Download the Oracle WebLogic Server installer from the Oracle website.

- Run the Installer: Execute the installer and follow the prompts. Choose the appropriate installation type, such as "Complete with Examples" or "WebLogic Server Only."

- Domain Creation: Create a new WebLogic domain for Oracle ERP. Configure the domain with the necessary administration server and managed servers.

3. Installing Oracle Fusion Middleware

- Download Middleware Components: Download the necessary Oracle Fusion Middleware components, such as Oracle HTTP Server, Oracle WebCenter, and Oracle SOA Suite.

- Run the Installers: Execute the installers for each component, following the on-screen instructions. Configure each component as required.

- Configure Middleware: Integrate the middleware components with the Oracle WebLogic Server domain. Ensure all services are running and properly configured.

4. Installing Oracle ERP Applications

- Download Application Files: Download the Oracle ERP application files from the Oracle Software Delivery Cloud.

- Extract Files: Extract the downloaded files to a suitable location on the server.

- Run the Installer: Navigate to the extracted directory and execute the installation script. Follow the installation wizard, providing inputs such as installation directory, database connection details, and administrative credentials.

- Module Selection: Select the Oracle ERP modules you want to install, such as Financial Management, Supply Chain Management, and Human Capital Management. Ensure you select only the modules you need to optimize system performance.

5. Post-Installation Configuration

- Patch Application: Apply any necessary patches to the installed Oracle ERP system. Oracle regularly releases patches to fix bugs and enhance functionality. Use Oracle's patch management tools to download and apply patches.

- Initial Configuration: Perform initial configuration tasks such as setting up users, defining roles and permissions, and configuring business units. Use the Oracle ERP Configuration Assistant to streamline this process.

- System Testing: Conduct thorough testing of the installed Oracle ERP system. Test all modules and functionalities to ensure they are working as expected. Identify and resolve any issues that arise during testing.

Detailed Steps

1. Setting Up the Database

a. Install Oracle Database Software:

  - Download the Oracle Database software from the Oracle website.

  - Run the installer and select the appropriate options for your environment.

  - Specify the installation directory and configure Oracle Base and Oracle Home.

  - Choose the database edition (Standard or Enterprise) and complete the installation.

b. Create a Database Instance:

  - Use the Database Configuration Assistant (DBCA) to create a new database instance.

  - Specify the database name, SID, and storage options.

  - Configure memory settings, specifying the amount of RAM to allocate to the database.

  - Set administrative passwords for SYS and SYSTEM users.

  - Configure database initialization parameters and create the database.

c. Configure the Listener:

  - Use the Net Configuration Assistant (NETCA) to configure the Oracle Net Listener.

  - Specify the listener name and the port number (default is 1521).

  - Start the listener service and ensure it is running.

2. Installing Oracle WebLogic Server

  a. Download and Install WebLogic Server:

  - Download the WebLogic Server installer from the Oracle website.

  - Run the installer and follow the on-screen instructions.

  - Choose the installation type (e.g., Complete with Examples).

  - Specify the installation directory and complete the installation.

  b. Create a WebLogic Domain:

  - Launch the Configuration Wizard to create a new WebLogic domain.

  - Specify the domain name and domain directory.

- Configure the administration server and managed servers.

- Set the administrative username and password.

- Complete the domain creation process and start the servers.

3. Installing Oracle Fusion Middleware

  a. Download Middleware Components:

    - Download the necessary Oracle Fusion Middleware components.

    - Extract the downloaded files to a suitable location.

  b. Run the Installers:

    - Execute the installers for each middleware component.

    - Follow the installation wizard and provide the necessary inputs.

    - Specify the installation directory and complete the installation.

  c. Configure Middleware:

    - Integrate the middleware components with the WebLogic Server domain.

    - Use the Fusion Middleware Configuration Wizard to configure each component.

    - Ensure all middleware services are running and properly configured.

4. Installing Oracle ERP Applications

  a. Download Application Files:

    - Download the Oracle ERP application files from the Oracle Software Delivery Cloud.

    - Extract the downloaded files to a suitable location on the server.

  b. Run the Installer:

    - Navigate to the extracted directory and execute the installation script.

    - Follow the installation wizard, providing necessary inputs.

    - Specify the installation directory and database connection details.

    - Set administrative credentials and complete the installation.

c. Module Selection:

- Select the Oracle ERP modules you want to install.

- Ensure you select only the modules you need to optimize system performance.

5. Post-Installation Configuration

a. Apply Patches:

- Use Oracle's patch management tools to download and apply patches.

- Ensure your system is up-to-date with the latest patches.

b. Initial Configuration:

- Perform initial configuration tasks such as setting up users and roles.

- Define business units and configure permissions.

- Use the Oracle ERP Configuration Assistant to streamline the process.

c. System Testing:

- Conduct thorough testing of the installed Oracle ERP system.

- Test all modules and functionalities to ensure they are working as expected.

- Identify and resolve any issues that arise during testing.

Detailed Walkthrough of Key Steps

1. Installing Oracle Database Software

a. Download Oracle Database Software:

- Visit the Oracle website and navigate to the Downloads section.

- Select the appropriate version of Oracle Database and download the installer.

b. Run the Installer:

- Extract the downloaded files and run the installer.

- Choose the installation type (e.g., Create and configure a database).

- Specify the Oracle Base and Oracle Home directories.

- Select the database edition (Standard or Enterprise) and proceed with the installation.

c. Configure Database Parameters:

- Use the Database Configuration Assistant (DBCA) to create a new database.

- Specify the database name, SID, and storage options.

- Configure memory settings and initialization parameters.

- Set administrative passwords for SYS and SYSTEM users.

- Complete the database creation process.

2. Installing Oracle WebLogic Server

a. Download WebLogic Server Installer:

- Visit the Oracle website and download the WebLogic Server installer.

- Choose the appropriate version and platform.

b. Run the Installer:

- Extract the downloaded files and run the installer.

- Follow the on-screen instructions and specify the installation directory.

- Choose the installation type (Complete with Examples or WebLogic Server Only).

- Complete the installation process.

c. Create a WebLogic Domain:

- Launch the Configuration Wizard to create a new WebLogic domain.

- Specify the domain name and domain directory.

- Configure the administration server and managed servers.

- Set the administrative username and password.

- Complete the domain creation process.

3. Installing Oracle Fusion Middleware

a. Download Middleware Components:

- Visit the Oracle website and download the necessary middleware components.

- Extract the downloaded files to a suitable location.

b. Run the Installers:

- Execute the installers for each middleware component.

- Follow the installation wizard and provide necessary inputs.

- Specify the installation directory and complete the installation.

c. Configure Middleware Components:

- Use the Fusion Middleware Configuration Wizard to configure each component.

- Integrate the middleware components with the WebLogic Server domain.

- Ensure all services are running and properly configured.

4. Installing Oracle ERP Applications

a. Download Application Files:

- Access the Oracle Software Delivery Cloud and download the Oracle ERP application files.

- Extract the downloaded files to a suitable location on the server.

b. Run the Installer:

- Navigate to the extracted directory and execute the installation script.

- Follow the installation wizard, providing necessary inputs.

- Specify the installation directory, database connection details, and administrative credentials.

- Complete the installation process.

c. Select Modules:

- Choose the Oracle ERP modules you want to install, such as Financial Management, Supply Chain Management, and Human Capital Management.

- Ensure you select only the modules you need to optimize system performance.

5. Post-Installation Configuration

a. Apply Patches:

- Use Oracle's patch management tools to download and apply the latest patches.

- Ensure your system is up-to-date with all necessary patches.

b. Initial Configuration:

- Perform initial configuration tasks such as setting up users, roles, and permissions.

- Define business units and configure organizational structures.

- Use the Oracle ERP Configuration Assistant to streamline the process.

c. System Testing:

- Conduct thorough testing of the installed Oracle ERP system.

- Test all modules and functionalities to ensure they are working as expected.

- Identify and resolve any issues that arise during testing.

Conclusion

Installing Oracle ERP is a detailed and meticulous process that requires careful planning, execution, and testing. By following the steps outlined in this guide, you can ensure a successful installation that sets the foundation for effective use of Oracle ERP in your organization. Remember to always refer to the latest Oracle documentation and support resources for additional guidance and updates during the installation process.

2.2.2 Initial Configuration

Introduction

After successfully installing Oracle ERP, the next critical step is the initial configuration. This phase is pivotal as it sets the foundation for how your ERP system will operate, ensuring it aligns with your business processes and requirements. Proper initial configuration guarantees that the system is tailored to support your organization's goals, enhance productivity, and optimize operations.

System Initialization

1. Setting Up the System Administrator

The first step in the initial configuration is setting up the system administrator. The system administrator plays a vital role in managing and maintaining the ERP system. This user has full access to all functions and modules within Oracle ERP and is responsible for setting up other users, configuring modules, and maintaining system security.

Steps:

1. Log in with the default system administrator credentials provided during installation.

2. Navigate to the "User Management" module.

3. Create a new user account for the system administrator.

4. Assign appropriate roles and responsibilities to this account to ensure it has full system access.

5. Update the password for security purposes.

2. Configuring Global System Settings

Global system settings influence the behavior of the entire ERP system. These settings include defining currencies, setting up fiscal calendars, and configuring company profiles.

Steps:

1. Define Currencies: Navigate to the "Financials" module. Select "Currencies" and define the base currency and any additional currencies your business will use.

2. Set Up Fiscal Calendars: In the "Financials" module, access the "Fiscal Calendars" section. Define the fiscal year, periods, and any adjustments required for your business cycle.

3. Configure Company Profile: Go to "System Settings" and input your company's information, such as name, address, contact details, and logo.

3. Security and Access Controls

Security is paramount in any ERP system. Oracle ERP allows detailed configuration of security settings to ensure data integrity and protection.

Steps:

1. Define User Roles: In the "User Management" module, create roles that reflect the different job functions within your organization (e.g., Finance Manager, HR Specialist, Inventory Clerk).

2. Assign Permissions: Assign appropriate permissions to each role, ensuring users have access only to the functionalities required for their job.

3. Set Up User Accounts: Create user accounts and assign them to the predefined roles. Ensure that strong passwords and password policies are enforced.

Configuring Core Modules

1. Financial Management Module

The Financial Management module is crucial as it handles the organization's financial operations, including general ledger, accounts payable, and accounts receivable.

Steps:

1. Chart of Accounts: Navigate to the "General Ledger" section. Define your chart of accounts, including account types, account numbers, and descriptions.

2. Bank Accounts: Set up your organization's bank accounts within the "Cash Management" section. Define account numbers, bank names, and routing information.

3. Tax Codes: Configure tax codes and rates relevant to your business operations. This setup is typically found in the "Tax Management" section.

2. Supply Chain Management Module

This module covers procurement, inventory, and order management processes.

Steps:

1. Procurement Configuration: In the "Procurement" section, set up supplier information, purchasing policies, and approval workflows.

2. Inventory Settings: Access the "Inventory" section. Define inventory locations, categories, and valuation methods.

3. Order Management: Configure order processing rules, pricing policies, and shipping methods within the "Order Management" section.

3. Human Capital Management Module

The Human Capital Management module helps manage employee information, payroll, and benefits.

Steps:

1. Employee Records: Navigate to the "Employee Management" section. Enter employee details such as personal information, job titles, and department assignments.

2. Payroll Configuration: In the "Payroll" section, set up payroll calendars, salary structures, and tax deductions.

3. Benefits Administration: Configure employee benefits, including health insurance, retirement plans, and other perks, in the "Benefits Management" section.

Customizing User Interface

1. Dashboard Configuration

Oracle ERP provides customizable dashboards that offer users quick access to critical information and tasks.

Steps:

1. Create Custom Dashboards: In the "Dashboard" section, design dashboards tailored to different roles. Add widgets and reports relevant to each user group.

2. Set Default Dashboards: Assign default dashboards to user roles, ensuring that each user sees the most relevant information upon logging in.

2. Personalizing Navigation

Personalizing the navigation improves user efficiency by providing quick access to frequently used functions.

Steps:

1. Favorites Menu: Encourage users to add frequently accessed modules and reports to their "Favorites" menu for easy navigation.

2. Shortcuts: Set up keyboard shortcuts for commonly used actions to speed up workflow processes.

3. Menu Layout: Customize the layout of the navigation menu to reflect the structure of your organization and the needs of its users.

Data Migration and Import

1. Preparing Data for Import

Data migration is a critical step in setting up your ERP system. Ensuring that your data is clean and accurately formatted before import is essential.

Steps:

1. Data Cleansing: Review existing data for accuracy and completeness. Remove duplicates and correct errors.

2. Data Mapping: Map your existing data fields to the corresponding fields in Oracle ERP. This step ensures that all data is correctly imported.

2. Importing Data

Oracle ERP provides tools for importing data from various sources, including spreadsheets and legacy systems.

Steps:

1. Use Data Import Tools: Access the "Data Management" module. Utilize import tools to upload data files.

2. Validate Data: After importing, run validation checks to ensure data integrity. Correct any issues identified during this process.

Testing and Validation

1. System Testing

Thorough testing is essential to ensure that the ERP system operates as expected and meets business requirements.

Steps:

1. Unit Testing: Test individual components of the ERP system to verify their functionality.

2. Integration Testing: Ensure that different modules and components work together seamlessly.

3. User Acceptance Testing (UAT): Conduct UAT with a group of end-users to validate that the system meets their needs and performs as expected.

2. Issue Resolution

During testing, you may encounter issues that need resolution before going live.

Steps:

1. Log Issues: Document any problems encountered during testing.

2. Prioritize and Resolve: Prioritize issues based on their impact on business operations. Work with your ERP support team to resolve these issues promptly.

3. Retest: After resolving issues, retest the affected areas to ensure they function correctly.

Training and Documentation

1. User Training

Proper training is crucial to ensure that users can effectively utilize the ERP system.

Steps:

1. Develop Training Materials: Create comprehensive training materials, including user guides, video tutorials, and hands-on exercises.

2. Conduct Training Sessions: Schedule training sessions for different user groups. Ensure that these sessions cover all aspects of the system relevant to each group.

3. Provide Ongoing Support: Establish a support system to assist users as they begin using the new ERP system.

2. System Documentation

Documenting your ERP configuration and processes is essential for future reference and troubleshooting.

Steps:

1. Create Configuration Documentation: Document all system settings, configurations, and customizations. Include screenshots and detailed descriptions.

2. Develop Process Documentation: Document key business processes and how they are implemented within the ERP system. This documentation should be accessible to all users.

3. Maintain Documentation: Regularly update documentation to reflect any changes or updates to the ERP system.

Go-Live Preparation

1. Final Checks

Before going live, conduct final checks to ensure everything is in place for a smooth transition.

Steps:

1. Review System Configuration: Double-check all configurations and settings to ensure accuracy.

2. Verify Data Integrity: Conduct final data validation to ensure all data is correctly imported and accurate.

3. Test Critical Processes: Run through critical business processes to ensure they function correctly in the live environment.

2. Go-Live Plan

Having a detailed go-live plan is essential to ensure a smooth transition.

Steps:

1. Create a Go-Live Checklist: Develop a checklist of tasks to be completed before, during, and after go-live.

2. Assign Responsibilities: Assign responsibilities to team members for each task on the go-live checklist.

3. Communicate with Stakeholders: Keep all stakeholders informed about the go-live plan and any potential impacts on business operations.

3. Post-Go-Live Support

After going live, provide ongoing support to ensure a smooth transition and address any issues that arise.

Steps:

1. Monitor System Performance: Regularly monitor system performance and address any issues promptly.

2. Provide User Support: Offer support to users as they adapt to the new system. This support can include a helpdesk, FAQs, and additional training sessions.

3. Collect Feedback: Gather feedback from users to identify any areas for improvement. Use this feedback to make necessary adjustments to the system.

Conclusion

The initial configuration of Oracle ERP is a critical step in ensuring the system meets your business needs and operates efficiently. By following these steps, you can set up a robust and effective ERP system that supports your organization's goals and enhances overall productivity. Proper planning, thorough testing, comprehensive training, and ongoing support are essential components of a successful ERP implementation.

2.3 User Interface Overview

2.3.1 Navigation Basics

Navigating through Oracle ERP is fundamental to leveraging its full potential. Understanding the navigation basics is crucial for users to interact effectively with the system, perform tasks efficiently, and minimize errors. This section will guide you through the primary components of the Oracle ERP interface, essential navigation techniques, and tips for efficient use.

Understanding the Main Dashboard

When you first log into Oracle ERP, you are greeted by the main dashboard. This dashboard serves as the central hub from which you can access various modules, tasks, and reports. The layout typically includes:

- Navigation Menu: Found on the left-hand side, this menu provides quick access to different modules such as Financials, Procurement, Inventory, and more. The menu is usually collapsible, allowing you to maximize your workspace.

- Task Panel: This panel displays the tasks that are relevant to your role and responsibilities. It helps you quickly navigate to commonly used functions without having to dig through multiple menus.

- Notifications and Alerts: Positioned at the top right, this section keeps you informed about important updates, approvals, and other notifications that require your attention.

- Search Bar: A powerful tool that allows you to search for specific records, transactions, or reports within the ERP system.

- User Profile: Located in the top right corner, this area provides access to user settings, preferences, and logout options.

Navigating Modules and Submodules

Oracle ERP is organized into modules, each covering a specific area of business operations. Within each module, there are submodules that break down the functionalities further. Here's how to navigate these:

- Accessing Modules: From the navigation menu, click on the desired module. For example, to manage financial transactions, you would click on the "Financials" module.

- Exploring Submodules: Once inside a module, the navigation menu will expand to show submodules. For instance, within the Financials module, you might see submodules like General Ledger, Accounts Payable, and Accounts Receivable.

- Using Breadcrumbs: Breadcrumbs are displayed at the top of the screen, showing your current location within the ERP. They allow you to backtrack easily by clicking on any of the previous steps.

Working with Forms and Fields

Forms are integral to Oracle ERP as they are used to enter and manage data. Here are some key points to understand:

- Mandatory Fields: These fields are marked with an asterisk () and must be filled out to proceed. Missing these will trigger error messages.

- Dropdown Menus: Many fields provide dropdown menus with predefined options, ensuring data consistency and reducing entry errors.

- Date Pickers: Date fields often come with a date picker tool that allows you to select dates from a calendar view.

- Validation and Error Messages: As you fill out forms, the system performs real-time validation. Error messages guide you to correct mistakes before submission.

Performing Common Actions

Several common actions are repeatedly performed within Oracle ERP. Mastering these will enhance your efficiency:

- Creating Records: To create a new record, navigate to the relevant module and submodule, then click on the "Create" or "New" button. Follow the prompts to fill out the necessary information and save the record.

- Editing Records: To edit an existing record, use the search bar or navigation menu to locate the record. Open it, make the necessary changes, and save.

- Deleting Records: Deleting is usually restricted to prevent data loss. If permitted, locate the record, open it, and select the "Delete" option. Confirm the deletion when prompted.

- Running Reports: Navigate to the reporting section of the relevant module, select the report type, set your parameters, and run the report. Reports can often be exported in various formats such as PDF, Excel, or CSV.

Utilizing Shortcuts and Hotkeys

Oracle ERP provides several shortcuts and hotkeys to streamline navigation and task completion:

- Keyboard Shortcuts: Familiarize yourself with common shortcuts such as Ctrl+S to save, Ctrl+F to find, and Tab to navigate between fields.

- Quick Access Toolbar: Customize this toolbar with frequently used commands for one-click access.

- Favorites: Mark frequently accessed records or reports as favorites for easy retrieval from the main dashboard.

Personalizing the Interface

Customization options allow you to tailor the Oracle ERP interface to your preferences:

- Themes and Layouts: Choose from different themes and layouts to enhance visual comfort and usability.

- Dashboards: Customize your dashboard by adding widgets, reports, and links that are relevant to your role.

- Saved Searches: Save common search criteria to avoid repetitive data entry.

Tips for Efficient Navigation

- Regular Training: Regularly attend training sessions and webinars to stay updated on new features and best practices.

- Help and Documentation: Utilize the in-built help and documentation for step-by-step guidance on various functions.

- Collaboration: Collaborate with colleagues and share tips and shortcuts that enhance efficiency.

- Feedback: Provide feedback to administrators about interface improvements or additional training needs.

Understanding and mastering the navigation basics in Oracle ERP sets the foundation for effective use of the system. With these skills, you can quickly access the information you need, perform tasks efficiently, and leverage the full capabilities of Oracle ERP to unlock business potential.

2.3.2 Customizing the Interface

Customizing the interface in Oracle ERP allows users to tailor the system to better meet their specific needs and preferences. This can improve usability, enhance efficiency, and ensure that the ERP system aligns with the unique workflows of the organization. Customization can range from simple adjustments like changing display settings to more complex modifications such as creating custom dashboards or reports.

Understanding the Importance of Customization

Customization plays a crucial role in maximizing the effectiveness of Oracle ERP. Each organization has unique requirements, and a one-size-fits-all approach may not be sufficient. By customizing the interface, users can create a more intuitive and streamlined experience, reduce the learning curve, and ensure that the most relevant information is readily accessible.

Basic Customization Options

Oracle ERP offers a variety of basic customization options that can be easily implemented by users without advanced technical knowledge. These options include:

1. Personalizing Homepages:

   - Users can personalize their homepages to display frequently used modules and reports. This helps in quick navigation and improves productivity.

   - Steps to personalize:

   1. Navigate to the homepage settings.

   2. Select the modules or widgets to display.

   3. Arrange them in the preferred order.

2. Adjusting Display Settings:

   - Display settings such as theme, font size, and color schemes can be customized to improve readability and reduce eye strain.

   - Steps to adjust display settings:

   1. Go to the user settings menu.

   2. Select display options.

   3. Choose the desired theme, font size, and color scheme.

3. Creating Shortcuts:

   - Users can create shortcuts to frequently accessed functions or reports. This reduces the time spent navigating through multiple menus.

   - Steps to create shortcuts:

   1. Identify the frequently accessed function.

   2. Add it to the shortcuts menu.

   3. Access it directly from the shortcuts menu in the future.

Advanced Customization Options

For users with more advanced technical knowledge or those working closely with IT professionals, Oracle ERP offers several advanced customization options. These include:

1. Custom Dashboards:

 - Custom dashboards allow users to consolidate relevant data and key performance indicators (KPIs) into a single view. This provides a quick overview of important metrics and supports better decision-making.

 - Steps to create a custom dashboard:

   1. Access the dashboard creation tool.

   2. Select the data sources and KPIs to include.

   3. Arrange the components in a visually appealing layout.

   4. Save and publish the dashboard.

2. Personalized Reports:

 - Users can design personalized reports to meet specific reporting requirements. This involves selecting relevant data fields, applying filters, and defining the report layout.

 - Steps to create a personalized report:

   1. Open the report builder tool.

   2. Choose the data fields to include in the report.

   3. Apply filters to refine the data.

   4. Define the layout and format of the report.

   5. Save and schedule the report for regular updates.

3. Custom Forms:

 - Custom forms can be created to capture specific data inputs that are not covered by standard forms. This ensures that all necessary information is collected accurately.

 - Steps to create a custom form:

1. Access the form creation tool.

2. Define the fields and data types required.

3. Arrange the fields in a logical order.

4. Validate and save the form for use.

4. Workflow Automation:

- Workflow automation enables users to streamline business processes by defining automated workflows. This reduces manual effort and ensures consistency in task execution.

- Steps to automate workflows:

1. Identify the business process to automate.

2. Define the workflow steps and conditions.

3. Configure the automation rules.

4. Test and deploy the automated workflow.

Customizing Navigation

Customizing navigation within Oracle ERP enhances the user experience by making it easier to find and access essential functions. This includes:

1. Modifying Menu Structures:

- Users can modify menu structures to group related functions together, reducing the time spent searching for specific options.

- Steps to modify menu structures:

1. Access the menu customization settings.

2. Drag and drop functions to the desired menu group.

3. Save the modified menu structure.

2. Creating Custom Menus:

- Custom menus can be created to provide quick access to frequently used functions, tailored to the user's role or department.

  - Steps to create a custom menu:

    1. Define the functions to include in the custom menu.

    2. Group them logically.

    3. Save and assign the custom menu to specific user roles.

User Roles and Permissions

Effective customization also involves managing user roles and permissions. This ensures that users have access to the functions they need while maintaining security and control over sensitive data.

1. Defining User Roles:

  - User roles define the permissions and access levels for different users within the organization. Properly defined roles ensure that users only access the functions relevant to their responsibilities.

  - Steps to define user roles:

    1. Identify the roles required within the organization.

    2. Define the permissions for each role.

    3. Assign roles to users based on their job functions.

2. Managing Permissions:

  - Permissions control the actions that users can perform within the ERP system. Fine-tuning permissions helps prevent unauthorized access and actions.

  - Steps to manage permissions:

    1. Review the default permissions for each role.

    2. Modify permissions as necessary to align with organizational policies.

    3. Regularly review and update permissions to ensure ongoing security.

Customization Best Practices

To ensure successful customization of the Oracle ERP interface, consider the following best practices:

1. Start with Standard Options:

   - Before implementing complex customizations, explore the standard options available within Oracle ERP. These options often meet many customization needs without requiring significant effort.

2. Involve Key Stakeholders:

   - Engage key stakeholders from different departments in the customization process. Their input ensures that the customizations meet the needs of all users and align with business objectives.

3. Document Customizations:

   - Documenting customizations helps maintain a clear record of changes made to the system. This is particularly important for troubleshooting, training, and future upgrades.

   - Steps to document customizations:

     1. Record the purpose and scope of each customization.

     2. Note the steps taken to implement the customization.

     3. Store the documentation in a central repository for easy access.

4. Test Thoroughly:

   - Thoroughly test all customizations in a controlled environment before deploying them to the live system. This helps identify and resolve any issues that may arise.

   - Steps to test customizations:

     1. Implement the customization in a test environment.

     2. Perform comprehensive testing to ensure functionality.

     3. Solicit feedback from end-users and make necessary adjustments.

5. Plan for Future Changes:

- Customizations should be designed with future changes in mind. This includes considering potential system upgrades and how customizations will be maintained over time.

   - Steps to plan for future changes:

      1. Keep customizations modular and well-documented.

      2. Regularly review and update customizations to align with system updates.

      3. Plan for periodic reviews to ensure customizations remain relevant.

Training and Support

Providing training and support for users is crucial to ensure they can effectively utilize the customized interface. Consider the following:

1. User Training:

   - Conduct training sessions to familiarize users with the customized interface. This helps them understand the changes and how to leverage the new features effectively.

   - Steps for user training:

      1. Develop training materials tailored to the customizations.

      2. Schedule training sessions for different user groups.

      3. Provide hands-on training and practice sessions.

2. Ongoing Support:

   - Establish a support system to address user queries and issues related to the customized interface. This ensures users can quickly resolve problems and continue working efficiently.

   - Steps to provide ongoing support:

      1. Set up a helpdesk or support team.

      2. Create a knowledge base with FAQs and troubleshooting guides.

3. Encourage users to provide feedback and report issues.

Conclusion

Customizing the interface in Oracle ERP is a powerful way to enhance the system's usability and align it with the specific needs of the organization. By understanding the available customization options, involving key stakeholders, and following best practices, organizations can create a tailored ERP experience that improves efficiency, supports business processes, and ultimately contributes to achieving strategic goals.

Regular review and updates, thorough testing, and providing adequate training and support are essential to ensure the customizations deliver the desired benefits and continue to meet the evolving needs of the organization.

CHAPTER III
Financial Management in Oracle ERP

3.1 General Ledger

3.1.1 Chart of Accounts

The Chart of Accounts (CoA) is the foundation of the financial structure within Oracle ERP. It provides a systematic way to organize and record financial transactions. The CoA is a list of all accounts used by an organization to define each class of items for which money or its equivalent is spent or received. These accounts are essential for reporting and analysis and must be carefully planned and maintained.

Understanding the Chart of Accounts

A well-structured CoA is crucial for accurate financial reporting and efficient business operations. It typically consists of the following components:

- Account Number: A unique identifier for each account, which helps in easy tracking and reporting.

- Account Name: A descriptive title of the account to ensure clarity and understanding.

- Account Type: This categorizes the account into assets, liabilities, equity, revenue, and expenses.

- Account Description: A detailed explanation of what the account represents.

The structure and format of the CoA can vary depending on the size and complexity of the organization. However, the primary goal remains the same: to provide a clear and consistent framework for recording financial transactions.

Creating a Chart of Accounts

Creating a CoA in Oracle ERP involves several steps:

1. Planning the Structure:

  - Determine the levels of detail needed for reporting and analysis.

  - Decide on the account numbering system, ensuring it is flexible enough to accommodate future growth.

  - Identify the primary segments that will make up your accounts (e.g., department, cost center, project).

2. Defining Segments:

  - In Oracle ERP, segments are parts of the account code that provide additional detail and dimensions for reporting. Typical segments include Company, Department, Account, Sub-account, and Project.

  - Each segment should have a clear purpose and should be consistent across the organization.

3. Setting Up the Account Hierarchy:

  - Define parent and child relationships among accounts to create a hierarchical structure. This helps in consolidating and reporting financial data at various levels.

- For example, you might have a parent account for "Office Expenses" with child accounts for "Office Supplies," "Utilities," and "Rent."

4. Entering Accounts into Oracle ERP:

  - Navigate to the General Ledger module in Oracle ERP.

  - Go to the CoA setup section and start entering the details for each account.

  - Ensure each account is assigned the correct segment values and is placed in the appropriate hierarchy.

5. Validating the CoA:

  - After entering all the accounts, validate the CoA to ensure there are no errors or inconsistencies.

  - Run test reports to check if the CoA structure meets the reporting requirements.

Best Practices for Chart of Accounts

To ensure the effectiveness and efficiency of your CoA, consider the following best practices:

- Consistency: Use a consistent naming convention and account numbering system throughout the CoA. This helps in maintaining clarity and ease of use.

- Scalability: Design the CoA with future growth in mind. Ensure there is enough flexibility to add new accounts and segments as the business evolves.

- Simplicity: Avoid over-complicating the CoA with too many segments or overly detailed account descriptions. Strive for a balance between detail and simplicity.

- Regular Review: Periodically review and update the CoA to reflect changes in the business environment and financial reporting requirements.

- User Training: Provide training for users who will interact with the CoA to ensure they understand its structure and how to use it effectively.

Implementing Chart of Accounts in Oracle ERP

Implementing the CoA in Oracle ERP requires a strategic approach to ensure it aligns with your business processes and reporting needs. Here's a step-by-step guide to implementing the CoA in Oracle ERP:

1. Define the Requirements:

   - Engage with key stakeholders, including finance, accounting, and management, to gather requirements and understand their reporting needs.

   - Document these requirements to ensure they are addressed during the CoA setup.

2. Design the CoA Structure:

   - Based on the requirements, design the CoA structure. Determine the number of segments and the hierarchy levels needed.

   - Create a draft version of the CoA and review it with stakeholders to ensure it meets their needs.

3. Configure Segments and Values:

   - In Oracle ERP, navigate to the General Ledger module and access the CoA setup section.

   - Define each segment, including its name, length, and values. For example, if you have a "Department" segment, list all the department codes and names.

   - Configure the segment value sets, which define the valid values for each segment.

4. Create Account Combinations:

   - Once the segments and values are defined, create account combinations. These are the valid combinations of segment values that form the complete account code.

   - For example, a combination might be "100-2000-300" where "100" is the company code, "2000" is the account code, and "300" is the department code.

5. Set Up Security Rules:

- Define security rules to control who can access and modify the CoA. This ensures that only authorized personnel can make changes, maintaining the integrity of the CoA.

- In Oracle ERP, navigate to the security rules section and configure the rules based on user roles and responsibilities.

6. Test the CoA Setup:

- Before going live, thoroughly test the CoA setup. Create test transactions and run financial reports to ensure the CoA functions as expected.

- Identify and resolve any issues that arise during testing to prevent problems during actual use.

7. Go Live and Monitor:

- Once testing is complete and any issues have been resolved, go live with the new CoA. Monitor its usage closely during the initial phase to ensure it meets all requirements.

- Provide support and training to users to help them transition smoothly to the new CoA.

Chart of Accounts Maintenance

Maintaining the CoA is an ongoing process. Regular maintenance ensures that the CoA remains accurate and relevant to the business. Key maintenance activities include:

- Periodic Reviews:

- Regularly review the CoA to ensure it continues to meet the organization's reporting needs. Adjust the structure as necessary to reflect changes in the business environment.

- Conduct annual reviews with key stakeholders to gather feedback and make improvements.

- Adding New Accounts:

- As the business grows, new accounts may need to be added to the CoA. Follow the established procedures to add new accounts and ensure they fit into the existing structure.

- Validate new accounts to ensure they are correctly configured and do not cause inconsistencies.

- Inactivating Obsolete Accounts:

- Over time, some accounts may become obsolete. Mark these accounts as inactive to prevent further use, but retain them in the system for historical reporting purposes.

- Ensure that inactivating accounts does not impact financial reporting or cause data loss.

- Ensuring Compliance:

- Ensure the CoA complies with accounting standards and regulatory requirements. Regularly review and update the CoA to reflect any changes in regulations.

- Engage with auditors to review the CoA and address any compliance issues.

Chart of Accounts Examples

To illustrate the concepts discussed, here are examples of CoA structures for different types of organizations:

Example 1: Small Business CoA

1000 - Cash

1010 - Accounts Receivable

1020 - Inventory

2000 - Accounts Payable

3000 - Sales Revenue

4000 - Cost of Goods Sold

5000 - Operating Expenses

Example 2: Manufacturing Company CoA

1000 - Assets

  1100 - Current Assets

    1110 - Cash

    1120 - Accounts Receivable

    1130 - Inventory

  1200 - Fixed Assets

    1210 - Equipment

    1220 - Buildings

2000 - Liabilities

  2100 - Current Liabilities

    2110 - Accounts Payable

    2120 - Short-Term Loans

  2200 - Long-Term Liabilities

    2210 - Long-Term Debt

3000 - Equity

  3100 - Common Stock

  3200 - Retained Earnings

4000 - Revenue

  4100 - Sales Revenue

  4200 - Service Revenue

5000 - Expenses

  5100 - Cost of Goods Sold

  5200 - Operating Expenses

   5210 - Salaries

   5220 - Rent

   5230 - Utilities

Example 3: Non-Profit Organization CoA

1000 - Assets

  1100 - Cash

  1200 - Grants Receivable

  1300 - Inventory

2000 - Liabilities

  2100 - Accounts Payable

  2200 - Deferred Revenue

3000 - Net Assets

  3100 - Unrestricted Net Assets

  3200 - Temporarily Restricted Net Assets

  3300 - Permanently Restricted Net Assets

4000 - Revenues

  4100 - Donations

  4200 - Grants

  4300 - Program Fees

5000 - Expenses

5100 - Program Expenses

    5110 - Salaries

    5120 - Supplies

5200 - Administrative Expenses

    5210 - Office Supplies

    5220 - Utilities

5300 - Fundraising Expenses

    5310 - Event Costs

    5320 - Advertising

These examples provide a basic framework that can be customized to fit the specific needs of any organization. The key is to ensure the CoA is well-organized, flexible, and aligned with the organization's reporting and operational requirements.

Conclusion

The Chart of Accounts is a critical component of financial management in Oracle ERP. A well-designed CoA provides the foundation for accurate financial reporting and effective decision-making. By following best practices and maintaining the CoA regularly, organizations can ensure they have a robust and flexible financial structure that supports their business goals. Whether you are setting up a new CoA or maintaining an existing one, careful planning and attention to detail are essential for success.

3.1.2 Journal Entries

Overview of Journal Entries

Journal entries are fundamental to any accounting system, serving as the primary method for recording all business transactions. In Oracle ERP, journal entries are used to record and track financial transactions across various accounts. This section will cover the following aspects of journal entries in Oracle ERP:

- Understanding Journal Entries

- Creating Journal Entries

- Types of Journal Entries

- Posting Journal Entries

- Reviewing and Approving Journal Entries

- Common Practices and Troubleshooting

Understanding Journal Entries

A journal entry typically consists of the following elements:

- Date: The date on which the transaction occurred.

- Description: A brief explanation of the transaction.

- Account: The specific ledger accounts that are affected by the transaction.

- Debit and Credit: The monetary amounts to be debited and credited to the respective accounts.

- Reference Number: A unique identifier for tracking the journal entry.

- Supporting Documentation: Attachments or references to documents that provide evidence of the transaction.

In Oracle ERP, journal entries ensure that every financial transaction is accurately recorded and maintained, facilitating seamless financial reporting and analysis.

Creating Journal Entries

To create a journal entry in Oracle ERP, follow these steps:

1. Navigate to the Journal Entries Page:

   - Log in to Oracle ERP.

   - Navigate to the General Ledger module.

   - Select the "Journals" option, followed by "Enter Journals".

2. Enter Journal Header Information:

   - Batch Name: Enter a name for the batch of journal entries.

   - Journal Name: Enter a name for the specific journal entry.

   - Ledger: Select the appropriate ledger for the entry.

   - Period: Select the accounting period in which the transaction occurred.

   - Currency: Choose the currency in which the transaction is denominated.

3. Enter Journal Lines:

   - Line Number: The system automatically generates this number.

   - Account: Select the ledger account to be debited or credited.

   - Debit or Credit: Enter the amount to be debited or credited.

   - Description: Provide a brief description of the transaction.

   - Reference: Enter any reference number or additional information.

4. Complete the Journal Entry:

   - After entering all necessary information, review the journal entry for accuracy.

   - Save the journal entry.

5. Post the Journal Entry:

   - Navigate to the "Post Journals" page.

- Select the journal entry batch.

- Click on the "Post" button to post the journal entry to the ledger.

Types of Journal Entries

Oracle ERP supports various types of journal entries to accommodate different business needs:

1. Manual Journal Entries: Created manually by users to record specific transactions.

2. Recurring Journal Entries: Used for transactions that occur regularly, such as monthly rent or utility expenses.

3. Reversing Journal Entries: Automatically reverses a journal entry in the following accounting period.

4. Auto-Reversing Journal Entries: Similar to reversing entries but scheduled to reverse automatically on a specific date.

5. Adjusting Journal Entries: Made at the end of an accounting period to adjust account balances before financial statements are prepared.

Posting Journal Entries

Posting journal entries is the process of updating the general ledger with the recorded transactions. This step is crucial as it ensures that the financial data is up-to-date and accurately reflects the company's financial position.

Steps to Post Journal Entries:

1. Review Journal Entries: Ensure that all journal entries are accurate and complete.

2. Navigate to Post Journals Page:

  - Go to the "General Ledger" module.

  - Select "Journals", then "Post Journals".

3. Select Journal Entries:

  - Choose the batch of journal entries to be posted.

  - Verify the details of each entry.

4. Post Journal Entries:

  - Click the "Post" button.

  - The system will update the ledger accounts and reflect the transactions.

Reviewing and Approving Journal Entries

Reviewing and approving journal entries is a critical control mechanism to ensure the accuracy and validity of financial transactions. Oracle ERP provides tools for managers and accountants to review and approve journal entries before they are posted.

Steps for Reviewing and Approving Journal Entries:

1. Access the Journal Approval Workflow:

  - Navigate to the "General Ledger" module.

  - Select "Journals", followed by "Journal Approval".

2. Review Journal Entries:

  - Open the journal entry batch.

  - Examine each entry for accuracy and completeness.

  - Verify the supporting documentation.

3. Approve or Reject Entries:

   - If the entries are accurate, click "Approve".

   - If there are issues, click "Reject" and provide feedback for corrections.

Common Practices and Troubleshooting

Effective journal entry management involves adhering to best practices and being prepared to troubleshoot common issues. Here are some tips and common troubleshooting steps:

Best Practices:

- Accuracy: Ensure that all data entered is accurate and complete.

- Supporting Documentation: Attach relevant documents to support the transaction.

- Segregation of Duties: Implement proper segregation of duties to prevent fraud and errors.

- Review and Approval: Regularly review and approve journal entries before posting.

Troubleshooting Common Issues:

- Unbalanced Journal Entries: Ensure that the total debits equal the total credits.

- Incorrect Account Codes: Verify that the correct ledger accounts are used.

- Missing Documentation: Attach all necessary supporting documents.

- Posting Errors: If an entry fails to post, review the error message and correct the issue.

Conclusion

Journal entries are the backbone of financial management in Oracle ERP. By understanding and mastering the process of creating, posting, reviewing, and approving journal entries, businesses can ensure accurate and reliable financial records. This section has provided a detailed guide to managing journal entries in Oracle ERP, equipping users with the knowledge needed to perform these tasks effectively.

3.2 Accounts Payable

Accounts Payable (AP) is a crucial module within Oracle ERP that handles the company's liabilities, ensuring that all vendor invoices are processed and paid accurately and on time. This section provides a comprehensive guide on how to manage the AP processes, starting with invoice processing.

3.2.1 Invoice Processing

Invoice processing is a critical function in the Accounts Payable module. It involves receiving, verifying, and recording supplier invoices, followed by the approval and payment process. This section will walk you through the steps required to effectively manage invoice processing in Oracle ERP.

1. Understanding the Invoice Processing Workflow

The invoice processing workflow typically includes the following steps:

1. Invoice Receipt

2. Invoice Validation

3. Invoice Approval

4. Invoice Payment

5. Invoice Accounting

Each of these steps is essential for ensuring that invoices are processed accurately and efficiently.

2. Invoice Receipt

The first step in the invoice processing workflow is receiving the invoice from the supplier. In Oracle ERP, invoices can be received through various channels:

- Manual Entry: Invoices can be manually entered into the system by AP clerks.

- Electronic Data Interchange (EDI): Invoices can be received electronically from suppliers.

- Scanning and OCR: Paper invoices can be scanned, and Optical Character Recognition (OCR) technology can be used to extract invoice data.

3. Invoice Entry

After receiving the invoice, the next step is to enter the invoice details into the Oracle ERP system. Here's how you can do it:

      1. Navigate to the Invoices Workbench:

- Go to the Oracle Payables responsibility.

- Navigate to Invoices > Entry > Invoices.

      2. Enter Invoice Header Information:

- Supplier Name: Select the supplier from whom the invoice was received.

- Invoice Number: Enter the unique invoice number provided by the supplier.

- Invoice Date: Enter the date on the invoice.

- Invoice Amount: Enter the total amount of the invoice.

- Invoice Type: Select the type of invoice (e.g., Standard, Credit Memo, Debit Memo).

      3. Enter Invoice Line Information:

- Line Type: Select the type of line (e.g., Item, Freight, Miscellaneous).

- Amount: Enter the amount for each line.

- Distribution: Assign the correct GL code for each line item.

      4. Save the Invoice: After entering all necessary information, save the invoice. This action will generate an invoice number in Oracle ERP.

4. Invoice Validation

Once the invoice is entered, it must be validated to ensure that all details are accurate and comply with the company's policies. Validation checks can include:

- Duplicate Invoice Check: Ensures the invoice has not been entered previously.

- PO Match: Verifies that the invoice matches the purchase order (if applicable).

- Tax Calculation: Ensures that the correct tax amount is applied.

- Accounting Distribution: Checks that all line items are correctly coded to the appropriate GL accounts.

To validate an invoice in Oracle ERP:

1. Navigate to the Invoices Workbench.

2. Query the Invoice: Use the search functionality to find the invoice that needs validation.

3. Validate the Invoice: Click on the 'Actions' button and select 'Validate'. The system will run the validation process and highlight any errors or issues.

5. Invoice Approval

After validation, the invoice may require approval before payment. Approval workflows can be configured in Oracle ERP to route the invoice to the appropriate approvers based on the amount, supplier, or other criteria.

1. Configure Approval Rules: Define the rules and conditions under which an invoice requires approval.

2. Approval Workflow: The system will automatically route the invoice to the designated approvers.

3. Approve or Reject: Approvers can review the invoice and either approve or reject it. If rejected, the invoice can be sent back to the initiator for corrections.

6. Invoice Payment

Once the invoice is validated and approved, it is ready for payment. Oracle ERP supports various payment methods, including checks, electronic funds transfer (EFT), and wire transfers.

 1. Create a Payment Batch:

  - Navigate to Payments > Entry > Payments.

  - Select 'Create Payment Batch' and enter the payment batch details (e.g., Payment Date, Bank Account, Payment Method).

 2. Select Invoices for Payment: The system will display a list of approved invoices. Select the invoices you wish to pay.

 3. Review and Submit the Payment Batch: Review the payment batch details and submit for processing.

 4. Generate Payments: The system will generate payments based on the selected method. For EFT and wire transfers, payment files will be created and sent to the bank.

7. Invoice Accounting

The final step in the invoice processing workflow is accounting for the invoice. This involves generating the necessary accounting entries in the General Ledger.

 1. Create Accounting Entries:

  - Navigate to Invoices > Entry > Accounting.

  - Select the invoice and click 'Create Accounting'.

 2. Review Accounting Entries: Review the generated accounting entries to ensure accuracy.

 3. Post to General Ledger: Once reviewed, post the accounting entries to the General Ledger.

8. Managing Invoice Holds and Releases

During the invoice validation process, some invoices might be placed on hold due to discrepancies or policy violations. Common types of holds include:

- Quantity Hold: The quantity invoiced exceeds the quantity received.

- Price Hold: The invoice price exceeds the purchase order price.

- Tax Hold: Incorrect tax amounts.

To manage holds:

1. Review Hold Details: Navigate to Invoices > Holds.

2. Resolve Issues: Investigate and resolve the issues causing the hold (e.g., match the invoice to the correct purchase order, correct tax amounts).

3. Release Hold: Once the issue is resolved, release the hold so the invoice can proceed through the workflow.

9. Reporting and Analytics

Oracle ERP provides robust reporting and analytics capabilities for Accounts Payable. Standard reports and custom queries can be used to monitor and analyze invoice processing performance.

1. Standard Reports:

- Aging Reports: Track overdue invoices and outstanding liabilities.

- Payment History: Review past payments and identify trends.

- Supplier Performance: Analyze supplier reliability and accuracy.

2. Custom Queries:

- Use Oracle's reporting tools (e.g., Oracle BI Publisher, SQL) to create custom reports tailored to your organization's needs.

10. Best Practices for Efficient Invoice Processing

Implementing best practices can help streamline the invoice processing workflow and improve efficiency:

1. Automate Invoice Capture: Use OCR and EDI to reduce manual data entry and errors.

2. Standardize Processes: Establish clear, standardized procedures for invoice entry, validation, and approval.

3. Implement Approval Workflows: Use automated approval workflows to speed up the approval process.

4. Regular Reconciliation: Conduct regular reconciliations to ensure that all invoices are accounted for and paid accurately.

5. Continuous Training: Provide ongoing training for AP staff to stay updated with system updates and process improvements.

11. Common Challenges and Solutions

Despite best efforts, organizations may encounter challenges in invoice processing. Some common challenges include:

1. Data Entry Errors: Mitigate by implementing automated data capture and validation rules.

2. Approval Delays: Address by optimizing approval workflows and setting clear approval thresholds.

3. Discrepancies: Reduce discrepancies by improving communication with suppliers and implementing robust matching rules.

4. Fraud Prevention: Implement controls such as segregation of duties, multi-factor authentication, and regular audits to prevent fraud.

By following these guidelines and utilizing the powerful features of Oracle ERP, organizations can achieve efficient and accurate invoice processing, ultimately improving their financial management and supplier relationships.

3.2.2 Payment Processing

Payment Processing is a crucial component of Accounts Payable (AP) in Oracle ERP. It involves the steps and procedures necessary to settle outstanding invoices with suppliers and vendors. Effective payment processing ensures that a business maintains good relationships with its suppliers, avoids late fees, and manages its cash flow efficiently. In this section, we will delve into the intricacies of payment processing within Oracle ERP, covering the end-to-end workflow, best practices, and practical tips for optimization.

Overview of Payment Processing

Payment processing in Oracle ERP involves several key steps:

1. Invoice Validation: Ensuring all supplier invoices are accurate and complete.

2. Payment Selection: Identifying which invoices are due for payment.

3. Payment Scheduling: Determining the timing of payments.

4. Payment Creation: Generating payment transactions.

5. Payment Approval: Approving the payments as per company policy.

6. Payment Execution: Disbursing funds to suppliers.

7. Payment Reconciliation: Matching payments with bank statements.

1. Invoice Validation

Before initiating payments, it is essential to validate the supplier invoices. Invoice validation ensures that all invoices are accurate, complete, and comply with the agreed-upon terms and conditions. In Oracle ERP, this process involves several checks:

- Verification of Invoice Details: Ensure that the invoice details, such as invoice number, date, amount, and supplier information, are correct.

- PO Matching: Match the invoice with the corresponding purchase order (PO) to verify that the goods or services were received as ordered.

- Three-Way Match: Compare the invoice with the purchase order and the receiving report to ensure consistency.

- Tax and Discount Calculations: Verify that the tax and discount calculations are correct as per the contractual agreement.

- Approval Workflow: Ensure that the invoice has gone through the necessary approval workflow and has been authorized for payment.

2. Payment Selection

Once the invoices are validated, the next step is to select which invoices should be paid. Oracle ERP provides a robust framework for payment selection based on several criteria:

- Due Date: Prioritize invoices that are nearing their due date to avoid late payment penalties.

- Discount Opportunities: Identify invoices that offer early payment discounts.

- Cash Flow Considerations: Consider the company's current cash flow situation and prioritize payments accordingly.

- Supplier Relationship: Prioritize payments to critical suppliers to maintain a good relationship.

In Oracle ERP, the Payment Selection process is typically managed through the Payment Process Request (PPR) feature, which allows users to specify selection criteria and generate a list of invoices to be paid.

3. Payment Scheduling

Payment scheduling involves determining the timing of payments. Effective payment scheduling can help optimize cash flow and take advantage of discounts offered by suppliers. In Oracle ERP, payment schedules can be created based on various parameters:

- Payment Terms: Define the payment terms for each supplier, such as Net 30, Net 60, or specific discount terms.

- Payment Date: Schedule payments based on the due date of invoices.

- Payment Frequency: Set up recurring payment schedules for regular suppliers.

- Batch Payments: Group multiple payments into batches to streamline processing and reduce transaction costs.

Oracle ERP's payment scheduling functionality allows for automated scheduling based on predefined rules, ensuring timely and accurate payments.

4. Payment Creation

Once the invoices are selected and scheduled for payment, the next step is to create the payment transactions. Oracle ERP offers various methods for creating payments, including checks, electronic funds transfers (EFT), and wire transfers. The payment creation process involves:

- Generating Payment Files: Create electronic payment files for EFT and wire transfers.

- Printing Checks: Generate and print checks for suppliers who prefer check payments.

- Payment Batch Processing: Process payments in batches to increase efficiency.

Oracle ERP provides templates and formats for various payment methods, ensuring compliance with banking and regulatory requirements.

5. Payment Approval

Before executing payments, it is important to go through an approval process to ensure that all payments are authorized. The approval process in Oracle ERP can be configured to include multiple levels of approval based on the payment amount, supplier, and other criteria. Key steps in the approval process include:

- Approval Hierarchies: Define approval hierarchies to route payments through the necessary approval levels.

- Notification and Alerts: Set up notifications and alerts to inform approvers of pending payments.

- Audit Trail: Maintain an audit trail of all approvals for compliance and auditing purposes.

The approval process helps mitigate the risk of fraudulent payments and ensures adherence to company policies.

6. Payment Execution

After the payments are approved, the next step is to execute the payments. Payment execution involves disbursing funds to the suppliers using the chosen payment method. In Oracle ERP, this process includes:

- EFT and Wire Transfers: Transmit electronic payment files to the bank for processing.

- Check Disbursement: Print and distribute checks to suppliers.

- Payment Confirmation: Receive confirmation from the bank that the payments have been processed.

Oracle ERP integrates with various banking systems to facilitate seamless payment execution, ensuring timely and accurate disbursement of funds.

7. Payment Reconciliation

The final step in the payment processing workflow is reconciliation. Payment reconciliation involves matching the payments recorded in Oracle ERP with the transactions on the bank statement. This step ensures that all payments have been processed correctly and helps identify any discrepancies. The reconciliation process includes:

- Bank Statement Import: Import bank statements into Oracle ERP for reconciliation.

- Matching Payments: Match the payments recorded in Oracle ERP with the transactions on the bank statement.

- Resolving Discrepancies: Investigate and resolve any discrepancies between the ERP records and the bank statement.

- Reconciliation Reports: Generate reconciliation reports to provide an overview of the reconciled and unreconciled transactions.

Oracle ERP provides tools for automated reconciliation, reducing the time and effort required for manual matching and ensuring accuracy.

Best Practices for Payment Processing

Implementing best practices in payment processing can help optimize the workflow, improve accuracy, and enhance efficiency. Here are some best practices to consider:

- Automate Where Possible: Use automation features in Oracle ERP to streamline payment processing, reduce manual effort, and minimize errors.

- Regularly Review Payment Terms: Regularly review and negotiate payment terms with suppliers to take advantage of discounts and improve cash flow.

- Maintain Accurate Supplier Information: Ensure that supplier information is accurate and up-to-date to avoid payment delays and errors.

- Implement Strong Approval Controls: Set up robust approval controls to prevent unauthorized payments and ensure compliance with company policies.

- Monitor Cash Flow: Continuously monitor cash flow to ensure that sufficient funds are available for scheduled payments and to optimize payment timing.

- Use Payment Analytics: Leverage payment analytics and reporting tools in Oracle ERP to gain insights into payment trends, identify opportunities for improvement, and make data-driven decisions.

Practical Tips for Optimization

Optimizing payment processing involves continuously seeking ways to improve efficiency and effectiveness. Here are some practical tips for optimizing payment processing in Oracle ERP:

- Leverage Electronic Payments: Wherever possible, use electronic payment methods such as EFT and wire transfers to speed up the payment process and reduce costs associated with printing and mailing checks.

- Set Up Payment Reminders: Use Oracle ERP's notification and alert features to set up payment reminders for due invoices, ensuring timely payments.

- Batch Payments Efficiently: Group payments into batches to process them more efficiently and reduce transaction costs.

- Reconcile Regularly: Perform regular reconciliation to promptly identify and resolve discrepancies, ensuring the accuracy of financial records.

- Train Staff: Provide training to staff on payment processing procedures, Oracle ERP functionalities, and best practices to enhance their skills and improve efficiency.

Conclusion

Effective payment processing is essential for managing Accounts Payable efficiently and maintaining good relationships with suppliers. Oracle ERP provides a comprehensive framework for managing the entire payment processing workflow, from invoice validation to payment reconciliation. By following best practices and optimizing the process, businesses can ensure timely and accurate payments, improve cash flow, and enhance operational efficiency.

In summary, payment processing in Oracle ERP is a multi-step process that requires careful planning, execution, and monitoring. By leveraging the powerful features of Oracle ERP and adhering to best practices, organizations can streamline their payment processing operations, minimize errors, and achieve better financial control.

3.3 Accounts Receivable

3.3.1 Customer Invoicing

Customer invoicing is a critical function within the Accounts Receivable (AR) module of Oracle ERP. It involves generating invoices for goods or services provided to customers, ensuring accurate billing, and maintaining records for financial reporting. This section will guide you through the entire process of customer invoicing in Oracle ERP, covering configuration, processing, and best practices.

Introduction to Customer Invoicing

Customer invoicing is the process of creating and issuing invoices to customers for the goods and services they have received. In Oracle ERP, this involves a series of steps that ensure the accuracy and efficiency of billing operations. Properly managed invoicing not only ensures timely payment but also helps maintain good customer relationships.

Configuring Invoicing Options

Before generating customer invoices, it is essential to configure the invoicing options in Oracle ERP. This setup ensures that invoices are created with the correct data and format.

Setting Up Invoicing Rules

1. Navigate to Receivables Manager:

   - Go to the Receivables Manager responsibility.

   - Select Setup > Transactions > Invoicing Rules.

2. Define Invoicing Rules:

   - Create invoicing rules based on your business requirements. Invoicing rules determine the timing and method of revenue recognition.

   - Examples of invoicing rules include:

- Bill in Advance: Revenue is recognized at the beginning of the invoicing period.

- Bill in Arrears: Revenue is recognized at the end of the invoicing period.

3. Save and Validate:

  - Save the newly created invoicing rules.

  - Validate to ensure they are correctly configured.

Configuring Payment Terms

Payment terms define the conditions under which invoices are paid. Setting up payment terms correctly ensures accurate due dates and helps manage cash flow.

1. Navigate to Payment Terms:

  - Go to Receivables Manager.

  - Select Setup > Transactions > Payment Terms.

2. Define Payment Terms:

  - Create payment terms with specific conditions, such as net 30, net 45, or cash on delivery.

  - Specify any discounts for early payment and penalties for late payment.

3. Save and Validate:

  - Save the payment terms and validate them for accuracy.

Creating Customer Invoices

Once the configuration is complete, you can start creating customer invoices. Oracle ERP provides several methods for creating invoices, including manual entry and automated processes.

Manual Invoice Entry

Manual invoice entry is useful for creating invoices on an ad-hoc basis or for specific customer transactions.

1. Navigate to Transactions:

   - Go to Receivables Manager.

   - Select Transactions > Transactions.

2. Enter Invoice Details:

   - Select the transaction type (e.g., Invoice).

   - Enter the customer information, including customer name, address, and contact details.

   - Input the invoice date and the payment terms.

3. Add Line Items:

   - Enter the details of the goods or services provided. This includes item description, quantity, unit price, and any applicable taxes.

   - Ensure the total amount is calculated correctly.

4. Review and Save:

   - Review the invoice for accuracy.

   - Save the invoice to generate a unique invoice number.

Automated Invoice Generation

For businesses with a high volume of transactions, automated invoice generation can significantly improve efficiency.

1. Set Up AutoInvoice Program:

   - Navigate to Receivables Manager.

   - Select Setup > Transactions > AutoInvoice.

2. Configure AutoInvoice:

   - Define the source of transaction data (e.g., Order Management).

   - Map the data fields to ensure correct import into the invoicing system.

3. Run AutoInvoice:

  - Schedule the AutoInvoice program to run at regular intervals.

  - Review the output for any errors or exceptions.

Managing Invoice Adjustments

In the real world, invoices may require adjustments due to errors, changes in customer orders, or other reasons. Oracle ERP allows for easy management of these adjustments.

Making Invoice Corrections

1. Navigate to Transactions:

  - Go to Receivables Manager.

  - Select Transactions > Transactions.

2. Find and Select Invoice:

  - Use the search function to find the invoice needing correction.

  - Select the invoice and open it for editing.

3. Edit Invoice Details:

  - Make the necessary corrections to the invoice, such as adjusting quantities, prices, or tax amounts.

  - Save the changes.

Applying Credit Memos

Credit memos are used to reduce the amount a customer owes, often due to returned goods or billing errors.

1. Create a Credit Memo:

  - Go to Receivables Manager.

  - Select Transactions > Transactions.

  - Choose Credit Memo as the transaction type.

2. Enter Credit Memo Details:

  - Enter the customer information and the reason for the credit.

  - Specify the amount to be credited.

3. Apply Credit Memo:

  - Link the credit memo to the original invoice.

  - Save and review the adjustments.

Monitoring and Reporting on Invoices

Effective monitoring and reporting are crucial for managing accounts receivable and ensuring timely collections.

Generating Invoice Reports

Oracle ERP offers various reporting tools to track invoice status and performance.

1. Access Reports:

  - Go to Receivables Manager.

  - Select Reports > Transactions.

2. Select Report Type:

  - Choose from standard reports such as Invoice Aging Report, Invoice Register, and Customer Balance Summary.

3. Run and Review Reports:

  - Customize the report parameters as needed.

  - Run the report and review the output for insights into invoicing performance.

Using Dashboards and Analytics

For a more dynamic view of your invoicing activities, Oracle ERP provides dashboards and analytics tools.

1. Access Dashboards:

- Navigate to the Receivables Manager Dashboard.

2. Customize Dashboard Views:

- Add widgets and graphs to track key metrics such as outstanding invoices, overdue payments, and collection rates.

3. Analyze Data:

- Use the dashboard to identify trends and areas for improvement in your invoicing process.

Best Practices for Customer Invoicing

To ensure an efficient and error-free invoicing process, consider the following best practices:

Standardize Invoicing Procedures

1. Develop Standard Operating Procedures (SOPs):

- Create detailed SOPs for the invoicing process, including step-by-step instructions and responsibilities.

- Ensure all team members are trained on these procedures.

2. Use Templates:

- Utilize standardized invoice templates to maintain consistency and reduce errors.

Ensure Data Accuracy

1. Regular Data Audits:

- Conduct regular audits of customer and transaction data to ensure accuracy and completeness.

- Correct any discrepancies promptly.

2. Automate Data Entry:

- Use automated systems and integrations to reduce manual data entry and minimize errors.

Improve Customer Communication

1. Clear and Timely Communication:

  - Send invoices promptly and ensure they are clear and easy to understand.

  - Communicate payment terms and deadlines clearly to avoid confusion.

2. Follow-Up on Overdue Invoices:

  - Implement a structured follow-up process for overdue invoices, including reminders and escalation procedures.

Monitor and Optimize Processes

1. Regular Performance Reviews:

  - Regularly review the performance of your invoicing process using reports and analytics.

  - Identify areas for improvement and implement changes as needed.

2. Stay Updated with Oracle ERP Enhancements:

  - Keep your Oracle ERP system updated with the latest features and enhancements to take advantage of new functionalities.

Conclusion

Customer invoicing is a vital component of the Accounts Receivable module in Oracle ERP. By configuring the system correctly, using automated processes, managing adjustments efficiently, and following best practices, you can ensure a smooth and effective invoicing process. This not only helps in maintaining accurate financial records but also improves cash flow and strengthens customer relationships.

3.3.2 Cash Receipts

Cash receipts processing is a crucial part of the Accounts Receivable (AR) function within Oracle ERP. It involves recording incoming payments from customers, ensuring that these payments are accurately applied to outstanding invoices, and maintaining up-to-date records of the company's receivables. This section provides a comprehensive guide to the steps, features, and best practices involved in managing cash receipts in Oracle ERP.

Understanding Cash Receipts

Cash receipts are payments received by a business from its customers. These payments can come in various forms, including checks, electronic funds transfers (EFTs), credit card payments, and cash. Efficient management of cash receipts is essential for maintaining healthy cash flow and accurate financial records.

Key Features of Cash Receipts in Oracle ERP

Oracle ERP provides several features to streamline the cash receipts process, including:

- Multiple Payment Methods: Support for various payment methods, including checks, EFTs, and credit card payments.

- Receipt Entry: Efficient data entry screens for recording cash receipts.

- Auto-Application: Automated matching and application of payments to outstanding invoices.

- Receipt Batching: Grouping of receipts into batches for easier management and reconciliation.

- Reconciliation: Tools for reconciling bank statements with recorded receipts.

- Reporting: Comprehensive reports to track and analyze cash receipts.

Steps to Process Cash Receipts

1. Receipt Creation

   - Navigation: Navigate to the Receivables module and select the Receipts entry screen.

   - Data Entry: Enter the details of the payment, including the customer name, payment amount, payment date, and payment method.

   - Reference Information: Enter any reference information such as invoice numbers or customer account numbers to facilitate the application of the payment.

2. Receipt Application

- Auto-Application: Use the auto-application feature to automatically match the payment to outstanding invoices based on reference information.

- Manual Application: For payments that cannot be auto-applied, manually select the invoices to apply the payment to. This involves reviewing the customer's account and selecting the appropriate invoices.

3. Receipt Batching

- Batch Creation: Group receipts into batches for easier management. This involves assigning receipts to a batch and providing batch details such as batch name, date, and total amount.

- Batch Approval: Submit the batch for approval. Depending on the organization's workflow, this may involve a review by a supervisor or manager.

4. Receipt Posting

- General Ledger Posting: Post the receipts to the General Ledger (GL) to update the financial records. This step ensures that the company's financial statements reflect the receipt of payments.

- Bank Reconciliation: Reconcile the recorded receipts with bank statements to ensure that all payments have been accurately recorded and deposited.

5. Reporting and Analysis

- Receipt Reports: Generate reports to review and analyze cash receipts. Key reports include the Cash Receipts Journal, which provides a detailed list of all receipts, and the Aging Report, which shows the status of outstanding invoices.

- Trend Analysis: Analyze trends in cash receipts to identify patterns and areas for improvement. This might involve reviewing payment methods, customer payment behaviors, and seasonal variations.

Best Practices for Managing Cash Receipts

1. Timely Processing

- Process cash receipts promptly to ensure accurate financial records and maintain healthy cash flow. Delayed processing can lead to discrepancies in financial statements and cash flow issues.

2. Accurate Data Entry

- Ensure accurate data entry by double-checking payment details and reference information. Errors in data entry can lead to misapplied payments and reconciliation issues.

3. Automation

- Utilize the automation features in Oracle ERP, such as auto-application and electronic data interchange (EDI), to streamline the cash receipts process. Automation reduces manual effort and the risk of errors.

4. Reconciliation

- Regularly reconcile cash receipts with bank statements to identify and resolve discrepancies. Reconciliation ensures that all payments have been accurately recorded and helps detect any potential issues early.

5. Customer Communication

- Maintain clear communication with customers regarding payment expectations and invoice details. Promptly address any customer inquiries or issues related to payments to ensure smooth cash flow.

6. Internal Controls

- Implement robust internal controls to prevent fraud and ensure the integrity of the cash receipts process. This includes segregating duties, conducting regular audits, and requiring approval for large transactions.

Example: Processing a Cash Receipt

Let's walk through an example of processing a cash receipt in Oracle ERP.

Scenario:

A customer, ABC Corporation, has sent a payment of $10,000 via check to settle outstanding invoices. The payment includes references to three invoice numbers: INV-1001 ($3,000), INV-1002 ($4,000), and INV-1003 ($3,000).

Step-by-Step Process:

1. Receipt Creation:

   - Navigate to the Receivables module and select the Receipts entry screen.

   - Enter the following details:

     - Customer Name: ABC Corporation

     - Payment Amount: $10,000

     - Payment Date: [Current Date]

     - Payment Method: Check

     - Check Number: [Check Number]

   - Enter reference information:

     - Invoice Numbers: INV-1001, INV-1002, INV-1003

2. Receipt Application:

   - Use the auto-application feature to match the payment to the referenced invoices.

   - Verify that the payment has been correctly applied to the following invoices:

     - INV-1001: $3,000

     - INV-1002: $4,000

     - INV-1003: $3,000

3. Receipt Batching:

- Create a batch for the receipt:

  - Batch Name: Batch-2024-06-28

  - Batch Date: [Current Date]

  - Total Amount: $10,000

- Add the receipt to the batch and submit for approval.

4. Receipt Posting:

  - Post the receipt to the General Ledger:

    - Navigate to the posting screen and select the batch Batch-2024-06-28.

    - Review the batch details and confirm posting.

  - Reconcile the receipt with the bank statement once the payment is deposited.

5. Reporting and Analysis:

  - Generate the Cash Receipts Journal to review the receipt details.

  - Review the Aging Report to ensure that the applied invoices are no longer outstanding.

Common Challenges and Solutions

1. Unapplied Cash Receipts:

  - Challenge: Sometimes, payments cannot be matched to specific invoices.

  - Solution: Place the payment in an unapplied receipts account and periodically review to apply the payment once the corresponding invoice is identified.

2. Discrepancies in Payment Amounts:

  - Challenge: The payment amount may not match the invoice amounts exactly due to partial payments or overpayments.

- Solution: Apply the partial payment to the invoice and follow up with the customer for the remaining balance. For overpayments, either apply the excess amount to future invoices or issue a refund.

3. Missing or Incorrect Reference Information:

- Challenge: Payments may arrive without proper reference information, making it difficult to apply them correctly.

- Solution: Reach out to the customer for clarification or use historical payment patterns to make an educated guess. Implement stricter guidelines for customers to include reference information with their payments.

4. Delayed Bank Deposits:

- Challenge: There may be delays in depositing checks, causing discrepancies between recorded receipts and bank statements.

- Solution: Implement a policy for timely deposit of checks and use EFT or other electronic payment methods to reduce delays.

5. Customer Disputes:

- Challenge: Customers may dispute invoices or payments, leading to delays in cash receipt application.

- Solution: Maintain clear records of all communications and promptly address any disputes. Establish a process for handling disputes efficiently.

Conclusion

Effective management of cash receipts is essential for maintaining accurate financial records and healthy cash flow. Oracle ERP provides robust tools and features to streamline the cash receipts process, from receipt creation and application to batching, posting, and reconciliation. By following best practices and leveraging automation, organizations can ensure timely and accurate processing of cash receipts, ultimately enhancing their financial management capabilities.

3.4 Fixed Assets

3.4.1 Asset Management

Asset management in Oracle ERP is a comprehensive process that involves tracking, managing, and accounting for fixed assets throughout their lifecycle, from acquisition to disposal. The Fixed Assets module in Oracle ERP facilitates the management of physical assets to ensure efficient utilization, compliance with financial regulations, and accurate financial reporting. This section will guide you through the essential steps and best practices for managing fixed assets in Oracle ERP.

Understanding Fixed Assets

Fixed assets are long-term tangible assets that a business owns and uses in its operations to generate income. Examples include buildings, machinery, vehicles, and office equipment. Proper management of these assets is crucial for maintaining operational efficiency, ensuring compliance with accounting standards, and optimizing financial performance.

Key Features of the Fixed Assets Module

- Asset Tracking: Maintain detailed records of all physical assets, including their location, condition, and usage.

- Depreciation Management: Automatically calculate depreciation using various methods to reflect the asset's declining value over time.

- Asset Transfers: Facilitate the movement of assets between different locations, departments, or entities.

- Retirement and Disposal: Manage the retirement or disposal of assets, ensuring accurate financial accounting and compliance with regulations.

- Integration with Other Modules: Seamlessly integrate with General Ledger, Accounts Payable, and other Oracle ERP modules for comprehensive financial management.

Setting Up Fixed Assets in Oracle ERP

1. Defining Asset Categories:

Asset categories are used to classify fixed assets for reporting and management purposes. Each category can have its own set of attributes, depreciation rules, and financial accounts. Common categories include machinery, vehicles, office equipment, and buildings.

  - Steps to Define Asset Categories:

  - Navigate to the Asset Categories setup screen.

  - Define the category name and description.

  - Assign the appropriate asset account, accumulated depreciation account, and expense account.

  - Specify the default depreciation method and life for the category.

2. Configuring Asset Books:

Asset books are used to manage the financial aspects of fixed assets, including depreciation calculations and financial reporting. Oracle ERP allows you to create multiple asset books to cater to different accounting standards, tax regulations, or internal reporting requirements.

  - Steps to Configure Asset Books:

  - Navigate to the Asset Books setup screen.

  - Define the book name and description.

  - Specify the calendar, currency, and depreciation conventions.

  - Assign the appropriate asset categories to the book.

3. Setting Up Depreciation Methods:

Depreciation methods determine how the value of an asset is expensed over time. Common methods include straight-line, declining balance, and sum-of-the-years-digits.

Oracle ERP provides flexibility to define and customize depreciation methods to meet your organization's needs.

- Steps to Set Up Depreciation Methods:

  - Navigate to the Depreciation Methods setup screen.

  - Define the method name and description.

  - Choose the calculation method (e.g., straight-line, declining balance).

  - Specify the parameters for the calculation, such as the rate and useful life.

Managing Fixed Assets Lifecycle

1. Asset Acquisition:

  Acquiring fixed assets involves adding new assets to the system, either through purchase, lease, or internal construction. The acquisition process ensures that all relevant information is recorded, and the asset is assigned to the correct category and book.

- Steps to Record Asset Acquisition:

  - Navigate to the Asset Acquisition screen.

  - Enter the asset details, such as name, description, category, and location.

  - Specify the acquisition date, cost, and vendor information.

  - Assign the asset to the appropriate asset book and category.

2. Asset Maintenance and Tracking:

  Ongoing maintenance and tracking of assets are essential to ensure their optimal performance and longevity. This includes scheduling regular maintenance, tracking asset movements, and updating asset records as needed.

- Steps to Track and Maintain Assets:

  - Use the Asset Maintenance module to schedule and record maintenance activities.

- Track asset movements using the Asset Transfer feature.

- Update asset details, such as location and condition, in the Asset Management screen.

3. Depreciation Processing:

Depreciation is the systematic allocation of the cost of an asset over its useful life. Oracle ERP automates the depreciation process, ensuring accurate calculations and financial reporting.

 - Steps to Process Depreciation:

  - Navigate to the Depreciation Run screen.

  - Select the asset book and period for which to run depreciation.

  - Review the depreciation projections and make any necessary adjustments.

  - Post the depreciation entries to the General Ledger.

4. Asset Transfers:

Assets may need to be transferred between different locations, departments, or entities within the organization. Properly recording these transfers ensures accurate asset tracking and financial reporting.

 - Steps to Transfer Assets:

  - Navigate to the Asset Transfer screen.

  - Select the asset to be transferred and specify the new location or department.

  - Enter the transfer date and any additional details.

  - Confirm and post the transfer.

5. Asset Retirement and Disposal:

Retiring or disposing of assets involves removing them from active use and recording the financial impact of their retirement. This process includes calculating any gains or losses on disposal and updating the asset records accordingly.

- Steps to Retire or Dispose of Assets:

  - Navigate to the Asset Retirement screen.

  - Select the asset to be retired and specify the retirement date.

  - Choose the retirement reason (e.g., sale, scrapping, donation).

  - Calculate any gains or losses on disposal and post the entries to the General Ledger.

Best Practices for Fixed Asset Management

1. Regularly Update Asset Records:

Keep asset records up-to-date by regularly reviewing and updating asset information. This includes recording new acquisitions, disposals, transfers, and maintenance activities.

2. Conduct Physical Inventories:

Periodically conduct physical inventories of fixed assets to verify their existence and condition. Reconcile physical counts with the records in the ERP system to identify and address discrepancies.

3. Implement Asset Tagging:

Use asset tags or barcodes to label and track assets. This helps streamline the process of locating and managing assets and reduces the risk of loss or theft.

4. Monitor Depreciation and Financial Impact:

Regularly monitor depreciation calculations and their impact on financial statements. Ensure that the chosen depreciation methods and rates are appropriate and reflect the actual usage and value of the assets.

5. Optimize Asset Utilization:

Analyze asset usage and performance to identify opportunities for improving utilization. This may involve reassigning underutilized assets, upgrading equipment, or disposing of obsolete assets.

Conclusion

Effective asset management is critical for optimizing the use of fixed assets, ensuring accurate financial reporting, and maintaining compliance with accounting standards. The Fixed Assets module in Oracle ERP provides a robust framework for managing the entire lifecycle of fixed assets, from acquisition to disposal. By following the guidelines and best practices outlined in this section, organizations can enhance their asset management processes, improve operational efficiency, and achieve better financial outcomes.

Understanding and implementing the comprehensive features of the Fixed Assets module in Oracle ERP will empower your organization to manage its fixed assets efficiently, reduce costs, and maximize asset utilization. Whether you are setting up new assets, tracking existing ones, or managing their depreciation and disposal, Oracle ERP offers the tools and flexibility needed to meet your asset management needs.

3.4.2 Depreciation Methods

Depreciation in Oracle ERP is a critical process that helps businesses manage the gradual reduction in value of their fixed assets over time. This section will guide you through the various depreciation methods available in Oracle ERP, their setup, and their application in financial management.

Understanding Depreciation

Depreciation is the accounting process of allocating the cost of tangible assets over their useful lives. This process allows businesses to match the expense of using the asset with the revenue it generates, ensuring accurate financial reporting. Oracle ERP supports several depreciation methods to cater to different business needs and regulatory requirements.

Depreciation Methods in Oracle ERP

Oracle ERP offers a variety of depreciation methods, including:

1. Straight-Line Depreciation

2. Declining Balance Depreciation

3. Sum-of-the-Years' Digits Depreciation

4. Units of Production Depreciation

Let's delve into each method in detail.

1. Straight-Line Depreciation

Straight-line depreciation is the simplest and most commonly used method. It spreads the cost of an asset evenly over its useful life.

Formula:

Depreciation Expense = [Cost of Asset - Salvage Value] / Useful Life

Example:

If a company purchases a machine for $10,000 with a salvage value of $1,000 and a useful life of 5 years, the annual depreciation expense would be:

Depreciation Expense = (10,000 - 1,000)/5 = $1,800

Setup in Oracle ERP:

1. Navigate to the Fixed Assets module.

2. Select the asset you wish to depreciate.

3. Choose the "Straight-Line" method from the depreciation methods list.

4. Enter the asset's cost, salvage value, and useful life.

5. Save the settings to apply the straight-line depreciation method.

2. Declining Balance Depreciation

The declining balance method accelerates depreciation, with higher expenses in the earlier years of an asset's life. This method is suitable for assets that lose value quickly.

Formula:

Depreciation Expense = Book Value at Beginning of Year / Depreciation Rate

The rate is often double the straight-line rate, known as the Double Declining Balance method.

Example:

For an asset costing $10,000 with a useful life of 5 years and using the double declining balance method:

Depreciation Rate 2/5 = 40%

First-year depreciation:

Depreciation Expense = 10,000 x 0.4 = $4,000

Setup in Oracle ERP:

1. Select the asset and choose the "Declining Balance" method.

2. Input the depreciation rate and other necessary values.

3. Confirm and save to apply the method.

3. Sum-of-the-Years' Digits Depreciation

This method accelerates depreciation by applying a decreasing fraction to the depreciable base each year.

Formula:

Depreciation Expense = (Cost of Asset - Salvage Value) x (Remaining Life /Sum of the Years' Digits)

Example:

For an asset costing $10,000 with a salvage value of $1,000 and a 5-year life:

Sum of the years' digits:

5 + 4 + 3 + 2 + 1 = 15

First-year fraction:

5 / 15

First-year depreciation:

(10,000 - 1,000) (5/15) = $3,000

Setup in Oracle ERP:

1. Choose the "Sum-of-the-Years' Digits" method.

2. Enter the cost, salvage value, and useful life.

3. Save the configuration.

4. Units of Production Depreciation

This method bases depreciation on the asset's usage, ideal for manufacturing equipment.

Formula:

Depreciation Expense = (Cost of Asset - Salvage Value) / (Total Units Expected to be Produced) Units Produced in Period

Example:

For a machine costing $10,000 with a salvage value of $1,000 and expected to produce 50,000 units:

Depreciation Expense per Unit = (10,000 - 1,000)/50,000 = $0.18

If 10,000 units are produced in a year:

Annual Depreciation Expense = 10,000 × 0.18 = $1,800

Setup in Oracle ERP:

1. Select "Units of Production" as the depreciation method.

2. Enter the total expected units and other relevant data.

3. Save to implement the method.

Depreciation Process in Oracle ERP

1. Asset Addition: Enter the asset details into the Fixed Assets module.

2. Depreciation Calculation: Oracle ERP automatically calculates depreciation based on the chosen method.

3. Depreciation Run: Schedule regular depreciation runs (monthly, quarterly, annually) to update asset values.

4. Journal Entries: Oracle ERP generates journal entries to record depreciation expenses in the General Ledger.

5. Review and Adjustments: Review depreciation reports and make necessary adjustments for accuracy.

Key Considerations

1. Regulatory Compliance: Ensure the chosen depreciation method complies with local accounting standards and regulations.

2. Asset Life Reassessment: Periodically review and reassess the useful life of assets to maintain accurate depreciation schedules.

3. Integration with Financial Modules: Depreciation impacts various financial statements. Ensure seamless integration with General Ledger, Accounts Payable, and other relevant modules.

4. Depreciation Reports: Utilize Oracle ERP's robust reporting tools to generate detailed depreciation reports for analysis and compliance purposes.

Practical Example

Scenario: A manufacturing company purchases a new piece of equipment for $50,000 with a salvage value of $5,000 and a useful life of 10 years. The company decides to use the straight-line method.

1. Setup:

  - Navigate to the Fixed Assets module.

  - Add the new equipment with the purchase price of $50,000.

  - Set the salvage value to $5,000 and useful life to 10 years.

  - Choose the "Straight-Line" depreciation method.

2. Depreciation Calculation:

Annual Depreciation Expense = (50,000 - 5,000)/10 = $4,500

3. Depreciation Run:

  - Schedule monthly depreciation runs.

  - Each month, Oracle ERP calculates:

4,500/12 = $375

- Oracle ERP updates the asset value and generates the necessary journal entries.

4. Journal Entries:

   - Oracle ERP posts a monthly journal entry:

   - Debit: Depreciation Expense $375

   - Credit: Accumulated Depreciation $375

5. Review and Reporting:

   - Generate monthly and annual depreciation reports.

   - Review asset values and ensure accuracy.

Advanced Depreciation Features

Oracle ERP offers advanced features to handle complex depreciation scenarios:

1. Mid-Month and Mid-Quarter Conventions: Customize depreciation calculations based on specific business conventions.

2. Depreciation Override: Manually adjust depreciation for unique situations.

3. Impairment Handling: Record asset impairments and adjust depreciation schedules accordingly.

4. Component Depreciation: Depreciate individual components of an asset separately for more accurate financial reporting.

Conclusion

Understanding and applying the appropriate depreciation methods in Oracle ERP is crucial for accurate financial management and compliance. By leveraging Oracle ERP's robust features, businesses can efficiently manage asset depreciation, ensuring precise financial reporting and optimal asset utilization.

This detailed section provides a comprehensive guide to the various depreciation methods available in Oracle ERP, their setup, and practical application. With this knowledge, users can effectively manage their fixed assets and maintain accurate financial records.

3.5 Cost Management

3.5.1 Standard Costing

Standard costing is a critical component of cost management in Oracle ERP, enabling organizations to maintain control over production costs, streamline their accounting processes, and improve decision-making through accurate cost data. This section will delve into the setup, management, and utilization of standard costing within Oracle ERP, offering detailed guidance on how to effectively implement and use this costing method.

Overview of Standard Costing

Standard costing involves setting predetermined costs for products or services, which are then compared to actual costs incurred during production. The variance between standard and actual costs provides valuable insights into production efficiency and cost control. Standard costing simplifies the process of inventory valuation and cost control by providing a consistent cost basis.

Key benefits of standard costing include:

- Improved Cost Control: By establishing standard costs, organizations can better monitor and manage deviations, enabling timely corrective actions.

- Simplified Inventory Valuation: Standard costs streamline the process of valuing inventory, as the same cost basis is used for similar products.

- Enhanced Decision Making: Variance analysis helps managers identify areas for improvement and make informed decisions based on cost performance.

Setting Up Standard Costing in Oracle ERP

To implement standard costing in Oracle ERP, follow these steps:

1. Define Cost Elements: Identify the various cost elements that will be included in the standard cost, such as materials, labor, and overhead. Cost elements should be detailed enough to provide meaningful insights but not so granular that they become difficult to manage.

2. Create Cost Categories: Group similar cost elements into cost categories. For example, direct materials, direct labor, and manufacturing overhead can be separate categories. This grouping helps in organizing and managing costs more effectively.

3. Set Standard Costs: Establish standard costs for each cost element within the defined categories. Standard costs can be based on historical data, industry benchmarks, or management expectations. Ensure that the standard costs are realistic and reflect the expected cost structure.

4. Define Cost Components: In Oracle ERP, cost components are used to define how cost elements are aggregated to form the total standard cost of a product. Set up cost components to represent each cost element and assign the relevant standard costs.

5. Configure Costing Methods: Oracle ERP supports multiple costing methods, such as standard costing, average costing, and FIFO. Ensure that the standard costing method is configured correctly in the system settings.

6. Assign Cost Types: Assign cost types to cost components to differentiate between fixed and variable costs. This classification helps in variance analysis and cost control.

7. Load Standard Costs: Load the standard costs into the system using Oracle ERP's standard cost update functionality. This step ensures that the system reflects the established standard costs for inventory valuation and cost management.

Managing Standard Costs

Once standard costs are set up, ongoing management is crucial to ensure accuracy and relevance. The following practices are essential for managing standard costs:

1. Periodic Review and Update: Regularly review and update standard costs to reflect changes in material prices, labor rates, and overhead costs. This ensures that standard costs remain accurate and useful for decision-making.

2. Variance Analysis: Perform regular variance analysis to compare standard costs with actual costs. Variances can be categorized into material variances, labor variances, and

overhead variances. Investigate significant variances to identify root causes and take corrective actions.

3. Cost Rollup: Periodically perform a cost rollup to aggregate individual cost components into the total standard cost of finished goods. This process ensures that any changes in component costs are accurately reflected in the overall product cost.

4. Reporting and Analysis: Utilize Oracle ERP's reporting and analysis tools to generate detailed cost reports. These reports provide insights into cost performance, variances, and trends, aiding in strategic decision-making.

5. Audit and Compliance: Ensure that standard costing processes comply with internal policies and external regulations. Regular audits of cost data and procedures help maintain accuracy and integrity.

Utilizing Standard Costing for Decision Making

Standard costing provides a wealth of data that can be leveraged for various decision-making processes:

1. Budgeting and Forecasting: Use standard costs as a basis for budgeting and forecasting. Accurate standard costs enable more reliable financial projections and resource planning.

2. Pricing Strategies: Determine product pricing strategies based on standard costs and desired profit margins. Understanding cost structures helps in setting competitive prices while maintaining profitability.

3. Performance Evaluation: Assess production efficiency and performance by analyzing cost variances. Identify areas where actual costs exceed standard costs and implement measures to improve efficiency.

4. Inventory Management: Optimize inventory levels by understanding the cost implications of holding and producing inventory. Standard costing aids in evaluating the cost-effectiveness of inventory policies.

5. Cost Reduction Initiatives: Identify opportunities for cost reduction by analyzing cost variances and trends. Implement targeted initiatives to reduce material waste, improve labor productivity, and optimize overhead costs.

Practical Example: Implementing Standard Costing in Oracle ERP

Consider a manufacturing company that produces electronic components. The company decides to implement standard costing to improve cost control and streamline inventory valuation. Here's how they go about it:

1. Define Cost Elements: The company identifies the following cost elements:

 - Direct materials: Raw materials used in production

 - Direct labor: Wages paid to production workers

 - Manufacturing overhead: Indirect costs such as utilities and depreciation

2. Create Cost Categories: The cost elements are grouped into three categories:

 - Direct Materials

 - Direct Labor

 - Manufacturing Overhead

3. Set Standard Costs: The company establishes the following standard costs based on historical data and industry benchmarks:

 - Direct materials: $5 per unit

 - Direct labor: $3 per hour

 - Manufacturing overhead: $2 per unit

4. Define Cost Components: Cost components are set up in Oracle ERP to represent each cost element, and the standard costs are assigned accordingly.

5. Configure Costing Methods: The standard costing method is selected in the system settings to ensure accurate inventory valuation and cost management.

6. Assign Cost Types: The company classifies direct materials and direct labor as variable costs, while manufacturing overhead is classified as a fixed cost.

7. Load Standard Costs: The standard costs are loaded into the system using Oracle ERP's standard cost update functionality.

Maintaining Standard Costs

The company implements the following practices to maintain and manage standard costs:

1. Periodic Review and Update: Standard costs are reviewed quarterly to reflect changes in raw material prices and labor rates. Adjustments are made as necessary to ensure accuracy.

2. Variance Analysis: Monthly variance analysis is conducted to compare standard costs with actual costs. Significant variances are investigated, and corrective actions are taken to address any issues.

3. Cost Rollup: A cost rollup is performed at the end of each month to aggregate individual cost components into the total standard cost of finished goods.

4. Reporting and Analysis: Detailed cost reports are generated using Oracle ERP's reporting tools, providing insights into cost performance and helping management make informed decisions.

5. Audit and Compliance: Regular audits are conducted to ensure compliance with internal policies and external regulations. Any discrepancies are addressed promptly.

Leveraging Standard Costing Data

The company uses standard costing data for various decision-making processes:

1. Budgeting and Forecasting: Standard costs serve as the basis for the annual budget and financial forecasts, enabling more accurate and reliable projections.

2. Pricing Strategies: Product pricing is determined based on standard costs and desired profit margins, ensuring competitiveness while maintaining profitability.

3. Performance Evaluation: Production efficiency is assessed through cost variance analysis, identifying areas for improvement and implementing measures to enhance performance.

4. Inventory Management: Inventory levels are optimized by evaluating the cost implications of holding and producing inventory, leading to more efficient inventory management.

5. Cost Reduction Initiatives: Cost variances and trends are analyzed to identify opportunities for cost reduction, such as reducing material waste and improving labor productivity.

Conclusion

Standard costing is an essential tool for cost management in Oracle ERP, providing a consistent and reliable basis for inventory valuation, cost control, and decision-making. By effectively setting up, managing, and utilizing standard costs, organizations can achieve better cost control, enhance operational efficiency, and make informed strategic decisions. Implementing the practices and strategies outlined in this section will help ensure that standard costing delivers maximum value to your organization.

3.5.2 Actual Costing

Actual costing is a crucial aspect of Oracle ERP's cost management module. It enables businesses to track and assign actual costs to products, services, and projects, providing a precise view of the financial performance. This section will delve into the intricacies of actual costing, including setup, data collection, cost calculation, and reporting.

Overview of Actual Costing

Actual costing, unlike standard costing, records the actual expenses incurred in producing goods or services. It captures real-time data, reflecting the true cost of materials, labor, and overheads. This method is particularly beneficial for industries with fluctuating costs, such as manufacturing and project-based industries.

Setting Up Actual Costing

1. Configuring Cost Elements:

 - Material Costs: Define the actual costs of raw materials. Ensure that purchase price variances are captured.

 - Labor Costs: Set up the actual labor rates based on payroll data.

 - Overhead Costs: Configure the overhead rates, which may include utilities, depreciation, and other indirect expenses.

2. Defining Cost Centers:

- Create Cost Centers: Group related expenses under specific cost centers, such as production, maintenance, and administration.

- Assign Resources: Allocate resources (labor, machines, etc.) to the appropriate cost centers.

3. Setting Up Cost Types and Subtypes:

  - Direct Costs: Identify direct costs, including materials and direct labor.

  - Indirect Costs: Classify indirect costs such as utilities, rent, and administrative expenses.

Data Collection for Actual Costing

1. Inventory Transactions:

  - Receiving Inventory: Capture the actual cost of materials received, including purchase price, taxes, and shipping.

  - Issuing Inventory: Track the actual cost of materials issued to production or projects.

2. Labor Transactions:

  - Timekeeping: Record actual labor hours worked, using timecards or timekeeping systems.

  - Payroll Integration: Ensure payroll data is integrated to reflect actual labor costs.

3. Overhead Allocation:

  - Cost Allocation Methods: Use methods such as activity-based costing (ABC) or traditional allocation methods to assign overhead costs accurately.

  - Data Integration: Integrate utility bills, maintenance expenses, and other overheads into the ERP system.

Calculating Actual Costs

1. Material Cost Calculation:

  - Perpetual Inventory System: Utilize a perpetual inventory system to maintain real-time updates of inventory costs.

- Weighted Average Cost: Calculate the weighted average cost for materials when multiple purchase prices are involved.

2. Labor Cost Calculation:

   - Actual Labor Rate: Apply the actual labor rate to the recorded hours worked.

   - Labor Efficiency Variance: Calculate variances between standard labor hours and actual hours worked.

3. Overhead Cost Calculation:

   - Allocate Overheads: Distribute overhead costs based on actual usage rates.

   - Overhead Absorption Rate: Determine the absorption rate by dividing total overheads by the total labor hours or machine hours.

Reporting and Analysis

1. Cost Reports:

   - Actual Cost Reports: Generate detailed reports showing the actual costs incurred for materials, labor, and overheads.

   - Variance Analysis Reports: Compare actual costs to standard costs and budgeted costs to identify variances and analyze their causes.

2. Profitability Analysis:

   - Product Profitability: Assess the profitability of each product by comparing its selling price to the actual cost of production.

   - Project Profitability: Evaluate the financial performance of projects by analyzing actual costs against project budgets.

3. Cost Control Reports:

   - Cost Overruns: Identify areas where actual costs have exceeded budgeted amounts.

   - Cost Savings: Highlight areas where actual costs are below budgeted amounts, indicating potential savings.

Best Practices for Implementing Actual Costing

1. Accurate Data Entry:

   - Ensure all transactions are recorded accurately and promptly to maintain the integrity of cost data.

2. Regular Audits:

   - Conduct regular audits of cost data to verify accuracy and identify discrepancies.

3. Training and Education:

   - Train employees on the importance of accurate data entry and the principles of actual costing.

   - Provide ongoing education to keep staff updated on any changes in costing procedures.

4. Integration with Other Modules:

   - Integrate actual costing with other Oracle ERP modules such as procurement, production, and finance for seamless data flow and accuracy.

5. Use of Technology:

   - Leverage advanced technologies such as IoT and AI to automate data collection and improve the accuracy of actual costing.

Challenges and Solutions

1. Data Accuracy:

   - Challenge: Ensuring the accuracy of data collected from various sources.

   - Solution: Implement automated data collection systems and regular data validation processes.

2. Complexity in Overhead Allocation:

   - Challenge: Allocating overhead costs accurately can be complex.

   - Solution: Use activity-based costing (ABC) to allocate overheads more precisely based on actual activities.

3. Integration Issues:

- Challenge: Integrating actual costing data with other ERP modules can be challenging.

- Solution: Ensure proper configuration and regular maintenance of integration points between modules.

4. Resource Intensive:

- Challenge: Actual costing can be resource-intensive in terms of data collection and processing.

- Solution: Utilize automated systems and technologies to streamline data collection and processing.

Conclusion

Implementing actual costing in Oracle ERP provides a detailed and accurate view of the costs associated with producing goods and services. By capturing real-time data on materials, labor, and overheads, businesses can make informed decisions, control costs, and enhance profitability. Proper setup, accurate data collection, and regular reporting are critical to the success of actual costing. With the right practices and technologies, businesses can effectively manage and optimize their costs using Oracle ERP.

3.5.3 Cost Allocation Methods

Cost allocation is a critical aspect of financial management within Oracle ERP, enabling organizations to distribute costs accurately across various departments, projects, or cost centers. This section delves into the details of cost allocation methods, explaining the concepts, processes, and best practices involved in efficiently managing and allocating costs in Oracle ERP.

Introduction to Cost Allocation

Cost allocation involves assigning indirect costs to different departments, projects, or cost centers based on specific criteria or allocation bases. Indirect costs, also known as overheads, include expenses that are not directly attributable to a single product or service but are necessary for overall operations, such as utilities, rent, and administrative salaries. Accurate cost allocation ensures that each department or project bears a fair share of these costs, leading to more precise financial reporting and better decision-making.

Oracle ERP provides various tools and methodologies for cost allocation, enabling organizations to implement complex allocation rules and ensure compliance with accounting standards.

Types of Cost Allocation Methods

Oracle ERP supports several cost allocation methods, each suited to different types of expenses and organizational structures. The primary methods include:

1. Direct Allocation

2. Step-Down Allocation

3. Reciprocal Allocation

4. Activity-Based Costing (ABC)

1. Direct Allocation

Direct allocation is the simplest method, where costs are directly assigned to a specific cost center or department based on predefined criteria. This method is used when the relationship between the cost and the cost center is straightforward and easily identifiable.

Steps for Direct Allocation in Oracle ERP:

1. Identify Costs: Determine the indirect costs that need to be allocated.

2. Select Cost Centers: Choose the cost centers or departments that will receive the allocations.

3. Define Allocation Bases: Establish the basis for allocation, such as square footage for rent or headcount for administrative salaries.

4. Apply Allocation Rules: Use Oracle ERP's allocation rules to distribute the costs accordingly.

Example:

An organization allocates office rent based on the square footage occupied by each department. If the total rent is $10,000 and the Marketing department occupies 20% of the office space, the direct allocation for Marketing would be $2,000.

2. Step-Down Allocation

Step-down allocation, also known as sequential allocation, involves allocating costs in a hierarchical order. Costs are first assigned to the primary cost centers and then allocated to secondary cost centers based on predefined criteria. This method recognizes the interdependencies between departments.

Steps for Step-Down Allocation in Oracle ERP:

1. List Departments in Order: Arrange departments in a sequence based on the hierarchy or level of service provided.

2. Allocate Primary Costs: Assign costs to primary departments first.

3. Secondary Allocations: Distribute the remaining costs to secondary departments.

Example:

A company allocates IT department costs first to the HR department (which benefits from IT services) and then allocates remaining HR and IT costs to production departments.

3. Reciprocal Allocation

Reciprocal allocation is a more complex method that fully recognizes the mutual services provided between departments. Unlike the step-down method, reciprocal allocation simultaneously allocates costs between departments that provide services to each other.

Steps for Reciprocal Allocation in Oracle ERP:

1. Identify Interdependent Departments: Determine departments that provide services to each other.

2. Set Up Allocation Equations: Create equations that represent the cost distribution among departments.

3. Solve Equations Simultaneously: Use Oracle ERP's cost allocation module to solve these equations and distribute the costs accurately.

Example:

Both the IT and HR departments provide services to each other. The IT department supports HR systems, and HR manages IT staff benefits. Reciprocal allocation calculates and assigns these costs simultaneously.

4. Activity-Based Costing (ABC)

Activity-Based Costing is a sophisticated method that allocates costs based on activities that drive costs rather than direct usage. ABC identifies cost drivers, assigns costs to activities, and then allocates these costs to products or services based on their consumption of activities.

Steps for ABC in Oracle ERP:

1. Identify Activities: Determine all the activities involved in the production process.

2. Assign Costs to Activities: Allocate overhead costs to these activities based on cost drivers.

3. Calculate Activity Rates: Establish rates for each activity by dividing total costs by the activity's cost driver units.

4. Allocate Costs to Products/Services: Use these rates to distribute costs to products or services based on their usage of activities.

Example:

An organization identifies activities like machine setups, quality inspections, and order processing. Costs are allocated to these activities, and then products are assigned costs based on the number of setups, inspections, and orders they require.

Implementing Cost Allocation in Oracle ERP

Implementing cost allocation methods in Oracle ERP involves several steps and the use of specific modules and functionalities. Here's a detailed guide on setting up and managing cost allocations:

1. Setting Up Cost Centers and Accounts

- Define cost centers in Oracle ERP to represent different departments or units within the organization.

- Create accounts for indirect costs and link them to the relevant cost centers.

2. Defining Allocation Rules

- Use Oracle ERP's Cost Allocation module to define allocation rules.

- Specify the allocation bases, such as square footage, headcount, or activity cost drivers.

3. Creating Allocation Sets

- Group related allocation rules into allocation sets for easier management and execution.

- Define the sequence of allocations, especially for step-down and reciprocal methods.

4. Executing Allocations

- Run allocation processes periodically (monthly, quarterly) to distribute costs.

- Review and adjust allocations as necessary to ensure accuracy.

5. Monitoring and Reporting

- Use Oracle ERP's reporting tools to monitor the results of cost allocations.

- Generate reports to analyze the impact of allocations on different cost centers and projects.

Best Practices for Cost Allocation

1. Accurate Data Collection: Ensure that the data used for allocations, such as headcounts or activity volumes, is accurate and up-to-date.

2. Regular Reviews: Periodically review allocation bases and rules to reflect changes in the organization's operations or cost structure.

3. Transparency: Maintain transparency in allocation processes by documenting methodologies and making them accessible to stakeholders.

4. Automation: Utilize Oracle ERP's automation capabilities to streamline allocation processes and reduce manual errors.

5. Alignment with Organizational Goals: Align cost allocation methods with the organization's strategic goals to ensure that resource distribution supports overall objectives.

Conclusion

Effective cost allocation is essential for accurate financial reporting and informed decision-making. Oracle ERP provides robust tools and methodologies to manage cost allocations, from simple direct allocations to complex activity-based costing. By understanding and implementing these methods, organizations can ensure that costs are fairly distributed, enhancing financial transparency and operational efficiency. Following best practices and leveraging Oracle ERP's capabilities, businesses can optimize their cost allocation processes, leading to better resource management and strategic planning.

CHAPTER IV
Supply Chain Management in Oracle ERP

4.1 Procurement Management

4.1.1 Purchase Orders

Introduction to Purchase Orders

A Purchase Order (PO) is a critical document in the procurement process within Oracle ERP. It serves as a formal request to a supplier to provide specified goods or services under agreed terms and conditions. Understanding how to create, manage, and process purchase orders efficiently is essential for optimizing procurement operations and ensuring smooth supply chain management.

Creating Purchase Orders

The process of creating a purchase order in Oracle ERP involves several key steps:

1. Initiating the Purchase Order: The first step is to initiate the purchase order creation process. This can be done by navigating to the "Purchasing" module and selecting the "Create Purchase Order" option. Users with the appropriate permissions can initiate this process.

2. Entering Supplier Information: Select the supplier from whom the goods or services will be procured. This involves entering the supplier's name, address, and contact details. If the supplier is not already in the system, they need to be added to the supplier master database.

3. Defining Purchase Order Lines: The next step is to define the purchase order lines. Each line represents a specific item or service being procured. Information such as item description, quantity, unit of measure, price, and delivery date must be entered accurately.

4. Specifying Terms and Conditions: Define the terms and conditions for the purchase order. This includes payment terms, delivery terms, and any other contractual obligations. These terms ensure that both parties are clear on their responsibilities and expectations.

5. Approvals and Workflow: Once the purchase order details are entered, it may need to go through an approval workflow. Oracle ERP allows configuring workflows to ensure that purchase orders are reviewed and approved by the appropriate personnel before being sent to the supplier.

6. Submitting the Purchase Order: After approval, the purchase order is submitted to the supplier. This can be done electronically through the Oracle ERP system or via traditional methods such as email or fax.

Managing Purchase Orders

Effective management of purchase orders involves tracking, modifying, and closing purchase orders as needed. Key aspects include:

1. Tracking Purchase Orders: Oracle ERP provides tools to track the status of purchase orders. Users can view the current status (e.g., pending, approved, rejected) and track the delivery status of the items or services ordered. This helps in ensuring that suppliers meet their delivery commitments.

2. Modifying Purchase Orders: Sometimes, it may be necessary to modify a purchase order after it has been issued. This could be due to changes in quantity, price, delivery dates, or other terms. Oracle ERP allows authorized users to make amendments to purchase orders while maintaining an audit trail of changes.

3. Receiving Goods and Services: Once the ordered goods or services are received, the receipt is recorded in the system. This involves verifying the received quantity and quality against the purchase order. Discrepancies, if any, can be flagged for resolution.

4. Closing Purchase Orders: After all items or services have been received and verified, the purchase order can be closed. This signifies the completion of the procurement transaction. Closed purchase orders are archived for record-keeping and auditing purposes.

Purchase Order Types

Oracle ERP supports various types of purchase orders to cater to different procurement needs:

1. Standard Purchase Orders: Used for one-time procurement of goods or services. Each line item specifies the details of the product or service, including quantity, price, and delivery date.

2. Blanket Purchase Orders: Used for long-term agreements with suppliers. They define the terms and conditions of the agreement and allow for multiple releases over a specified period.

3. Contract Purchase Orders: Similar to blanket purchase orders, but with a focus on specific contracts or projects. They outline the contractual terms and allow for periodic releases.

4. Planned Purchase Orders: Used for future procurements. They provide a forecast of requirements and allow for scheduling releases based on projected needs.

Best Practices for Managing Purchase Orders

Implementing best practices can enhance the efficiency and effectiveness of purchase order management:

1. Standardize Processes: Develop and enforce standard procedures for creating, approving, and managing purchase orders. This ensures consistency and reduces errors.

2. Utilize Approval Workflows: Configure approval workflows to ensure that purchase orders are reviewed by the appropriate personnel. This enhances accountability and compliance with procurement policies.

3. Monitor Supplier Performance: Track supplier performance in terms of delivery times, quality of goods or services, and adherence to contractual terms. Use this information to make informed decisions about future procurement.

4. Leverage Automation: Utilize Oracle ERP's automation capabilities to streamline the purchase order process. Automated alerts, reminders, and approvals can reduce manual intervention and speed up the process.

5. Maintain Accurate Records: Ensure that all purchase orders and related documents are accurately recorded in the system. This facilitates auditing, reporting, and analysis.

Troubleshooting Common Issues

Despite best efforts, issues can arise in the purchase order process. Common issues and their resolutions include:

1. Discrepancies in Received Goods: If there is a mismatch between the received goods and the purchase order, initiate a discrepancy resolution process. This may involve contacting the supplier, inspecting the goods, and updating the purchase order or receipt records.

2. Delayed Approvals: Delays in the approval process can impact procurement timelines. Ensure that approval workflows are optimized and that approvers are notified promptly of pending approvals.

3. System Errors: Technical issues with the Oracle ERP system can disrupt the purchase order process. Work with the IT team to resolve system errors and ensure that the system is regularly maintained and updated.

4. Supplier Non-Compliance: If a supplier fails to meet the terms of the purchase order, address the issue promptly. This may involve renegotiating terms, seeking alternative suppliers, or implementing penalties as per the contract.

Conclusion

Managing purchase orders effectively is crucial for the success of the procurement process and overall supply chain management. Oracle ERP provides robust tools and features to create, manage, and track purchase orders, ensuring that organizations can procure goods and services efficiently and cost-effectively. By adhering to best practices and leveraging the capabilities of Oracle ERP, businesses can optimize their procurement operations, maintain strong supplier relationships, and achieve their operational goals.

4.1.2 Supplier Management

Effective supplier management is crucial for any organization aiming to optimize its procurement processes. In Oracle ERP, supplier management involves a comprehensive approach to managing supplier relationships, performance, and compliance. This section provides a detailed guide on how to manage suppliers within Oracle ERP, covering setup, maintenance, performance monitoring, and strategic utilization.

Introduction to Supplier Management

Supplier management encompasses all activities related to the selection, evaluation, and ongoing management of suppliers. It ensures that the procurement process is efficient, cost-effective, and aligned with organizational goals. Oracle ERP provides robust tools to streamline supplier management, enhance collaboration, and ensure compliance with procurement policies.

Setting Up Suppliers in Oracle ERP

Supplier Registration

The first step in supplier management is supplier registration. Oracle ERP allows organizations to capture detailed information about each supplier. This includes:

- Supplier Profile: Basic information such as supplier name, address, contact details, and tax information.

- Supplier Classification: Categorizing suppliers based on criteria like goods/services provided, geographical location, and business size.

- Supplier Sites: Defining different locations where the supplier operates, which is useful for large suppliers with multiple branches.

Steps to Register a Supplier:

1. Navigate to Supplier Management Module:

   Go to the Supplier Management module in Oracle ERP.

2. Create Supplier Profile:

   - Click on 'Create Supplier'.

   - Fill in the necessary details such as supplier name, tax registration number, and address.

3. Define Supplier Sites:

   - Add supplier sites by entering site-specific information like site address and contact person.

4. Classify Supplier:

   - Assign the supplier to relevant categories to facilitate easy identification and reporting.

5. Save and Approve:

   - Save the supplier profile.

   - Route the profile for approval if necessary, based on organizational workflow.

Supplier Approval Workflow

Oracle ERP supports an approval workflow for supplier registration, ensuring that only vetted suppliers are added to the system. This workflow can be customized to include multiple approval levels based on the organization's policies.

Steps to Configure Supplier Approval Workflow:

1. Define Approval Rules:

   - Navigate to the Workflow Configuration section.

   - Define approval rules based on criteria like supplier category or spend threshold.

2. Assign Approvers:

   - Assign approvers for each level of the workflow.

   - Specify conditions under which each approver is required.

3. Activate Workflow:

   - Activate the workflow and test it with sample supplier registrations to ensure it functions as expected.

Maintaining Supplier Information

Regular maintenance of supplier information is essential to keep the data accurate and up-to-date. Oracle ERP provides functionalities to update supplier details, manage supplier documents, and handle supplier communications.

Updating Supplier Details

Changes in supplier information, such as address updates or changes in contact persons, should be promptly reflected in the system. Oracle ERP allows easy modification of supplier details.

Steps to Update Supplier Information:

1. Search for Supplier:

  - Use the search functionality to locate the supplier whose details need updating.

2. Edit Supplier Profile:

  - Select the supplier and click on 'Edit'.

  - Update the necessary information such as new address or contact details.

3. Save Changes:

  - Save the changes and notify relevant stakeholders if needed.

 Document Management

Managing supplier documents, such as contracts, certifications, and compliance documents, is critical. Oracle ERP offers a centralized repository for storing and managing these documents.

Steps to Manage Supplier Documents:

1. Upload Documents:

  - Navigate to the supplier's profile.

  - Use the document upload feature to add new documents.

2. Categorize Documents:

  - Categorize documents for easy retrieval, using tags like 'Contracts', 'Certifications', etc.

3. Set Expiry Alerts:

- Set alerts for documents that have expiration dates, ensuring timely renewals.

Supplier Communication

Oracle ERP facilitates efficient communication with suppliers through integrated messaging and notifications.

Steps to Communicate with Suppliers:

1. Send Messages:

- Use the messaging feature within the Supplier Management module to send messages directly to suppliers.

2. Set Notification Preferences:

- Set up notification preferences for important events like contract renewals or compliance updates.

3. Track Communication History:

- Maintain a history of communications within the supplier profile for reference.

Monitoring Supplier Performance

Monitoring supplier performance is essential to ensure that suppliers meet the agreed-upon standards and deliver value to the organization. Oracle ERP includes tools for performance evaluation and reporting.

Performance Metrics

Define key performance metrics to evaluate suppliers. Common metrics include:

- Delivery Timeliness: Measure how often suppliers deliver on or before the agreed delivery dates.

- Quality of Goods/Services: Assess the quality of goods or services received from suppliers.

- Compliance: Ensure that suppliers comply with contractual terms and regulatory requirements.

- Cost Management: Evaluate the cost-effectiveness of the supplier's offerings.

 Performance Evaluation Process

Steps to Evaluate Supplier Performance:

1. Define Evaluation Criteria:

   - Set up criteria and weightage for each performance metric in the Supplier Performance module.

2. Collect Data:

   - Collect performance data from purchase orders, receipts, and quality checks.

3. Analyze Performance:

   - Use built-in analytics tools to assess supplier performance against defined criteria.

4. Generate Reports:

   - Generate performance reports to identify top-performing and underperforming suppliers.

5. Feedback and Improvement:

   - Provide feedback to suppliers based on performance evaluations and work on improvement plans if necessary.

Performance Improvement Plans

For underperforming suppliers, develop and implement performance improvement plans. This includes setting targets, timelines, and regular review meetings.

Steps to Implement Performance Improvement Plans:

1. Identify Issues:

 - Analyze performance data to identify specific areas where the supplier is underperforming.

2. Develop Improvement Plan:

 - Collaborate with the supplier to develop a realistic improvement plan.

3. Monitor Progress:

 - Regularly monitor progress against the improvement plan and provide ongoing feedback.

4. Re-evaluate Performance:

 - Re-evaluate the supplier's performance after the improvement period to determine effectiveness.

Strategic Supplier Management

Strategic supplier management goes beyond day-to-day transactions and focuses on long-term partnerships, innovation, and risk management.

Supplier Segmentation

Segment suppliers based on their strategic importance and performance. This helps prioritize efforts and resources on key suppliers.

Steps to Segment Suppliers:

1. Define Segmentation Criteria:

  - Criteria may include spend volume, criticality of goods/services, and supplier performance.

2. Categorize Suppliers:

  - Use Oracle ERP's segmentation tools to categorize suppliers into strategic, preferred, and transactional segments.

3. Manage Segments:

  - Develop specific strategies for managing each segment to maximize value and mitigate risks.

Collaborative Planning and Innovation

Engage with strategic suppliers in collaborative planning and innovation initiatives to drive mutual growth and efficiency.

Steps to Foster Collaboration:

1. Joint Planning Sessions:

  - Hold regular planning sessions with strategic suppliers to align on goals and strategies.

2. Innovation Projects:

- Partner with suppliers on innovation projects, sharing insights and resources.

3. Performance Incentives:

- Offer performance-based incentives to encourage continuous improvement and innovation.

Risk Management

Identify and mitigate risks associated with supplier relationships. This includes financial stability, supply continuity, and compliance risks.

Steps to Manage Supplier Risks:

1. Conduct Risk Assessments:

- Regularly assess risks associated with key suppliers using Oracle ERP's risk management tools.

2. Develop Mitigation Strategies:

- Develop strategies to mitigate identified risks, such as diversifying the supplier base or holding safety stock.

3. Monitor Risks:

- Continuously monitor supplier risk indicators and update mitigation plans as needed.

Conclusion

Effective supplier management in Oracle ERP is a critical component of the procurement process, enabling organizations to build strong supplier relationships, ensure quality and compliance, and drive strategic value. By leveraging Oracle ERP's comprehensive supplier management features, organizations can achieve greater efficiency, cost savings, and innovation in their supply chain operations.

4.2 Inventory Management

4.2.1 Inventory Tracking

Introduction to Inventory Tracking

Inventory tracking is a critical component of effective inventory management within Oracle ERP. It involves the systematic process of monitoring and managing stock levels, locations, and movements to ensure accurate records and optimal stock levels. This section will guide you through the essential aspects of inventory tracking, including setting up inventory locations, using tracking methods, managing inventory transactions, and utilizing Oracle ERP tools to streamline these processes.

Setting Up Inventory Locations

Inventory locations are the physical or logical places where inventory is stored. Proper setup and management of these locations are crucial for accurate inventory tracking. In Oracle ERP, inventory locations can be configured in the following ways:

- *Defining Subinventories:* Subinventories are logical divisions of inventory within an organization. Each subinventory can represent a physical location, such as a warehouse, or a logical grouping of items, such as damaged goods or quality control.

  - Navigate to the Inventory module and select 'Subinventories'.

  - Click on 'Create Subinventory'.

  - Enter the subinventory name, description, and other relevant details.

  - Assign the subinventory to an organization and specify any relevant parameters, such as locator control and cost group.

- *Creating Locators:* Locators are specific locations within a subinventory, such as shelves or bins. They provide a more granular level of inventory tracking.

  - Within the subinventory setup, select 'Locators'.

  - Click on 'Create Locator'.

  - Define the locator structure, such as row, rack, and bin.

- Assign the locator to a subinventory and specify its capacity and dimensions if necessary.

- *Defining Inventory Organizations*: Inventory organizations represent different entities within an organization, such as a manufacturing plant or a distribution center.

  - Navigate to the Inventory module and select 'Inventory Organizations'.

  - Click on 'Create Organization'.

  - Enter the organization name, type, and other relevant details.

  - Specify the default subinventory and other parameters, such as cost method and valuation accounts.

Inventory Tracking Methods

Oracle ERP provides various methods for tracking inventory, each suitable for different business needs. The primary tracking methods include:

- *Serial Number Tracking:* Used for high-value items or products that require unique identification.

  - Navigate to the Item Master and select the item to be tracked.

  - Enable 'Serial Control' and specify the serial generation method (predefined or at receipt).

  - During inventory transactions, enter or scan the serial numbers to track the movement and location of each item.

- *Lot Number Tracking:* Suitable for items that are produced or purchased in batches.

  - In the Item Master, enable 'Lot Control' and define the lot attributes, such as expiration date and lot status.

  - During inventory transactions, assign lot numbers to items and record the quantity associated with each lot.

- *Revision Control:* Applicable for items with different versions or revisions, such as products that undergo design changes.

  - In the Item Master, enable 'Revision Control' and specify the revision format.

- During inventory transactions, enter the appropriate revision number to track the version of the item.

- *Locator Control:* Ensures that items are stored in specific locations within a subinventory.

  - In the Subinventory setup, enable 'Locator Control' and specify the locator format.

  - During inventory transactions, assign locators to items to track their precise storage location.

Managing Inventory Transactions

Inventory transactions encompass various activities, such as receiving, issuing, transferring, and adjusting inventory. Oracle ERP provides robust tools to manage these transactions effectively:

- *Receiving Inventory:* The process of accepting goods into inventory from suppliers or other sources.

  - Navigate to the 'Receiving' module and create a 'Receipt'.

  - Enter the purchase order or shipment details and record the quantity received.

  - Specify the subinventory and locator where the items will be stored.

  - Save and confirm the receipt to update inventory levels.

- *Issuing Inventory:* The process of removing goods from inventory for sales, production, or other purposes.

  - Navigate to the 'Inventory' module and select 'Issue'.

  - Enter the item details, quantity to be issued, and the destination subinventory or department.

  - Specify the lot, serial number, or locator if applicable.

  - Save and confirm the issue transaction to update inventory levels.

- *Transferring Inventory:* The process of moving goods between subinventories, locators, or organizations.

  - Navigate to the 'Inventory' module and select 'Transfer'.

- Enter the source and destination subinventory or locator details.

- Specify the item details and quantity to be transferred.

- Save and confirm the transfer to update inventory records.

- *Adjusting Inventory:* The process of correcting discrepancies in inventory records due to errors, damage, or other reasons.

  - Navigate to the 'Inventory' module and select 'Adjustment'.

  - Enter the item details, the quantity to be adjusted, and the reason for adjustment.

  - Specify the subinventory and locator if applicable.

  - Save and confirm the adjustment to update inventory levels.

Utilizing Oracle ERP Tools for Inventory Tracking

Oracle ERP offers several tools and features to enhance inventory tracking, ensuring accuracy and efficiency:

- *Cycle Counting:* A method of periodically counting a subset of inventory items to verify accuracy and update records.

  - Navigate to the 'Inventory' module and select 'Cycle Counting'.

  - Define a cycle count schedule and specify the items to be counted.

  - Record the count results and compare them with system records.

  - Adjust inventory levels based on discrepancies found during the cycle count.

- *Physical Inventory:* A comprehensive count of all inventory items to ensure complete accuracy of inventory records.

  - Navigate to the 'Inventory' module and select 'Physical Inventory'.

  - Create a physical inventory and define the items and locations to be counted.

  - Perform the physical count and record the results.

  - Reconcile the count results with system records and adjust inventory levels accordingly.

- *Inventory Transactions Interface*: An interface for importing and exporting inventory transactions to and from external systems.

  - Navigate to the 'Inventory' module and select 'Transactions Interface'.

  - Define the transaction source and format for importing or exporting data.

  - Use the interface to load transactions from external systems or export transactions for reporting and analysis.

- *Inventory Reports and Inquiries:* Tools for generating detailed reports and conducting inquiries to monitor inventory status and performance.

  - Navigate to the 'Inventory' module and select 'Reports' or 'Inquiries'.

  - Choose the desired report or inquiry type, such as stock status, transaction history, or valuation.

  - Generate the report or conduct the inquiry to obtain detailed information on inventory levels, movements, and performance metrics.

Best Practices for Inventory Tracking

To ensure effective inventory tracking in Oracle ERP, consider the following best practices:

- Regularly Review and Update Inventory Records: Conduct periodic reviews of inventory records to identify and correct discrepancies.

- Implement Robust Training Programs: Train employees on inventory tracking procedures and the use of Oracle ERP tools to ensure accuracy and consistency.

- Utilize Barcode and RFID Technologies: Implement barcode or RFID systems to automate inventory tracking and reduce manual errors.

- Maintain Clear and Consistent Procedures: Establish clear procedures for inventory transactions and ensure they are consistently followed across the organization.

- Leverage Advanced Analytics: Use Oracle ERP's analytics tools to gain insights into inventory performance and make data-driven decisions to optimize stock levels and reduce carrying costs.

Conclusion

Effective inventory tracking is essential for maintaining accurate inventory records, optimizing stock levels, and ensuring efficient operations. By leveraging the powerful tools and features provided by Oracle ERP, organizations can streamline their inventory tracking processes, improve accuracy, and enhance overall inventory management. This section has provided a detailed guide on setting up inventory locations, using tracking methods, managing inventory transactions, and utilizing Oracle ERP tools for inventory tracking. Implementing these practices will help organizations unlock the full potential of their Oracle ERP system and achieve better inventory control and visibility.

4.2.2 Stock Management

Effective stock management is crucial for maintaining the balance between supply and demand, optimizing inventory levels, reducing costs, and ensuring timely availability of products. In Oracle ERP, stock management encompasses various functions and processes designed to streamline and control the movement, storage, and handling of inventory. This section provides a comprehensive guide on how to manage stock effectively using Oracle ERP.

Overview of Stock Management

Stock management involves the administration of stock levels to ensure that the right amount of inventory is available at the right time. It includes tasks such as inventory tracking, stock replenishment, cycle counting, and inventory reconciliation. Oracle ERP offers a robust suite of tools and functionalities to help organizations manage their stock efficiently.

Key Components of Stock Management in Oracle ERP

1. Inventory Organization Setup

- Defining Inventory Organizations: Setting up inventory organizations, which are the logical entities where inventory is stored and managed. This includes defining parameters such as organization codes, locations, and inventory costing methods.

- Subinventories and Locators: Configuring subinventories (logical separations within an inventory organization) and locators (specific storage locations within subinventories) to organize and track inventory at a granular level.

2. Inventory Transactions

- Receipts and Issues: Recording inventory transactions such as receiving stock from suppliers (receipts) and issuing stock for sales or production (issues). This helps maintain accurate inventory records.

- Transfers: Managing internal transfers of inventory between different subinventories or locators within the same organization or across different organizations.

3. Inventory Tracking and Visibility

- Lot and Serial Control: Implementing lot and serial control to track inventory items at the lot or serial number level, providing enhanced traceability and control over individual items.

- Item Attributes: Utilizing item attributes to classify and manage inventory items based on characteristics such as item category, status, and revision.

4. Stock Replenishment

- Reorder Point Planning: Setting reorder points and reorder quantities to trigger stock replenishment when inventory levels fall below predefined thresholds.

- Min-Max Planning: Using min-max planning to define minimum and maximum stock levels for each item and automate replenishment based on these parameters.

- Kanban: Implementing Kanban-based replenishment systems to manage inventory in a just-in-time (JIT) manner, particularly useful for manufacturing environments.

5. Cycle Counting and Physical Inventory

- Cycle Counting: Conducting regular cycle counts to verify inventory accuracy without disrupting daily operations. Cycle counting involves counting a subset of inventory items on a scheduled basis.

- Physical Inventory: Performing full physical inventory counts periodically to reconcile system records with actual stock on hand, ensuring data accuracy and identifying discrepancies.

6. Inventory Valuation and Costing

- Costing Methods: Applying different costing methods (such as FIFO, LIFO, or Average Cost) to value inventory and calculate the cost of goods sold (COGS).

- Inventory Valuation Reports: Generating reports to provide insights into inventory valuation, cost variances, and inventory turnover ratios.

Step-by-Step Guide to Stock Management in Oracle ERP

1. Setting Up Inventory Organizations

- Define Inventory Organizations: Navigate to the Inventory Organizations window in Oracle ERP. Define the inventory organization by specifying its code, name, and relevant parameters.

- Create Subinventories: Within each inventory organization, create subinventories to further categorize and manage inventory. Define attributes such as subinventory name, type, and default locator.

- Configure Locators: Set up locators within subinventories to identify specific storage locations. Assign locators to items to enhance tracking and retrieval.

2. Managing Inventory Transactions

- Receipts: Use the Receiving Transactions window to record incoming stock. Specify details such as item number, quantity, and supplier information. Verify the receipt against purchase orders.

- Issues: Record inventory issues through the Transaction Entry window. Enter details such as item number, quantity, and reason for the issue (e.g., sales order fulfillment).

- Transfers: Perform inventory transfers using the Transfer Transactions window. Select the source and destination subinventories/locators, and enter the items and quantities to be transferred.

3. Implementing Lot and Serial Control

- Enable Lot Control: In the Item Master, enable lot control for items that require batch tracking. Specify lot generation methods and assign lot numbers during receiving and issuing transactions.

- Enable Serial Control: Enable serial control for items that require unique identification. Assign serial numbers during receiving, and track them through the item's lifecycle.

4. Stock Replenishment Planning

- Reorder Point Planning: Define reorder points and quantities in the Item Master. Set up automatic replenishment triggers based on current stock levels.

- Min-Max Planning: Configure min-max planning parameters for each item. Run the Min-Max Planning report to generate replenishment recommendations and create purchase requisitions or internal orders.

- Kanban: Set up Kanban cards for items managed using JIT principles. Monitor stock levels visually and replenish based on Kanban signals.

5. Conducting Cycle Counting and Physical Inventory

- Cycle Counting Setup: Define cycle counting classes and assign items to each class. Schedule cycle counts based on item importance and movement frequency.

- Performing Cycle Counts: Execute cycle counts using the Cycle Count Entries window. Record count results and reconcile discrepancies with system records.

- Physical Inventory Preparation: Schedule physical inventory counts. Freeze transactions during the count to ensure data integrity.

- Conducting Physical Counts: Perform physical counts and enter results in the Physical Inventory window. Reconcile discrepancies and adjust inventory records accordingly.

6. Inventory Valuation and Reporting

- Applying Costing Methods: Choose and apply the appropriate costing method in the Cost Management module. Configure costing rules and policies.

- Generating Valuation Reports: Access inventory valuation reports through the Reports window. Analyze reports such as Inventory Valuation Summary, Cost Variance Report, and Inventory Turnover Report to gain insights into inventory performance.

Best Practices for Stock Management in Oracle ERP

1. Accurate Data Entry: Ensure all inventory transactions are recorded accurately and promptly to maintain data integrity and avoid discrepancies.

2. Regular Cycle Counts: Implement regular cycle counting schedules to continuously validate inventory accuracy without disrupting operations.

3. Effective Replenishment Planning: Use reorder point and min-max planning to automate replenishment and maintain optimal stock levels.

4. Lot and Serial Tracking: Enable lot and serial tracking for high-value or regulated items to enhance traceability and compliance.

5. Timely Reconciliation: Regularly reconcile physical inventory counts with system records to identify and address discrepancies promptly.

6. Comprehensive Reporting: Utilize inventory reports to monitor stock levels, valuation, and performance metrics, aiding in informed decision-making.

Conclusion

Effective stock management within Oracle ERP involves a combination of robust setup, efficient transaction processing, precise tracking, and proactive planning. By leveraging the comprehensive tools and functionalities offered by Oracle ERP, organizations can achieve optimal inventory control, reduce costs, and ensure timely availability of products. Implementing best practices and regularly reviewing inventory performance will further enhance the efficiency and effectiveness of stock management processes.

4.3 Order Management

4.3.1 Sales Order Processing

Sales order processing is a critical component of Order Management in Oracle ERP. It involves a series of steps that manage the lifecycle of a sales order, from creation to fulfillment. This section will provide a detailed guide on how to effectively manage sales order processing within Oracle ERP, including step-by-step instructions, best practices, and key features.

Overview of Sales Order Processing

Sales order processing in Oracle ERP involves the following main steps:

1. Order Entry: Capturing the customer's order details.

2. Order Booking: Confirming and validating the order.

3. Order Fulfillment: Picking, packing, and shipping the order.

4. Invoicing: Generating and sending the invoice to the customer.

5. Order Closure: Closing the order after fulfillment and payment.

Each step is crucial to ensure a seamless order management process, improve customer satisfaction, and maintain operational efficiency.

Step-by-Step Guide to Sales Order Processing

Order Entry

1. Customer Information:

 - Navigate to the Sales Orders module.

- Enter the customer's information, such as name, address, and contact details. Oracle ERP allows for quick selection of existing customers from the customer master data or the creation of new customer profiles.

2. Order Details:

  - Specify the order details, including product items, quantities, and prices.

  - Use the item master to select products. The item master contains a comprehensive list of all products, including their descriptions, prices, and availability.

  - Apply any applicable discounts or promotions.

3. Delivery Information:

  - Enter the shipping method, delivery address, and delivery date.

  - Confirm the shipping terms and conditions.

4. Order Validation:

  - Validate the order to ensure all required fields are completed and the order meets all necessary criteria.

  - Oracle ERP will automatically check for inventory availability and alert if any items are out of stock.

 Order Booking

1. Order Confirmation:

  - Once the order details are validated, proceed to book the order.

  - Booking an order involves confirming the order details and reserving the inventory.

2. Order Number Generation:

  - Oracle ERP will generate a unique order number for tracking and reference purposes.

  - The order number is crucial for future order tracking, fulfillment, and reporting.

3. Credit Check:

  - Conduct a credit check if necessary. Oracle ERP can be configured to automatically perform credit checks based on customer credit limits and payment history.

- If the credit check is successful, proceed to the next step. If not, address the credit issues before proceeding.

Order Fulfillment

1. Pick Release:

  - Initiate the pick release process to generate pick slips.

  - Pick slips guide warehouse staff on which items to pick and where they are located within the warehouse.

2. Picking:

  - Warehouse staff use the pick slips to locate and pick the items.

  - Oracle ERP can integrate with warehouse management systems (WMS) to streamline the picking process and update inventory levels in real-time.

3. Packing:

  - After picking, the items are packed for shipment.

  - Generate packing slips that detail the contents of the package, shipping information, and any special instructions.

4. Shipping:

  - Ship the packed items to the customer.

  - Update the order status in Oracle ERP to reflect that the order has been shipped.

  - Provide tracking information to the customer if available.

Invoicing

1. Invoice Generation:

  - Generate an invoice for the shipped order.

  - Ensure that the invoice includes all relevant details such as order number, item descriptions, quantities, prices, discounts, taxes, and total amount due.

2. Invoice Delivery:

  - Send the invoice to the customer via email or other preferred methods.

  - Oracle ERP supports electronic invoicing (e-invoicing) for faster and more efficient invoice delivery.

3. Payment Processing:

  - Record the payment once received from the customer.

  - Apply the payment to the corresponding invoice to update the accounts receivable.

Order Closure

1. Review Order Status:

  - Verify that the order has been fulfilled and the payment has been received.

  - Ensure all transactions related to the order are complete and accurate.

2. Close the Order:

  - Close the order in Oracle ERP to finalize the order processing cycle.

  - Closed orders are typically moved to an archive for historical reference and reporting purposes.

3. Customer Follow-Up:

  - Follow up with the customer to confirm satisfaction with the order.

  - Address any issues or concerns the customer may have.

Best Practices for Sales Order Processing

1. Automation:

  - Utilize Oracle ERP's automation capabilities to streamline repetitive tasks such as order validation, credit checks, and invoicing. Automation reduces errors and improves efficiency.

2. Real-Time Inventory Management:

- Maintain accurate and real-time inventory data to ensure that stock levels are correctly reflected during order entry and fulfillment.

3. Customer Communication:

- Keep customers informed at every stage of the order process, from order confirmation to shipment tracking. Effective communication enhances customer satisfaction and loyalty.

4. Order Tracking and Reporting:

- Use Oracle ERP's robust tracking and reporting features to monitor order status, fulfillment performance, and sales metrics. Regular reporting helps identify bottlenecks and areas for improvement.

5. Training and Support:

- Provide comprehensive training to staff on Oracle ERP's order management functionalities. Ensure that support resources are available to address any issues that may arise during order processing.

Key Features of Oracle ERP for Sales Order Processing

1. Order Management Dashboard:

- A centralized dashboard provides a real-time view of all orders, their statuses, and any pending actions. The dashboard helps manage orders efficiently and prioritize tasks.

2. Integration with CRM:

- Oracle ERP integrates seamlessly with Customer Relationship Management (CRM) systems, enabling better management of customer interactions and order history.

3. Advanced Pricing Engine:

- The advanced pricing engine allows for complex pricing rules, discounts, and promotions to be applied automatically during order entry.

4. Configurable Workflows:

- Oracle ERP supports customizable workflows that can be tailored to fit the specific needs of the business. This flexibility ensures that order processing aligns with internal processes and policies.

5. Mobile Access:

- Mobile access to Oracle ERP enables sales and warehouse staff to manage orders on-the-go, enhancing productivity and responsiveness.

6. Audit Trail:

- A comprehensive audit trail tracks all changes and actions taken on an order, providing transparency and accountability.

Conclusion

Effective sales order processing is essential for maintaining customer satisfaction and operational efficiency. Oracle ERP provides a comprehensive suite of tools and features to manage the entire sales order lifecycle, from entry to fulfillment and invoicing. By following best practices and leveraging Oracle ERP's capabilities, businesses can streamline their order management processes, reduce errors, and improve overall performance.

This detailed guide on sales order processing within Oracle ERP should equip users with the knowledge and skills needed to efficiently handle orders and enhance their business operations.

4.3.2 Shipping and Delivery

Efficient shipping and delivery processes are crucial for maintaining customer satisfaction and optimizing supply chain operations. Oracle ERP offers comprehensive tools to manage shipping and delivery effectively, ensuring that products are delivered to customers on time and in good condition. This section will cover the various aspects of managing shipping and delivery in Oracle ERP, including setup, process execution, tracking, and reporting.

Overview of Shipping and Delivery Processes

Shipping and delivery processes in Oracle ERP encompass several key activities:

1. Shipping Setup: Configuring the shipping methods, carriers, and related parameters.

2. Order Fulfillment: Picking, packing, and shipping products.

3. Shipment Tracking: Monitoring the progress of shipments and delivery status.

4. Delivery Confirmation: Ensuring the products reach their destination and confirming receipt.

Each of these steps is crucial for ensuring a seamless delivery process and minimizing delays or errors.

1. Shipping Setup

1.1 Defining Shipping Methods

Shipping methods refer to the different ways products can be shipped to customers. Oracle ERP allows businesses to define multiple shipping methods based on customer requirements and business logistics.

1. Navigate to the Shipping Methods setup screen in Oracle ERP.

2. Click on "New" to create a new shipping method.

3. Enter the details such as shipping method name, description, and associated carrier.

4. Specify the transit time and cost associated with the shipping method.

5. Save the shipping method and ensure it is available for selection during the order fulfillment process.

1.2 Setting Up Carriers

Carriers are the logistics providers responsible for transporting goods from the warehouse to the customer. Oracle ERP enables businesses to define and manage carrier information.

1. Access the Carriers setup screen in Oracle ERP.

2. Click "New" to add a new carrier.

3. Enter the carrier's name, contact information, and service areas.

4. Assign shipping methods to the carrier, indicating which methods they can handle.

5. Save the carrier details.

1.3 Configuring Shipping Parameters

Shipping parameters are settings that control various aspects of the shipping process, such as packaging rules, handling charges, and delivery schedules.

1. Go to the Shipping Parameters configuration screen.

2. Define packaging rules, including box sizes, weight limits, and packing materials.

3. Set handling charges based on shipping method, order value, or other criteria.

4. Configure delivery schedules, specifying cutoff times for same-day shipping and delivery windows.

5. Save the shipping parameters.

 2. Order Fulfillment

2.1 Picking and Packing

Picking and packing are critical steps in the order fulfillment process. Oracle ERP provides tools to streamline these activities and ensure accuracy.

Picking:

1. Access the Picking screen in Oracle ERP.

2. Generate pick lists based on customer orders.

3. Assign pick lists to warehouse staff.

4. Track the progress of picking activities and ensure all items are picked correctly.

Packing:

1. Navigate to the Packing screen.

2. Use the packing workbench to pack items into appropriate containers.

3. Verify that the items match the pick list.

4. Print packing slips and shipping labels.

5. Seal the packages and prepare them for shipping.

2.2 Shipping Products

Once items are picked and packed, they are ready to be shipped. Oracle ERP facilitates the shipping process through integration with carriers and automated documentation.

1. Access the Shipping screen.

2. Select the orders ready for shipping.

3. Generate shipping documents, including shipping labels, bills of lading, and customs forms.

4. Schedule pickups with carriers.

5. Confirm shipment and update the order status in Oracle ERP.

 3. Shipment Tracking

Shipment tracking is essential for keeping customers informed about the status of their orders and for internal monitoring of delivery performance.

3.1 Tracking Shipments in Oracle ERP

Oracle ERP integrates with carrier tracking systems to provide real-time updates on shipment status.

1. Access the Shipment Tracking screen.

2. Enter the tracking number or order number.

3. View the current status of the shipment, including location and estimated delivery date.

4. Set up automated notifications to inform customers about shipment progress.

3.2 Handling Exceptions

Occasionally, shipments may encounter issues such as delays, lost packages, or damaged goods. Oracle ERP provides tools to handle these exceptions efficiently.

1. Monitor shipment status for any alerts or exceptions.

2. Investigate the cause of the issue, contacting the carrier if necessary.

3. Update the customer on the status and resolution plan.

4. Record the exception in Oracle ERP for reporting and analysis.

4. Delivery Confirmation

Delivery confirmation is the final step in the shipping process, ensuring that customers receive their orders as expected.

4.1 Confirming Delivery in Oracle ERP

Oracle ERP allows businesses to confirm delivery and capture proof of delivery.

1. Access the Delivery Confirmation screen.

2. Enter the tracking number or order number.

3. Confirm that the package has been delivered and received by the customer.

4. Capture proof of delivery, such as a signed delivery receipt or photo evidence.

4.2 Handling Delivery Discrepancies

If there are discrepancies between the shipped items and what the customer received, Oracle ERP helps manage these issues.

1. Record the discrepancy in Oracle ERP.

2. Investigate the cause, checking shipping records and packaging details.

3. Communicate with the customer to resolve the issue, offering replacements or refunds as necessary.

4. Update the order status and inventory records accordingly.

Best Practices for Shipping and Delivery in Oracle ERP

1. Optimize Shipping Routes

Using advanced algorithms, Oracle ERP can optimize shipping routes to minimize transit time and cost.

1. Analyze historical shipping data to identify common routes.

2. Use route optimization tools to plan efficient delivery paths.

3. Adjust routes based on real-time traffic and weather conditions.

2. Ensure Accurate Order Fulfillment

Accuracy in picking, packing, and shipping is crucial for customer satisfaction.

1. Implement barcode scanning to verify items during picking and packing.

2. Use automated weight checks to ensure packages are correctly packed.

3. Conduct regular audits of shipping processes to identify and correct errors.

3. Provide Excellent Customer Service

Keeping customers informed and handling issues promptly enhances the overall experience.

1. Set up automated email notifications for order status updates.

2. Offer multiple shipping options to meet different customer needs.

3. Have a dedicated team to handle shipping-related customer inquiries and issues.

4. Monitor Performance and Continuous Improvement

Regularly reviewing shipping and delivery performance helps identify areas for improvement.

1. Generate reports on shipping times, delivery accuracy, and customer feedback.

2. Use key performance indicators (KPIs) to measure success and identify trends.

3. Implement changes based on performance data to enhance shipping efficiency and customer satisfaction.

Conclusion

Efficient shipping and delivery are critical components of order management in Oracle ERP. By properly setting up shipping methods and carriers, managing the order fulfillment process, tracking shipments, and confirming deliveries, businesses can ensure timely and accurate delivery of products to customers. Implementing best practices and continuously monitoring performance will further enhance the effectiveness of the shipping and delivery processes, leading to improved customer satisfaction and operational efficiency.

CHAPTER V
Human Capital Management in Oracle ERP

5.1 Employee Information Management

5.1.1 Employee Records

Effective management of employee records is crucial for any organization, and Oracle ERP offers a comprehensive solution to streamline this process. Employee records in Oracle ERP encompass a wide range of data points, including personal details, employment history, qualifications, and more. This section provides a detailed guide on how to manage employee records within Oracle ERP.

Introduction to Employee Records

Employee records are the cornerstone of human capital management, serving as the primary repository of all relevant information about employees. These records support various HR functions, including payroll processing, benefits administration, performance management, and compliance reporting.

Setting Up Employee Records

The process of setting up employee records in Oracle ERP involves several steps:

1. Defining Employee Record Fields: Oracle ERP allows customization of employee record fields to cater to the specific needs of the organization. Standard fields typically include

personal information (name, date of birth, contact details), job details (position, department, manager), and employment terms (hire date, contract type).

2. Configuring Organizational Structures: Before entering employee data, it's essential to configure the organizational structure. This includes defining departments, job roles, and reporting hierarchies. Proper configuration ensures that employee records are accurately linked to their respective departments and managers.

3. Data Entry and Import: Employee data can be entered manually or imported from external sources. Oracle ERP supports data import from various file formats, enabling bulk upload of employee records. This is particularly useful during initial implementation or when migrating from another HR system.

Managing Personal Information

Oracle ERP provides a centralized platform to manage personal information securely:

1. Personal Details: Record personal details such as name, address, contact numbers, and emergency contacts. Ensure that this information is regularly updated to reflect any changes.

2. Identification and Documentation: Store copies of identification documents like passports, driving licenses, and work permits. Oracle ERP allows attaching digital copies to employee records, facilitating easy access and verification.

3. Compliance and Legal Requirements: Maintain records to comply with legal and regulatory requirements. This includes storing data on work authorization, tax identification numbers, and other statutory information.

Employment History and Job Details

Tracking employment history and job details is essential for managing an employee's career progression within the organization:

1. Job Assignments: Record details of current and past job assignments, including job title, department, manager, and employment dates. This information helps track career progression and is vital for succession planning.

2. Employment Terms: Document employment terms such as contract type (permanent, temporary, contract), work hours, and salary information. This data is crucial for payroll processing and benefits administration.

3. Promotions and Transfers: Record details of any promotions, transfers, or changes in job responsibilities. Oracle ERP provides workflows to manage these changes, ensuring that employee records are updated promptly.

Qualifications and Skills

Maintaining accurate records of employee qualifications and skills is vital for talent management and development:

1. Educational Background: Record details of educational qualifications, including degrees, certifications, and institutions attended. This information helps in assessing the qualifications of employees for various roles.

2. Professional Skills: Maintain a skills inventory for each employee. Oracle ERP allows tracking of technical skills, soft skills, and any other competencies relevant to the organization.

3. Training and Development: Document participation in training programs, workshops, and other professional development activities. This information supports performance reviews and career development planning.

Performance Management

Performance management is an integral part of employee records, influencing compensation, promotions, and development opportunities:

1. Performance Reviews: Record details of performance reviews, including review dates, performance ratings, and feedback. Oracle ERP facilitates the scheduling and management of regular performance reviews.

2. Goals and Objectives: Track employee goals and objectives, aligning them with organizational targets. Oracle ERP allows setting and monitoring progress towards these goals, providing a basis for performance evaluations.

3. Recognition and Rewards: Document any recognition, awards, or incentives received by employees. This information is valuable for performance appraisals and motivation.

Leave and Attendance

Managing leave and attendance records ensures accurate tracking of employee availability and compliance with leave policies:

1. Leave Balances: Track leave balances for various types of leave (e.g., vacation, sick leave, parental leave). Oracle ERP automatically updates leave balances based on approved leave requests.

2. Leave Requests: Manage leave requests through Oracle ERP's workflow system. Employees can submit leave requests, which are routed to managers for approval, and the system updates records accordingly.

3. Attendance Records: Maintain records of attendance, including clock-in and clock-out times. This data supports payroll processing and helps monitor employee punctuality and presence.

Compensation and Benefits

Accurate management of compensation and benefits records is essential for ensuring fair and timely remuneration:

1. Salary Details: Record salary information, including base salary, bonuses, and other compensation elements. Oracle ERP supports various salary structures and allows for adjustments based on performance and other factors.

2. Benefits Enrollment: Manage employee enrollment in benefit programs such as health insurance, retirement plans, and other perks. Oracle ERP facilitates the administration of these programs, ensuring that employee records are updated with benefit selections.

3. Payroll Integration: Integrate compensation records with the payroll module to ensure accurate and timely payroll processing. Oracle ERP automates payroll calculations based on the data in employee records.

Compliance and Reporting

Ensuring compliance with labor laws and regulations is a critical aspect of managing employee records:

1. Regulatory Compliance: Maintain records in compliance with local, state, and federal labor laws. Oracle ERP helps manage compliance requirements, such as maintaining records for minimum wage, overtime, and employment eligibility.

2. Audit Trails: Oracle ERP provides audit trails for all changes made to employee records. This feature ensures transparency and accountability, allowing organizations to track who made changes and when.

3. Reporting and Analytics: Generate reports on various aspects of employee records, such as headcount, turnover rates, and diversity metrics. Oracle ERP's reporting tools provide insights to support strategic decision-making.

Security and Privacy

Protecting the privacy and security of employee records is paramount:

1. Data Security: Oracle ERP employs robust security measures to protect employee data. This includes encryption, access controls, and regular security audits.

2. Access Control: Define roles and permissions to control who can access and modify employee records. Ensure that only authorized personnel have access to sensitive information.

3. Data Privacy: Comply with data privacy regulations, such as GDPR and CCPA. Oracle ERP supports data anonymization and provides tools for managing data subject access requests.

Conclusion

Managing employee records efficiently is crucial for the effective operation of any HR department. Oracle ERP offers a comprehensive solution that ensures accurate, secure, and compliant management of employee data. By leveraging Oracle ERP's capabilities, organizations can streamline HR processes, improve data accuracy, and support strategic decision-making.

This detailed guide provides a solid foundation for understanding and managing employee records within Oracle ERP. By following these best practices, HR professionals can ensure that their organization's employee records are well-maintained, up-to-date, and secure.

5.1.2 Organizational Structures

Organizational Structures in Oracle ERP's Human Capital Management (HCM) module form the backbone of how a company's workforce is managed, categorized, and utilized. Properly defining and managing organizational structures is crucial for ensuring that HR processes align with business goals, comply with regulatory requirements, and support operational efficiency. This section will provide a detailed guide on how to effectively configure and manage organizational structures in Oracle ERP.

Understanding Organizational Structures

Organizational structures in Oracle ERP HCM are hierarchical representations of a company's internal structure. They define the relationships between different departments, roles, and employees, and help in streamlining processes such as reporting, payroll, and performance management. The primary components of organizational structures include:

1. Legal Entities: Represent the legal business units that are legally recognized and responsible for transactions.

2. Business Units: Organizational units that are responsible for specific business functions.

3. Departments: Smaller units within business units that focus on particular operational areas.

4. Positions: Specific roles within departments, which are held by employees.

5. Jobs: Categories of roles that may encompass multiple positions.

Setting Up Organizational Structures

To set up organizational structures in Oracle ERP, follow these steps:

Step 1: Define Legal Entities

1. Navigate to Legal Entities Setup:

   - Go to the Setup and Maintenance work area.

   - Search for the task "Manage Legal Entity."

2. Create Legal Entities:

   - Click on the "Create" button.

   - Enter the required information such as Legal Entity Name, Legal Address, and Country.

   - Save and Close.

Step 2: Configure Business Units

1. Navigate to Business Units Setup:

   - In the Setup and Maintenance work area, search for "Manage Business Unit."

2. Create Business Units:

   - Click on the "Create" button.

   - Enter the Business Unit Name and assign it to the appropriate Legal Entity.

   - Define the primary ledger, default legal entity, and other mandatory fields.

   - Save and Close.

Step 3: Define Departments

1. Navigate to Departments Setup:

   - Access the task "Manage Departments" from the Setup and Maintenance work area.

2. Create Departments:

   - Click on "Create" to add new departments.

- Fill in details like Department Name, Business Unit association, and Manager.

- Specify the locations and other relevant attributes.

- Save and Close.

Step 4: Create Jobs and Positions

1. Define Jobs:

   - Navigate to "Manage Jobs."

   - Create new jobs by specifying Job Name, Code, and Description.

   - Define job characteristics like job family, grade, and role.

2. Define Positions:

   - Go to "Manage Positions."

   - Click on "Create" and enter the Position Name, associated Job, and Department.

   - Set the position attributes such as FTE (Full-Time Equivalent), location, and incumbent information.

   - Save and Close.

Best Practices for Managing Organizational Structures

1. Standardize Naming Conventions:

   - Use consistent naming conventions for entities, business units, departments, jobs, and positions to ensure clarity and avoid duplication.

2. Regular Audits and Updates:

   - Periodically review and update organizational structures to reflect any changes in the business environment, such as restructuring or expansion.

3. Define Clear Reporting Lines:

   - Ensure that reporting lines are clearly defined and maintained within the system to facilitate accurate reporting and performance management.

4. Utilize Role-Based Access:

 - Assign role-based access to manage who can create, update, or delete organizational structures to maintain data integrity and security.

5. Integration with Other Modules:

 - Ensure that organizational structures are integrated with other Oracle ERP modules like Financials and Supply Chain Management for seamless data flow and process efficiency.

Case Scenario: Configuring Organizational Structures

Let's consider a hypothetical scenario where a company, ABC Corporation, needs to configure its organizational structures in Oracle ERP HCM.

Company Profile:

- Legal Entity: ABC Corporation

- Business Units: North America Sales, Europe Sales, Asia Sales

- Departments: Marketing, Sales, Customer Support

- Jobs: Marketing Manager, Sales Representative, Customer Support Specialist

- Positions: North America Sales Manager, Europe Sales Manager, Asia Sales Manager

Steps for Configuration:

1. Create Legal Entity - ABC Corporation:

 - Navigate to "Manage Legal Entity" and create ABC Corporation with the relevant legal information.

2. Create Business Units:

 - Navigate to "Manage Business Unit" and create three business units: North America Sales, Europe Sales, and Asia Sales.

 - Assign each business unit to ABC Corporation.

3. Define Departments:

 - Create Marketing, Sales, and Customer Support departments under each business unit.

- Assign managers to each department.

4. Define Jobs:

- Create jobs for Marketing Manager, Sales Representative, and Customer Support Specialist with appropriate job families and grades.

5. Create Positions:

- Define positions like North America Sales Manager, Europe Sales Manager, and Asia Sales Manager under the Sales department.

- Link each position to the corresponding job and department.

By following these steps, ABC Corporation can establish a clear and functional organizational structure that supports its business operations across different regions.

Maintaining Organizational Structures

Regular Reviews:

- Conduct periodic reviews of organizational structures to ensure they align with current business strategies and operations.

Update Processes:

- Implement processes for updating organizational structures as changes occur, such as new departments, job roles, or business units.

Training and Documentation:

- Provide training for HR personnel on managing organizational structures within Oracle ERP.

- Maintain documentation of organizational structure configurations and any changes made over time.

Conclusion

Organizational structures are a fundamental component of Oracle ERP HCM, enabling businesses to manage their workforce effectively. By properly configuring and maintaining these structures, organizations can streamline HR processes, improve reporting accuracy, and ensure alignment with business goals. This section has provided a comprehensive guide to setting up and managing organizational structures, from defining legal entities to creating jobs and positions, ensuring that your organization can fully leverage the capabilities of Oracle ERP HCM.

5.2 Payroll Management

Effective payroll management is critical for maintaining employee satisfaction and ensuring compliance with various legal and tax regulations. Oracle ERP's Payroll Management module is a comprehensive tool that automates and streamlines the payroll process. This section provides an in-depth guide to setting up and managing payroll within Oracle ERP, focusing on Payroll Processing and Tax Management.

5.2.1 Payroll Processing

Payroll processing in Oracle ERP involves several steps, from gathering employee data to calculating and distributing payments. The following guide details each step, ensuring accurate and timely payroll management.

1. Setting Up Payroll Elements

Before processing payroll, you need to define various payroll elements, which include earnings, deductions, and other components of employee compensation.

- Earnings: Define different types of earnings such as base salary, overtime, bonuses, and commissions. Navigate to the Payroll Manager responsibility, and under Elements, create new earnings elements.

- Deductions: Set up deductions like taxes, health insurance, retirement contributions, and other benefits. Each deduction type must be configured to reflect the appropriate calculation rules and statutory requirements.

- Additional Elements: Other elements like allowances, reimbursements, and fringe benefits can also be defined based on organizational policies.

2. Maintaining Employee Payroll Information

Accurate employee data is essential for payroll processing. Ensure that all employee records are up-to-date and include necessary payroll-related information.

- Personal Information: Verify that each employee's personal details, including name, address, and social security number, are correct.

- Employment Details: Confirm employment type (full-time, part-time, contract), job role, department, and reporting structure.

- Compensation Details: Ensure that salary, wage rates, and any applicable bonuses or commissions are correctly entered into the system.

3. Defining Payroll Calendars

A payroll calendar outlines the pay periods and processing dates for the year.

- Create a Payroll Calendar: In Oracle ERP, navigate to the Payroll Manager responsibility. Under the Payroll Definitions section, create a new payroll calendar, specifying the start and end dates for each pay period.

- Assign Payroll Calendar: Assign the created payroll calendar to the relevant employee groups or departments, ensuring that all employees are linked to the appropriate payroll schedule.

4. Running Payroll Processes

Running the payroll process involves several key steps: pre-payroll activities, payroll calculation, and post-payroll activities.

- Pre-Payroll Activities: Before calculating payroll, complete the following:

 - Data Verification: Ensure all timesheets, leave records, and attendance data are accurately captured and approved.

 - Element Entries: Verify that all earnings, deductions, and other payroll elements are correctly entered for each employee.

- Payroll Calculation: This is the core of payroll processing where the system calculates gross pay, deductions, and net pay.

 - Initiate Payroll Run: In Oracle ERP, navigate to the Payroll Process section. Select the appropriate payroll definition and pay period, then initiate the payroll run.

- Review Payroll Results: After the payroll run, review the results to ensure accuracy. Check for any discrepancies in gross pay, deductions, and net pay.

- Resolve Errors: If errors are found, correct the data and re-run the payroll process for the affected employees.

5. Post-Payroll Activities

After calculating payroll, complete the following activities to finalize the payroll process:

- Generate Pay Slips: Oracle ERP can automatically generate pay slips for employees. These can be distributed electronically or printed as per organizational policy.

- Payments: Process payments through direct deposit or checks. Ensure all payments are correctly issued and recorded in the financial system.

- Statutory Reporting: Generate and submit required statutory reports to government agencies, including tax filings and social security contributions.

6. Payroll Reconciliation and Auditing

Regular reconciliation and auditing ensure the integrity of the payroll process and compliance with financial regulations.

- Reconciliation: Compare payroll records with financial statements to ensure accuracy. This includes reconciling payroll expenses, tax withholdings, and benefits contributions.

- Auditing: Conduct periodic audits of payroll processes to identify and rectify discrepancies or fraudulent activities. Ensure compliance with internal policies and external regulations.

7. Managing Payroll Adjustments

Occasionally, adjustments may be necessary due to errors, retroactive pay changes, or employee status changes.

- Retroactive Adjustments: If salary changes are applied retroactively, update the payroll system to reflect these changes and reprocess payroll as needed.

- Error Corrections: Correct any errors identified in previous payroll runs. This may involve adjusting individual employee records and recalculating payroll.

- Status Changes: Update the payroll system for changes in employee status, such as terminations, new hires, or transfers, ensuring that payroll processing reflects these changes.

8. Integrating Payroll with Other Modules

Oracle ERP's Payroll Management module integrates seamlessly with other modules, enhancing overall efficiency and data accuracy.

- Human Resources: Integration with the HR module ensures that employee information is consistently updated across the system, facilitating accurate payroll processing.

- Financials: Payroll expenses are automatically posted to the general ledger, ensuring real-time financial reporting and analysis.

- Time and Labor: Integration with the Time and Labor module allows automatic transfer of attendance and leave data to the payroll system, reducing manual data entry and errors.

9. Utilizing Self-Service and Mobile Solutions

Oracle ERP offers self-service and mobile solutions for payroll, empowering employees and reducing administrative workload.

- Employee Self-Service: Employees can access their pay slips, update personal information, and manage direct deposit preferences through a self-service portal.

- Mobile Access: Mobile solutions enable employees to view their payroll information, submit timecards, and manage leave requests on the go.

10. Ensuring Compliance and Security

Maintaining compliance and security is crucial for payroll management.

- Compliance: Stay updated with changing tax laws and regulatory requirements. Ensure the payroll system is configured to comply with local, state, and federal regulations.

- Security: Implement robust security measures to protect sensitive payroll data. This includes user access controls, data encryption, and regular security audits.

11. Continuous Improvement and Updates

Regularly updating and improving payroll processes ensures efficiency and accuracy.

- System Updates: Keep the Oracle ERP system updated with the latest patches and upgrades to leverage new features and improvements.

- Process Improvement: Continuously review and refine payroll processes to enhance accuracy, reduce processing time, and improve employee satisfaction.

Conclusion

Effective payroll processing in Oracle ERP involves meticulous setup, accurate data maintenance, and diligent monitoring of payroll activities. By following the detailed steps outlined in this guide, organizations can ensure smooth and compliant payroll operations, leading to enhanced employee satisfaction and operational efficiency.

5.2.2 Tax Management

Introduction to Tax Management in Payroll

Tax management is a critical component of payroll management in Oracle ERP. It involves the accurate calculation, deduction, and remittance of various taxes from employee salaries to the relevant tax authorities. Proper tax management ensures compliance with local, state, and federal tax regulations, helping organizations avoid legal penalties and maintain good standing with tax authorities.

Understanding Tax Components

In Oracle ERP, tax management within payroll covers several key components, including:

1. Income Tax: The primary tax deducted from an employee's salary, based on their income bracket.

2. Social Security Tax: Contributions to social security funds, usually a fixed percentage of the employee's salary.

3. Medicare Tax: A healthcare-related tax applicable in some regions.

4. Local Taxes: Additional taxes that may be imposed by local governments or municipalities.

Setting Up Tax Management in Oracle ERP

Step 1: Define Tax Authorities

Tax authorities must be defined in Oracle ERP to manage tax deductions accurately. This setup includes specifying the tax authority's details and the corresponding tax codes.

- Navigate to: Payroll -> Tax Management -> Define Tax Authorities.

- Enter the necessary information: Name, address, contact information, and tax codes.

- Save the details.

Step 2: Configure Tax Codes

Tax codes represent different types of taxes that need to be deducted from employees' salaries. Each tax code must be configured with the applicable tax rates and rules.

- Navigate to: Payroll -> Tax Management -> Define Tax Codes.

- Create a new tax code: Provide a unique code and description.

- Set the tax rate: Define whether the tax is a flat amount, a percentage of the salary, or based on income brackets.

- Specify applicability: Determine if the tax applies to all employees or specific groups.

- Save the configuration.

Step 3: Assign Tax Codes to Employees

After defining tax codes, they must be assigned to employees based on their tax obligations. This can be done individually or by group.

- Navigate to: Payroll -> Employee Tax Information.

- Select an employee: Search for and select the employee to assign tax codes.

- Assign tax codes: Choose the appropriate tax codes from the list and assign them to the employee.

- Save the assignment.

Step 4: Tax Calculation and Withholding

Oracle ERP automates the tax calculation process based on the predefined tax codes and employee information. During each payroll run, the system calculates the required tax deductions and withholds the amounts from the employees' salaries.

- Initiate payroll run: Payroll -> Payroll Processing -> Run Payroll.

- Verify tax calculations: Review the payroll summary report to ensure all taxes are correctly calculated.

- Approve and finalize payroll: Confirm the payroll run and process the payments.

Step 5: Generating Tax Reports

Accurate reporting is essential for compliance and auditing purposes. Oracle ERP provides various tax reports that can be generated to review and submit to tax authorities.

- Navigate to: Payroll -> Reports -> Tax Reports.

- Select report type: Choose from predefined tax reports such as Income Tax Report, Social Security Contributions, etc.

- Specify parameters: Define the reporting period and any other relevant criteria.

- Generate and review the report: Ensure all details are correct before submission.

- Export and submit: Export the report in the required format and submit it to the relevant tax authorities.

Advanced Tax Management Features

Oracle ERP also offers advanced features for managing complex tax scenarios, including:

1. Multiple Tax Jurisdictions: Managing employees working in different regions with varying tax laws.

2. Tax Credits and Deductions: Applying applicable tax credits and additional deductions.

3. Exemptions and Allowances: Handling exemptions for specific employees or income types.

4. Year-End Tax Processing: Managing annual tax calculations, adjustments, and issuing tax documents to employees.

Handling Tax Audits and Compliance

Regular audits are necessary to ensure ongoing compliance with tax regulations. Oracle ERP's audit and compliance features help in:

- Audit Trails: Maintaining detailed records of all tax-related transactions.

- Compliance Checks: Automated checks to ensure all tax calculations and filings are compliant with the latest regulations.

- Documentation: Keeping all necessary documentation readily available for internal and external audits.

Best Practices for Tax Management

To maximize the efficiency and accuracy of tax management in Oracle ERP, consider the following best practices:

1. Stay Updated: Regularly update the system with the latest tax rates and regulations.

2. Regular Audits: Conduct periodic internal audits to verify the accuracy of tax deductions and filings.

3. Employee Training: Ensure that payroll and HR staff are well-trained in using the tax management features of Oracle ERP.

4. Use Automation: Leverage Oracle ERP's automation capabilities to minimize manual errors and streamline tax processes.

5. Maintain Communication: Keep open communication channels with tax authorities to stay informed about any changes in tax laws or filing requirements.

Conclusion

Effective tax management within payroll is crucial for maintaining compliance and ensuring accurate salary disbursements. By leveraging Oracle ERP's robust tax management features, organizations can streamline their tax processes, reduce the risk of errors, and ensure timely and accurate tax filings. This not only helps in avoiding legal penalties but also enhances the overall efficiency of payroll management.

5.3 Time and Labor Management

Effective management of time and labor is crucial for the smooth operation of any organization. Oracle ERP's Time and Labor Management module provides comprehensive tools to track, manage, and optimize employee time and labor costs. This section will cover the essential features and functionalities of the Time and Labor Management module, focusing on Time Tracking.

5.3.1 Time Tracking

Time tracking is a vital component of the Time and Labor Management module in Oracle ERP. It allows organizations to record and monitor employee work hours accurately, ensuring proper payroll processing, compliance with labor laws, and effective resource management. This section will guide you through the detailed process of setting up and using the time tracking features in Oracle ERP.

Overview of Time Tracking

Time tracking in Oracle ERP involves capturing employee work hours, leave, and overtime in a systematic manner. This data is essential for various business processes, including payroll, project management, and labor cost analysis. The time tracking module integrates seamlessly with other HR and payroll functions, providing a comprehensive view of employee time and attendance.

Setting Up Time Tracking

Configuring Time Entry Rules

1. Define Time Categories: Time categories represent different types of work hours, such as regular hours, overtime, and leave. In Oracle ERP, you can customize these categories based on your organization's policies.

- Navigate to the Time Management setup.

- Select Time Categories and define the necessary categories.

- Assign each category a unique code and description.

2. Establish Time Entry Policies: Time entry policies govern how time is recorded and approved. Policies can include rules for rounding, grace periods, and submission deadlines.

- Go to Time Entry Policies under the Time Management module.

- Create policies for different employee groups, specifying rules for each category of time.

Configuring Time Clocks and Devices

Oracle ERP supports integration with various time clocks and biometric devices to automate time capture.

1. Device Integration: Integrate physical time clocks or biometric devices with Oracle ERP to streamline time entry.

- In the Time Management module, select Device Integration.

- Configure the connection settings for each device, ensuring secure data transfer.

2. Employee Registration: Register employees on the time clocks or biometric devices.

- Access the Employee Registration section.

- Follow the prompts to add employee details and link them to the corresponding devices.

Creating Timecards

Timecards are the primary means of recording employee work hours. Oracle ERP allows employees to create and submit timecards electronically.

1. Template Creation: Create timecard templates to standardize time entry.

- Navigate to Timecard Templates.

- Define the structure of the template, including time categories, fields, and validation rules.

2. Timecard Submission: Employees can submit their timecards for approval.

 - Employees access the Time Entry portal.

 - Select the appropriate template and enter their work hours.

 - Submit the timecard for managerial approval.

Managing Time Entries

Time Entry Validation

Time entries must be validated to ensure accuracy and compliance with organizational policies.

1. Automated Validation: Configure validation rules to automate the process.

 - Go to Time Entry Validation Rules.

 - Define rules such as maximum allowable hours, mandatory fields, and acceptable time ranges.

2. Manual Review: Managers can review and approve time entries.

 - Access the Time Approval section.

 - Review submitted timecards, making corrections if necessary.

 - Approve or reject time entries based on the validation results.

Handling Exceptions

Exception handling is crucial for managing irregularities in time entries, such as missed punches or incorrect entries.

1. Identifying Exceptions: Use exception reports to identify discrepancies.

 - Navigate to Exception Reports.

 - Generate reports to highlight time entries that deviate from standard rules.

2. Resolving Exceptions: Managers can resolve exceptions by adjusting time entries.

  - In the Time Entry section, select the entry with exceptions.

  - Make the necessary adjustments and provide justifications.

Reporting and Analytics

Oracle ERP's reporting tools provide insights into time and labor data, helping organizations make informed decisions.

1. Standard Reports: Generate predefined reports to analyze time and labor data.

  - Go to Time Management Reports.

  - Select from a variety of standard reports, such as daily time summaries, overtime reports, and attendance trends.

2. Custom Reports: Create custom reports to meet specific business needs.

  - Use the Report Builder tool.

  - Define report criteria, including filters, groupings, and data fields.

3. Data Visualization: Utilize data visualization tools to present time and labor data graphically.

  - Access the Data Visualization module.

  - Create dashboards and charts to visualize trends and patterns in time tracking data.

Integrations with Other Modules

Time tracking data is valuable across various business functions. Oracle ERP facilitates seamless integration with other modules, ensuring comprehensive data utilization.

1. Payroll Integration: Integrate time tracking with the Payroll Management module for accurate payroll processing.

   - Ensure time entries are approved and validated.

   - Transfer the data to the Payroll module for processing.

2. Project Management Integration: Use time tracking data for project costing and resource management.

   - Link time entries to specific projects and tasks.

   - Generate project time reports to analyze labor costs and resource utilization.

3. Compliance and Audit Integration: Maintain compliance with labor laws and internal policies.

   - Use audit trails to track changes and approvals in time entries.

   - Generate compliance reports to ensure adherence to regulations.

Best Practices for Effective Time Tracking

To maximize the benefits of time tracking in Oracle ERP, consider implementing the following best practices:

1. Regular Training: Provide training to employees and managers on time entry policies and procedures.

2. Clear Communication: Clearly communicate time tracking policies and deadlines to employees.

3. Periodic Audits: Conduct regular audits of time entries to ensure accuracy and compliance.

4. Continuous Improvement: Continuously review and improve time tracking processes based on feedback and changing business needs.

By following these guidelines and leveraging the robust features of Oracle ERP's Time and Labor Management module, organizations can achieve accurate time tracking, enhance productivity, and ensure effective labor cost management. This concludes the section on Time Tracking. Next, we will explore Labor Costing in detail.

5.3.2 Labor Costing

Labor costing is a crucial aspect of managing an organization's workforce expenses. In Oracle ERP, labor costing helps organizations accurately calculate and allocate labor costs to various projects, departments, or cost centers. This ensures that the financial statements reflect the true cost of labor, which is essential for budgeting, forecasting, and financial analysis. This section will provide a detailed guide on how to manage labor costing in Oracle ERP.

Introduction to Labor Costing

Labor costing involves tracking the costs associated with employees' work hours and allocating these costs appropriately. This includes direct labor costs, such as wages and salaries, as well as indirect costs like benefits, taxes, and overheads. Accurate labor costing enables organizations to understand the true cost of their workforce and make informed decisions regarding staffing, project pricing, and overall financial management.

Setting Up Labor Costing in Oracle ERP

To set up labor costing in Oracle ERP, follow these steps:

1. Define Cost Components: Identify and define the various cost components that make up the total labor cost. These components can include base wages, overtime, bonuses, benefits, taxes, and other indirect costs.

   - Base Wages: Regular hourly or salaried pay.

   - Overtime: Additional pay for hours worked beyond the standard workweek.

   - Bonuses: Performance-related or other incentive payments.

   - Benefits: Health insurance, retirement contributions, and other employee benefits.

   - Taxes: Payroll taxes, including Social Security, Medicare, and unemployment taxes.

- Indirect Costs: Allocated overhead costs related to labor, such as training and development expenses.

2. Create Cost Groups: Organize employees into cost groups based on similar labor cost structures. This could be by department, job role, or project team. Cost groups facilitate easier management and allocation of labor costs.

  - Example Cost Groups:

  - Sales Team

  - Production Workers

  - Administrative Staff

  - Project A Team

  - Project B Team

3. Set Up Cost Rates: Define the cost rates for each cost component within the cost groups. Cost rates can be fixed or variable, depending on the nature of the cost component.

  - Fixed Rates: Static costs such as base wages and standard benefits.

  - Variable Rates: Costs that fluctuate, such as overtime pay and performance bonuses.

4. Configure Cost Allocation Rules: Establish rules for allocating labor costs to specific projects, departments, or cost centers. These rules can be based on time worked, employee roles, or predefined allocation percentages.

  - Examples of Allocation Rules:

  - Allocate 50% of administrative staff costs to General Administration and 50% to Customer Support.

  - Allocate project team costs based on hours logged against each project.

5. Integrate Time Tracking Systems: Ensure that the time tracking system is integrated with Oracle ERP to capture accurate data on employee work hours. This data is essential for calculating labor costs.

  - Integration Points:

  - Time clock systems

  - Employee time sheets

- Project management tools

Managing Labor Costs

Once the setup is complete, managing labor costs involves continuous monitoring, analysis, and adjustment to ensure accuracy and alignment with organizational goals.

1. Collecting Time Data: Regularly collect and review time data from integrated systems. Ensure that employees accurately record their work hours, including regular time, overtime, and project-specific hours.

  - Best Practices:

    - Conduct regular audits of time entries to identify discrepancies.

    - Implement automated reminders for employees to submit time sheets.

2. Calculating Labor Costs: Use Oracle ERP's built-in functionalities to calculate labor costs based on the collected time data and predefined cost rates. The system should automatically apply the relevant cost rates to the recorded hours.

  - Calculation Example:

    - Employee A works 40 regular hours and 5 overtime hours in a week.

    - Base wage rate: $20/hour, Overtime rate: $30/hour.

    - Total labor cost: (40 hours x $20) + (5 hours x $30) = $950.

3. Allocating Labor Costs: Apply the cost allocation rules to distribute labor costs across projects, departments, or cost centers. This ensures that each unit reflects the true labor costs in its financial reports.

  - Allocation Example:

    - Project A requires 60% of Employee A's time, and Project B requires 40%.

    - Allocate 60% of $950 to Project A and 40% to Project B.

4. Monitoring and Adjusting Costs: Continuously monitor labor costs to identify any variances from budgeted amounts. Adjust cost rates, allocation rules, or workforce planning as needed to address any discrepancies.

  - Monitoring Tools:

- Labor cost reports

- Variance analysis tools

- Real-time dashboards

5. Reporting and Analysis: Generate detailed labor cost reports to analyze the cost structure, identify trends, and make informed decisions. Reports can include labor cost summaries, cost variances, and allocation breakdowns.

  - Common Reports:

  - Total labor costs by department

  - Project-specific labor cost analysis

  - Labor cost trends over time

Best Practices for Labor Costing

Implementing effective labor costing practices in Oracle ERP can significantly enhance financial management and operational efficiency. Here are some best practices to consider:

1. Regularly Review and Update Cost Rates: Labor cost rates can change due to wage adjustments, benefit changes, or new tax regulations. Regularly review and update cost rates to ensure accuracy.

  - Annual Review: Conduct a comprehensive review of all cost rates at least once a year.

  - Mid-Year Adjustments: Make necessary adjustments for significant changes in labor costs.

2. Automate Data Collection and Integration: Minimize manual data entry by automating the collection and integration of time data. This reduces errors and ensures timely updates.

  - Automation Tools: Use time tracking software and integration tools to streamline data flow.

3. Implement Strong Internal Controls: Establish robust internal controls to ensure the accuracy and integrity of labor cost data. This includes regular audits, approval workflows, and access controls.

- Audit Trails: Maintain detailed audit trails for all labor cost transactions.

- Approval Workflows: Implement approval processes for time entries and cost allocations.

4. Provide Training and Support: Ensure that employees and managers are trained on the importance of accurate time tracking and labor costing. Provide ongoing support to address any issues or questions.

- Training Programs: Conduct regular training sessions for new hires and refresher courses for existing employees.

- Help Desk Support: Offer dedicated support channels for labor costing queries.

5. Leverage Advanced Analytics: Use Oracle ERP's advanced analytics capabilities to gain deeper insights into labor costs. This can help identify cost-saving opportunities and improve decision-making.

- Predictive Analytics: Utilize predictive analytics to forecast future labor costs and plan accordingly.

- Dashboard Reporting: Create interactive dashboards to monitor labor costs in real-time.

Conclusion

Labor costing is a vital component of effective workforce management and financial control. By accurately tracking and allocating labor costs, organizations can ensure that their financial statements reflect the true cost of their workforce. Oracle ERP provides robust tools and functionalities to streamline labor costing, from initial setup to ongoing management and reporting.

By following the detailed guide outlined in this section, organizations can optimize their labor costing processes, improve financial accuracy, and make informed decisions that drive business success. With the right setup, continuous monitoring, and adherence to best practices, labor costing can become a powerful tool for enhancing operational efficiency and financial performance.

CHAPTER VI
Reporting and Analytics in Oracle ERP

6.1 Standard Reports

6.1.1 Financial Reports

Financial reports in Oracle ERP are crucial for providing insights into the financial health and performance of an organization. These reports help stakeholders make informed decisions by offering a comprehensive view of financial data. In this section, we will cover the various types of financial reports available in Oracle ERP, how to generate them, and the best practices for using these reports effectively.

Overview of Financial Reports

Financial reports in Oracle ERP typically include the following:

- Balance Sheet

- Income Statement

- Cash Flow Statement

- Trial Balance

- Accounts Receivable Aging Report

- Accounts Payable Aging Report

Each of these reports serves a specific purpose and provides different insights into the financial operations of the organization.

Generating Financial Reports

Generating financial reports in Oracle ERP involves the following steps:

1. Accessing the Reporting Module

   - Navigate to the Oracle ERP homepage.

   - Select the "Financial Reporting" module from the menu.

2. Selecting the Report Type

   - Choose the type of financial report you wish to generate (e.g., Balance Sheet, Income Statement).

   - Each report type will have a predefined template that includes standard fields and layout.

3. Configuring Report Parameters

   - Set the parameters for the report, such as the date range, account segments, and specific entities or departments to include.

   - Use filters to customize the report according to your needs.

4. Running the Report

   - Click the "Run Report" button.

   - The system will process the data and generate the report.

5. Reviewing and Exporting the Report

   - Review the report in the ERP system.

   - Export the report to various formats (e.g., PDF, Excel) if needed.

Detailed Walkthrough of Key Financial Reports

Balance Sheet

The Balance Sheet provides a snapshot of the organization's financial position at a specific point in time. It includes assets, liabilities, and equity.

- Assets: This section lists the company's resources, including current assets (cash, accounts receivable, inventory) and non-current assets (property, equipment, intangible assets).

- Liabilities: This section lists the company's obligations, including current liabilities (accounts payable, short-term loans) and long-term liabilities (long-term debt, deferred tax liabilities).

- Equity: This section shows the owner's interest in the company, including retained earnings and common stock.

Income Statement

The Income Statement, also known as the Profit and Loss Statement, shows the company's financial performance over a specific period. It includes revenues, expenses, and profits or losses.

- Revenues: This section lists all income generated from the company's core business operations.

- Expenses: This section lists all costs incurred in generating revenue, including operating expenses (salaries, rent, utilities) and non-operating expenses (interest, taxes).

- Net Profit/Loss: This is the difference between total revenues and total expenses, indicating the company's profitability.

Cash Flow Statement

The Cash Flow Statement provides insights into the company's cash inflows and outflows over a specific period. It includes operating, investing, and financing activities.

- Operating Activities: This section shows cash generated or used in core business operations.

- Investing Activities: This section shows cash used in or generated from investing activities, such as purchasing or selling assets.

- Financing Activities: This section shows cash flows related to financing, such as issuing shares, borrowing, and repaying loans.

Trial Balance

The Trial Balance is a summary of all ledger accounts at a specific point in time. It ensures that the total debits equal the total credits, indicating the accounts are balanced.

- Debits and Credits: This section lists all accounts with their respective debit or credit balances.

- Error Detection: Any discrepancies indicate errors that need to be corrected before finalizing financial statements.

Accounts Receivable Aging Report

This report provides a detailed view of outstanding receivables and their aging. It helps in managing credit risk and collections.

- Customer Balances: Lists all outstanding balances by customer.

- Aging Buckets: Categorizes receivables into aging buckets (e.g., 0-30 days, 31-60 days) to highlight overdue accounts.

Accounts Payable Aging Report

This report provides a detailed view of outstanding payables and their aging. It helps in managing cash flow and supplier relationships.

- Supplier Balances: Lists all outstanding balances by supplier.

- Aging Buckets: Categorizes payables into aging buckets (e.g., 0-30 days, 31-60 days) to highlight overdue payments.

Best Practices for Using Financial Reports

1. Regular Review and Analysis

   - Schedule regular intervals (monthly, quarterly) to review financial reports.

   - Analyze trends and variances to understand the financial performance and make informed decisions.

2. Customization and Filtering

   - Customize reports to focus on specific departments, entities, or time periods.

   - Use filtering options to drill down into details and identify key areas of interest.

3. Cross-Report Comparisons

   - Compare different reports (e.g., Balance Sheet and Income Statement) to get a comprehensive view of financial health.

   - Use cross-report comparisons to validate data accuracy and consistency.

4. Automation and Scheduling

   - Automate report generation and scheduling to ensure timely availability of financial information.

   - Use ERP system features to schedule regular report runs and distribute them to relevant stakeholders.

5. Security and Access Control

   - Ensure that only authorized personnel have access to sensitive financial reports.

   - Implement access controls and audit trails to track report usage and maintain data security.

Using Oracle ERP Reporting Tools

Oracle ERP provides several tools to enhance the reporting and analysis capabilities:

BI Publisher

BI Publisher is a reporting tool that allows users to create, manage, and deliver reports. It supports various data sources and output formats.

- Creating Reports: Use BI Publisher to design custom reports with a wide range of formatting options.

- Data Sources: Integrate data from multiple sources, including Oracle databases, XML files, and Web services.

- Delivery Options: Schedule and distribute reports via email, FTP, or web services.

Data Visualization

Oracle ERP includes data visualization tools to help users interpret complex data through graphical representations.

- Dashboards: Create interactive dashboards that provide a visual summary of key financial metrics.

- Charts and Graphs: Use charts and graphs to highlight trends, patterns, and outliers in financial data.

Conclusion

Financial reports are a vital component of Oracle ERP, providing essential insights into the financial health and performance of an organization. By understanding the various types of financial reports and how to generate and use them effectively, organizations can make informed decisions, manage risks, and optimize their financial operations. Leveraging Oracle ERP's reporting tools and best practices ensures that financial information is accurate, timely, and actionable, contributing to the overall success and growth of the business.

6.1.2 Operational Reports

Operational reports in Oracle ERP provide crucial insights into the day-to-day activities of a business. These reports help in monitoring, analyzing, and managing the operational performance and efficiency across various departments. This section provides a detailed guide on how to generate, customize, and utilize operational reports in Oracle ERP to ensure optimal business performance.

Understanding Operational Reports

Operational reports are designed to track and monitor the ongoing activities within an organization. They provide real-time data and insights into various operational aspects, such as inventory levels, production schedules, procurement processes, sales orders, and customer service metrics. These reports are essential for managers and decision-makers to ensure that operations are running smoothly and efficiently.

Types of Operational Reports

1. Inventory Reports: Track inventory levels, movements, and stock status.

2. Procurement Reports: Monitor purchase orders, supplier performance, and procurement cycles.

3. Sales and Order Reports: Analyze sales order processing, order fulfillment, and customer demand.

4. Production Reports: Assess production schedules, work order status, and manufacturing efficiency.

5. Customer Service Reports: Evaluate customer service performance, response times, and issue resolution.

Generating Operational Reports in Oracle ERP

Oracle ERP provides a user-friendly interface for generating operational reports. The following steps outline the process of creating standard operational reports:

Step 1: Access the Reporting Module

1. Log in to Oracle ERP.

2. Navigate to the "Reports and Analytics" module.

3. Select the "Operational Reports" section.

Step 2: Choose the Report Type

1. From the list of available reports, choose the specific operational report you need (e.g., Inventory Report, Procurement Report).

2. Click on the report name to open the report generation interface.

Step 3: Set Report Parameters

1. Date Range: Specify the date range for the report. This could be daily, weekly, monthly, or for a custom period.

2. Departments: Select the departments or business units for which you want to generate the report.

3. Metrics: Choose the specific metrics and data points you want to include in the report (e.g., inventory levels, purchase order status).

Step 4: Generate the Report

1. After setting the parameters, click on the "Generate Report" button.

2. Oracle ERP will process the request and generate the report based on the specified parameters.

Customizing Operational Reports

Oracle ERP allows users to customize operational reports to meet their specific needs. Customization can be done through the report builder interface:

1. Add/Remove Fields: Modify the report to include or exclude certain data fields.

2. Apply Filters: Use filters to narrow down the data to specific criteria (e.g., filter inventory reports by item category).

3. Group Data: Group data by specific attributes, such as department, supplier, or product category, for better analysis.

4. Sort Data: Sort the report data in ascending or descending order based on specific fields, such as order date or stock levels.

Utilizing Operational Reports

Operational reports are not just for viewing; they are essential tools for making informed decisions and improving business processes. Here are some ways to utilize operational reports effectively:

Monitoring Inventory Levels

1. Real-Time Inventory Tracking: Use inventory reports to monitor stock levels in real-time, ensuring that there are no shortages or excesses.

2. Reorder Points: Identify items that are below their reorder points and take action to replenish them.

3. Stock Movement Analysis: Analyze stock movement patterns to optimize inventory storage and reduce holding costs.

Improving Procurement Efficiency

1. Supplier Performance: Use procurement reports to evaluate supplier performance based on delivery times, order accuracy, and quality.

2. Purchase Order Status: Track the status of purchase orders to ensure timely receipt of goods and avoid delays in production.

3. Cost Management: Analyze procurement costs and identify opportunities for cost savings through better supplier negotiations or alternative sourcing strategies.

Enhancing Sales and Order Processing

1. Order Fulfillment: Monitor the order fulfillment process to ensure timely delivery to customers and improve customer satisfaction.

2. Sales Trends: Analyze sales trends to identify popular products, seasonal demand, and sales performance by region or sales team.

3. Customer Insights: Use sales and order reports to gain insights into customer behavior, preferences, and purchasing patterns.

Optimizing Production Schedules

1. Work Order Tracking: Use production reports to track the status of work orders and ensure that production schedules are on track.

2. Resource Allocation: Analyze production data to optimize resource allocation, such as labor and machinery, to improve manufacturing efficiency.

3. Production Costs: Monitor production costs and identify areas for cost reduction, such as minimizing waste or improving process efficiency.

Enhancing Customer Service

1. Response Times: Use customer service reports to monitor response times and ensure that customer inquiries and issues are resolved promptly.

2. Issue Resolution: Track the resolution of customer issues and identify recurring problems that need to be addressed.

3. Customer Feedback: Analyze customer feedback and satisfaction scores to improve service quality and customer experience.

Best Practices for Operational Reporting

To maximize the value of operational reports, consider the following best practices:

1. Regular Monitoring: Schedule regular generation and review of operational reports to stay updated on key performance metrics.

2. Actionable Insights: Focus on actionable insights that can lead to improvements in business processes and performance.

3. Collaboration: Share operational reports with relevant stakeholders and collaborate on strategies to address identified issues.

4. Continuous Improvement: Use operational reports as a basis for continuous improvement initiatives, such as process optimization and efficiency gains.

Conclusion

Operational reports in Oracle ERP are powerful tools that provide valuable insights into the day-to-day activities of a business. By understanding how to generate, customize, and utilize these reports, businesses can improve their operational efficiency, make informed decisions, and ultimately unlock their full potential. With the detailed guidance provided in this section, users can effectively leverage operational reports to drive business success.

6.2 Custom Reports

Custom reports in Oracle ERP provide the flexibility to design and generate reports tailored to specific business needs. This section will guide you through the process of creating custom reports using the Report Builder tool in Oracle ERP.

6.2.1 Report Builder

The Report Builder in Oracle ERP is a powerful tool that allows users to create custom reports by defining the data sources, layouts, and formatting options. Whether you need a detailed financial report or a summary of operational performance, the Report Builder offers a user-friendly interface and robust functionality to meet your reporting requirements.

Introduction to Report Builder

The Report Builder is an integrated tool within Oracle ERP designed to facilitate the creation of custom reports. It enables users to select data from various modules, apply filters and sorting criteria, and design the layout and formatting of the report.

Key Features

- Data Source Selection: Choose from a wide range of data sources within Oracle ERP.

- Layout Design: Customize the layout using drag-and-drop features.

- Formatting Options: Apply various formatting options to enhance the report's readability.

- Preview and Testing: Preview the report before finalizing to ensure accuracy.

- Scheduling and Distribution: Schedule automated report generation and distribute reports to stakeholders.

Step-by-Step Guide to Creating a Custom Report

Step 1: Accessing the Report Builder

To access the Report Builder, navigate to the Reports module within Oracle ERP. Select the 'Create Report' option to open the Report Builder interface.

Step 2: Selecting Data Sources

The first step in creating a custom report is selecting the data sources. Oracle ERP provides a comprehensive list of data sources, including tables, views, and predefined queries. You can choose multiple data sources and join them to fetch the required data.

1. Open Data Source Selection: Click on the 'Data Source' tab.

2. Add Data Source: Click the 'Add' button to select the required data source.

3. Configure Joins: If multiple data sources are selected, configure the joins between them to ensure accurate data retrieval.

Step 3: Defining Data Fields

After selecting the data sources, define the data fields you want to include in the report. Data fields represent the columns that will be displayed in the report.

1. Select Fields: In the 'Fields' section, select the required fields from the data sources.

2. Rename Fields: Optionally, rename the fields to make them more descriptive.

3. Add Calculated Fields: Create calculated fields by applying formulas to the selected fields.

Step 4: Applying Filters

Filters allow you to narrow down the data to include only the relevant information in the report.

1. Add Filters: Click on the 'Filters' tab and add the necessary filters.

2. Configure Filter Conditions: Specify the conditions for each filter, such as 'equals', 'contains', 'greater than', etc.

3. Combine Filters: Use logical operators (AND, OR) to combine multiple filters.

Step 5: Designing the Layout

The layout design is a crucial step in creating a custom report. It involves arranging the data fields and adding headers, footers, and other elements to enhance the report's readability.

1. Open Layout Designer: Click on the 'Layout' tab to open the layout designer.

2. Drag-and-Drop Fields: Drag the data fields from the 'Fields' section to the layout area.

3. Add Headers and Footers: Add headers and footers to the report for titles, dates, and page numbers.

4. Group Data: Group the data by specific fields to create summaries and sub-totals.

5. Insert Charts and Graphs: Use the 'Insert' menu to add charts and graphs to visualize the data.

Step 6: Formatting the Report

Formatting options allow you to enhance the visual appeal and readability of the report.

1. Text Formatting: Apply font styles, sizes, and colors to the text elements.

2. Conditional Formatting: Use conditional formatting to highlight specific data based on defined criteria.

3. Borders and Shading: Add borders and shading to the report elements for better separation and emphasis.

Step 7: Previewing the Report

Before finalizing the report, preview it to ensure that the data is accurate and the layout is as desired.

1. Click Preview: Click the 'Preview' button to generate a preview of the report.

2. Verify Data: Check the data for accuracy and completeness.

3. Adjust Layout: Make any necessary adjustments to the layout and formatting based on the preview.

Step 8: Saving and Running the Report

Once the report is designed and formatted, save it and run it to generate the final output.

1. Save Report: Click the 'Save' button and provide a name and description for the report.

2. Run Report: Click the 'Run' button to generate the report.

3. Export Options: Export the report in various formats such as PDF, Excel, or HTML.

Step 9: Scheduling and Distributing the Report

Oracle ERP allows you to schedule automated report generation and distribute the reports to stakeholders.

1. Schedule Report: Click on the 'Schedule' button to set up a schedule for automatic report generation.

2. Set Frequency: Define the frequency (daily, weekly, monthly) and time for the report generation.

3. Email Distribution: Add email addresses of the stakeholders to distribute the report automatically.

Best Practices for Creating Custom Reports

- Define Objectives: Clearly define the objectives of the report before starting the design process.

- Simplify Data: Keep the data simple and relevant to avoid clutter.

- Use Visuals: Incorporate charts and graphs to make the data more comprehensible.

- Test Thoroughly: Test the report with different data sets to ensure accuracy and reliability.

- Document the Process: Document the report creation process for future reference and updates.

By following these steps and best practices, you can effectively utilize the Report Builder in Oracle ERP to create custom reports that meet your specific business needs. The flexibility and functionality of the Report Builder make it a valuable tool for generating insightful and actionable reports.

6.2.2 Customization Techniques

Custom reports in Oracle ERP offer the flexibility to tailor the reporting to meet specific business needs. This customization ensures that the data presented is relevant, accurate, and actionable. In this section, we will explore various customization techniques that can be used to enhance the utility and functionality of reports in Oracle ERP.

1. Understanding Report Customization Requirements

Before diving into the customization process, it is crucial to understand the specific requirements of the custom report. This involves:

- Identifying the Audience: Determine who will be using the report and what their specific needs are.

- Defining Objectives: Clarify what the report aims to achieve, such as tracking performance metrics, monitoring compliance, or analyzing financial data.

- Data Sources: Identify the data sources that will be used in the report, including modules, tables, and fields within Oracle ERP.

2. Using Oracle BI Publisher for Customization

Oracle BI Publisher is a powerful tool for creating and customizing reports. Here are the key steps to customize reports using BI Publisher:

Step 1: Creating a Data Model

- Data Source Selection: Choose the appropriate data source, which could be a database, Excel file, Web service, or another format.

- SQL Query Design: Write SQL queries to extract the necessary data. Use joins and subqueries to fetch data from multiple tables if required.

- Parameters: Define parameters to allow users to filter data dynamically when running the report.

Step 2: Designing the Report Layout

- Layout Templates: Choose from existing templates or create a new layout using the BI Publisher layout editor. You can use different formats such as RTF, PDF, Excel, and HTML.

- Inserting Data Fields: Drag and drop data fields from the data model into the layout template. Use placeholders to dynamically insert data.

- Styling and Formatting: Customize fonts, colors, and other styling elements to match corporate branding guidelines.

Step 3: Testing and Validation

- Previewing the Report: Generate a preview to ensure that data is correctly displayed and formatted.

- Validation: Check for data accuracy and consistency. Make sure the report meets the initial requirements.

Step 4: Deployment and Scheduling

- Publishing: Deploy the report to the appropriate users or groups. Ensure that access permissions are correctly set.

- Scheduling: Set up a schedule to run the report at regular intervals. Configure delivery options such as email or saving to a network location.

3. Advanced Customization Techniques

To further enhance the functionality of custom reports, consider using these advanced customization techniques:

3.1. Adding Calculations and Formulas

- Calculated Fields: Create calculated fields within the data model to perform on-the-fly calculations.

- Excel-like Functions: Use functions similar to those in Excel, such as SUM, AVERAGE, and IF, to perform complex data manipulations.

3.2. Conditional Formatting

- Highlighting Data: Apply conditional formatting to highlight data based on certain conditions. For example, use color-coding to show high and low values.

- Rules and Conditions: Define rules for conditional formatting in the layout editor to dynamically change the appearance of data.

3.3. Sub-Reports and Nested Reports

- Sub-Reports: Create sub-reports to display related data within a main report. This is useful for showing detailed information alongside summary data.

- Linking Reports: Link multiple reports to provide a comprehensive view. Users can drill down from summary reports to detailed reports.

3.4. Data Visualization

- Charts and Graphs: Enhance reports with visual elements such as bar charts, pie charts, and line graphs. Visualizations help in better understanding trends and patterns.

- Interactive Elements: Add interactive elements like dropdown menus and clickable links to navigate between different sections of the report.

3.5. Integrating External Data Sources

- External Data: Incorporate data from external sources such as other databases, web services, or cloud applications.

- Data Blending: Blend data from Oracle ERP with external data to create comprehensive reports that provide a complete view of business operations.

4. Customization Best Practices

To ensure effective and efficient report customization, follow these best practices:

4.1. Planning and Design

- Requirement Gathering: Thoroughly gather and document requirements before starting the customization process.

- Prototyping: Create prototypes or mock-ups of the report to get feedback from stakeholders early in the process.

4.2. Performance Optimization

- Efficient Queries: Write efficient SQL queries to minimize the load on the database. Avoid complex joins and unnecessary calculations within the query.

- Indexing: Use database indexing to speed up data retrieval. Ensure that frequently queried columns are indexed.

4.3. Security and Access Control

- Data Security: Ensure that sensitive data is protected. Use role-based access control to restrict access to authorized users.

- Audit Trails: Maintain audit trails to track changes made to reports and data models. This helps in troubleshooting and maintaining data integrity.

4.4. Documentation and Training

- User Documentation: Provide comprehensive documentation for users to understand how to use and customize reports.

- Training Sessions: Conduct training sessions to educate users on customization techniques and best practices.

5. Real-World Examples and Use Cases

To illustrate the customization process, here are some real-world examples and use cases:

Example 1: Financial Performance Dashboard

- Objective: Create a dashboard to monitor key financial metrics such as revenue, expenses, and profit margins.

- Customization: Use BI Publisher to design interactive charts and tables. Add calculated fields for profit margin calculations. Apply conditional formatting to highlight variances from targets.

Example 2: Inventory Management Report

- Objective: Develop a report to track inventory levels, reorder points, and stock movement.

- Customization: Create a data model with SQL queries to fetch inventory data. Design a layout with tables and graphs to show current stock levels and trends. Add parameters for dynamic filtering by product category or warehouse.

Example 3: Employee Performance Report

- Objective: Generate a report to evaluate employee performance based on key metrics such as attendance, productivity, and goal achievement.

- Customization: Use BI Publisher to create a layout with detailed employee profiles. Add sub-reports to show individual performance metrics. Use conditional formatting to highlight top performers and areas needing improvement.

Conclusion

Customization of reports in Oracle ERP using techniques outlined in this section allows organizations to create tailored, meaningful reports that meet specific business needs. By leveraging tools like Oracle BI Publisher and following best practices, users can enhance the functionality, accuracy, and usability of their reports, ultimately driving better decision-making and business outcomes.

6.3 Data Analysis Tools

Data analysis tools play a crucial role in leveraging the data stored within Oracle ERP systems to derive meaningful insights and facilitate informed decision-making. Among these tools, BI Publisher stands out as a powerful reporting solution that enhances the capabilities of Oracle ERP users to generate, customize, and distribute reports efficiently.

6.3.1 BI Publisher

BI Publisher, part of Oracle's Business Intelligence Suite, is a robust reporting tool designed to meet diverse reporting needs within Oracle ERP environments. This section explores the functionalities, implementation, and best practices associated with BI Publisher.

Introduction to BI Publisher

BI Publisher enables users to create highly formatted reports from various data sources including Oracle databases, XML data sources, web services, and more. Unlike standard reports, BI Publisher offers extensive customization options, allowing users to design reports that meet specific business requirements without extensive IT involvement.

Key Features of BI Publisher

BI Publisher provides several key features that enhance reporting capabilities within Oracle ERP:

- Template-Based Reporting: Utilize pre-built templates or create custom templates to define the layout, formatting, and data sources for reports.

- Data Source Flexibility: Connect seamlessly to multiple data sources including Oracle databases, XML files, web services, and Excel spreadsheets.

- Parameterized Reports: Enable users to define parameters that allow for dynamic filtering and customization of report outputs based on user inputs.

- Multi-channel Delivery: Distribute reports via various channels such as email, FTP, printer, and portals, ensuring timely access to critical business information.

- Integration Capabilities: Integrate with other Oracle applications and third-party tools to enhance functionality and extend reporting capabilities.

Implementing BI Publisher in Oracle ERP

Implementing BI Publisher requires careful planning and configuration to ensure optimal performance and alignment with business needs:

1. Installation and Setup: Guide on installing BI Publisher within the Oracle ERP environment, including system requirements and prerequisites.

2. Configuration: Steps to configure BI Publisher settings, including defining data connections, security settings, and administrative configurations.

3. Creating Reports:

  - Template Design: Detailed instructions on designing report templates using BI Publisher's layout editor.

  - Data Model Creation: Define data models to retrieve and structure data from Oracle ERP tables and other sources.

  - Parameter Setup: Configure parameters to enable user-driven customization and filtering options in reports.

4. Customization Techniques:

  - Advanced Layout Options: Explore advanced formatting techniques such as conditional formatting, grouping, and aggregations.

  - Using Functions and Expressions: Leveraging BI Publisher's built-in functions and expressions to manipulate and calculate data within reports.

  - Incorporating Charts and Graphs: Integrate visual elements like charts and graphs to enhance data visualization and analysis.

5. Security and Access Control: Implement security measures to control access to sensitive data and ensure compliance with organizational policies.

Best Practices for Using BI Publisher

To maximize the effectiveness of BI Publisher within Oracle ERP, consider the following best practices:

- Standardize Report Templates: Develop standardized report templates to maintain consistency in reporting across departments and processes.

- Performance Optimization: Optimize report performance by tuning data queries, leveraging caching mechanisms, and minimizing data retrieval overhead.

- User Training and Support: Provide comprehensive training to users on BI Publisher's functionalities and reporting capabilities.

- Regular Maintenance: Schedule regular maintenance tasks such as database cleanup, server upgrades, and software updates to ensure smooth operation.

Conclusion

BI Publisher stands as a versatile tool within Oracle ERP, empowering organizations to transform raw data into actionable insights through flexible and customizable reporting capabilities. By mastering BI Publisher, users can streamline reporting processes, enhance decision-making, and drive business growth in today's competitive landscape.

6.3.2 Data Visualization

Data visualization in Oracle ERP encompasses a range of tools and capabilities designed to transform raw data into interactive visual representations. These visualizations include charts, graphs, dashboards, and other graphical elements that facilitate intuitive data exploration and analysis. Oracle provides several tools and features to support robust data visualization practices:

Overview of Data Visualization Tools in Oracle ERP

Oracle ERP integrates several tools and technologies to facilitate effective data visualization:

1. Oracle Business Intelligence (BI) Publisher

Oracle BI Publisher is a powerful reporting tool that enables users to create highly formatted reports, including pixel-perfect reports and operational reports. While primarily known for its reporting capabilities, BI Publisher also supports basic data visualization through charts and graphs embedded within reports.

- Creating Charts and Graphs: Users can leverage BI Publisher to generate charts and graphs directly within reports, allowing for visual representation of data trends and patterns.

- Integration with Oracle ERP Data Sources: BI Publisher seamlessly integrates with Oracle ERP data sources, ensuring real-time data visualization capabilities that reflect the most current information.

2. Oracle Data Visualization (DV)

Oracle Data Visualization (DV) is a comprehensive data visualization tool that empowers users to explore, analyze, and visualize data from multiple sources within Oracle ERP. DV offers interactive dashboards, predictive analytics, and advanced visualizations to support data-driven decision-making.

- Interactive Dashboards: DV allows users to create personalized dashboards with drag-and-drop functionality, enabling quick insights into key performance indicators (KPIs) and business metrics.

- Advanced Visualizations: Users can choose from a wide range of visualizations, including bar charts, line graphs, scatter plots, heat maps, and geographic maps, to represent data in the most meaningful way.

- Data Exploration Capabilities: DV provides robust data exploration capabilities, such as drill-downs, filters, and hierarchies, to uncover hidden insights and correlations within complex datasets.

3. Oracle Analytics Cloud (OAC)

Oracle Analytics Cloud is a cloud-based analytics platform that extends Oracle ERP's data visualization capabilities to the cloud environment. OAC offers advanced analytics, machine learning, and augmented analytics features alongside powerful data visualization tools.

- Augmented Analytics: OAC leverages machine learning algorithms to automate data analysis and generate actionable insights, reducing the reliance on manual data exploration.

- Collaborative Analytics: Users can share interactive dashboards and visualizations with stakeholders, fostering collaboration and data-driven decision-making across the organization.

- Integration with Oracle ERP Cloud: OAC seamlessly integrates with Oracle ERP Cloud applications, ensuring seamless data connectivity and synchronization for accurate and timely visualizations.

Best Practices for Effective Data Visualization in Oracle ERP

To maximize the effectiveness of data visualization in Oracle ERP, consider the following best practices:

- Define Clear Objectives: Identify the key business questions and objectives that data visualization aims to address. Tailor visualizations to communicate specific insights that support decision-making processes.

- Choose Appropriate Visualizations: Select visualizations that best represent the data patterns and relationships. Consider factors such as data type, audience preferences, and the story you want to convey through visuals.

- Ensure Data Accuracy and Consistency: Validate data sources and ensure data quality before visualizing. Consistent data definitions and cleansing practices are essential to avoid misinterpretation of visual insights.

- Empower User Interactivity: Enable interactive features such as drill-downs, filters, and tooltips to encourage exploration and discovery. User-driven analysis enhances engagement and facilitates deeper understanding of data trends.

- Optimize Performance: Design visualizations with performance in mind, especially when dealing with large datasets. Utilize aggregation, caching mechanisms, and data compression techniques to improve dashboard responsiveness.

Conclusion

Effective data visualization in Oracle ERP is instrumental in transforming raw data into actionable insights that drive business growth and operational excellence. By leveraging tools like Oracle BI Publisher, Oracle Data Visualization, and Oracle Analytics Cloud, organizations can empower users to make informed decisions based on clear, visually compelling data representations. Adopting best practices in data visualization ensures that insights are accurate, accessible, and impactful, supporting strategic initiatives and fostering a data-driven culture within the enterprise.

CHAPTER VII
Advanced Features and Customization

7.1 Workflow Automation

7.1.1 Creating Workflows

Workflow automation is a key feature of Oracle ERP that enables organizations to streamline and standardize business processes, ensuring efficiency and consistency. Creating workflows in Oracle ERP involves designing a series of steps that automate various business functions, such as approval processes, task assignments, and notifications. This section provides a detailed guide on how to create workflows in Oracle ERP.

Understanding Workflows

Workflows in Oracle ERP are defined sequences of tasks that are triggered based on specific conditions. These tasks can involve multiple users, systems, and data elements. The primary components of a workflow include:

- Tasks: Individual units of work that need to be completed.

- Transitions: The flow between tasks, often dependent on conditions or triggers.

- Notifications: Alerts and messages sent to users involved in the workflow.

- Approvals: Steps where certain tasks require authorization before proceeding.

Steps to Create a Workflow in Oracle ERP

1. Identify the Business Process

Before creating a workflow, it is essential to thoroughly understand the business process you intend to automate. Identify the key tasks, participants, decision points, and the desired outcomes. Documenting this process flow helps in visualizing the workflow and ensuring all critical steps are included.

2. Access the Workflow Builder

Oracle ERP provides a Workflow Builder tool, a graphical interface that allows users to design and manage workflows. To access the Workflow Builder:

- Navigate to the Oracle ERP main menu.

- Select the "Workflow" module.

- Open the "Workflow Builder" application.

3. Create a New Workflow

Once in the Workflow Builder:

- Click on "File" and select "New" to create a new workflow.

- Enter a name and description for the workflow. This helps in identifying the workflow and its purpose.

4. Define Workflow Attributes

Attributes are variables that store data related to the workflow. These can include user information, document details, or other process-specific data. To define attributes:

- Go to the "Attributes" tab in the Workflow Builder.

- Click on "New Attribute" and specify the name, type (e.g., string, number, date), and default value (if any).

5. Design the Workflow Diagram

The workflow diagram visually represents the sequence of tasks and transitions. To design the diagram:

- Drag and drop tasks from the palette onto the canvas.

- Connect tasks using arrows to define the transitions.

- Double-click on each task to configure its properties, such as name, performer, and conditions.

6. Configure Task Properties

Each task in the workflow has specific properties that need to be configured:

- Name: Enter a meaningful name for the task.

- Performer: Specify the user or role responsible for completing the task.

- Function: Define the action or function that the task will perform. This could be a manual task, an automated script, or an integration with another system.

- Conditions: Set conditions that determine when the task will be executed. These can include time-based triggers, data changes, or user actions.

7. Set Up Transitions

Transitions define the flow between tasks. To set up transitions:

- Click on the arrow connecting two tasks.

- Define the conditions under which the transition occurs. For example, a transition might be based on the approval or rejection of a document.

- Specify any actions that need to be performed during the transition, such as sending notifications or updating data.

8. Implement Notifications

Notifications are used to inform users about tasks, approvals, or any other relevant events within the workflow. To implement notifications:

- Go to the "Notifications" tab in the Workflow Builder.

- Create a new notification and specify the message content, recipients, and delivery method (e.g., email, system message).

- Link notifications to relevant tasks or transitions to ensure they are triggered at the appropriate points in the workflow.

9. Add Approvals

Many workflows require approval steps where certain tasks need to be authorized before proceeding. To add approvals:

- Create an approval task and assign it to the appropriate user or role.

- Define the approval criteria and any conditions that need to be met.

- Configure the transition based on the approval outcome (e.g., approved or rejected).

10. Test the Workflow

Before deploying the workflow, it is crucial to test it thoroughly to ensure it behaves as expected. To test the workflow:

- Use the Workflow Builder's simulation tools to run through the workflow steps.

- Check for any errors or issues in task execution, transitions, notifications, and approvals.

- Make necessary adjustments based on the test results.

11. Deploy the Workflow

Once the workflow has been tested and validated:

- Save the workflow and close the Workflow Builder.

- Navigate to the Workflow module in Oracle ERP and select "Deploy Workflow."

- Choose the workflow you created and follow the prompts to deploy it to the live environment.

12. Monitor and Maintain the Workflow

After deployment, it is important to monitor the workflow's performance and make any necessary adjustments. To monitor the workflow:

- Use Oracle ERP's workflow monitoring tools to track task completion, approval statuses, and any errors.

- Review user feedback and performance metrics to identify areas for improvement.

- Update the workflow as needed to adapt to changing business processes or requirements.

Best Practices for Creating Workflows

- Keep It Simple: Start with a simple workflow and gradually add complexity as needed. Avoid overcomplicating the workflow with unnecessary steps or conditions.

- Involve Stakeholders: Engage relevant stakeholders in the workflow design process to ensure it meets their needs and expectations.

- Document Everything: Maintain detailed documentation of the workflow, including the process flow, task definitions, conditions, and any customizations. This aids in troubleshooting and future updates.

- Use Templates: Leverage existing workflow templates provided by Oracle ERP to speed up the creation process and ensure best practices are followed.

- Regular Reviews: Periodically review and update workflows to keep them aligned with evolving business processes and objectives.

Creating workflows in Oracle ERP can significantly enhance operational efficiency and ensure standardized processes across the organization. By following this guide, users can design effective workflows that automate routine tasks, improve collaboration, and reduce the risk of errors.

7.1.2 Managing Workflows

Managing workflows in Oracle ERP is a crucial component in automating and streamlining business processes. Efficient management ensures that tasks are executed correctly, deadlines are met, and resource utilization is optimized. This section provides a comprehensive guide to managing workflows within Oracle ERP, detailing each step and best practices to ensure successful workflow management.

Understanding Workflow Management

Workflow management involves overseeing the creation, execution, and monitoring of workflows. In Oracle ERP, workflows can automate a variety of business processes, from approval processes to data entry and report generation. Effective workflow management ensures that these processes run smoothly and efficiently, reducing manual intervention and minimizing errors.

Key Components of Workflow Management

1. Workflow Design

  - Workflow Engine: The engine that drives the workflow, executing tasks, and managing transitions.

  - Tasks and Activities: Individual units of work within a workflow, such as approvals, data entry, or notifications.

  - Transitions: Pathways that dictate the flow from one task to another based on certain conditions or rules.

  - Roles and Responsibilities: Defines who is responsible for each task within the workflow.

2. Workflow Monitoring

  - Dashboards: Provide real-time visibility into the status of workflows.

  - Alerts and Notifications: Automated messages that inform users of pending tasks, delays, or errors.

  - Audit Trails: Logs that record the history of workflow execution for compliance and troubleshooting.

3. Workflow Optimization

  - Performance Metrics: KPIs that measure the efficiency and effectiveness of workflows.

  - Continuous Improvement: Strategies to refine and enhance workflows based on performance data and user feedback.

Managing Workflows in Oracle ERP

1. Accessing Workflow Management Tools

  - Oracle Workflow Builder: The primary tool for creating and managing workflows.

- Oracle Workflow Monitor: A tool for tracking and monitoring the status of workflows in real-time.

2. Creating a Workflow

- Defining the Workflow Process: Start by mapping out the business process you want to automate.

- Designing the Workflow: Use Oracle Workflow Builder to create the workflow diagram, adding tasks, transitions, and conditions.

- Assigning Roles: Define who will perform each task within the workflow.

- Setting Up Notifications: Configure automated messages to alert users about task assignments and deadlines.

- Testing the Workflow: Before deployment, test the workflow to ensure it functions as expected.

3. Deploying and Executing Workflows

- Workflow Deployment: Deploy the workflow in the Oracle ERP environment.

- Executing Workflows: Once deployed, workflows will begin executing according to the defined process and conditions.

4. Monitoring Workflow Execution

- Real-Time Monitoring: Use Oracle Workflow Monitor to view the status of active workflows.

- Handling Errors and Exceptions: Identify and resolve any issues that arise during workflow execution.

- Reviewing Audit Trails: Regularly review audit logs to ensure compliance and track any anomalies.

5. Optimizing Workflows

- Analyzing Performance: Use performance metrics to identify bottlenecks and inefficiencies.

- Implementing Improvements: Modify workflows based on analysis to improve efficiency.

- Continuous Monitoring: Regularly review workflows to ensure they remain optimized and effective.

Best Practices for Workflow Management

1. Thoroughly Define Business Processes

- Ensure that all steps, roles, and responsibilities are clearly defined before creating a workflow.

2. Keep Workflows Simple and Manageable

- Avoid overly complex workflows. Simplify where possible to enhance maintainability and reduce the likelihood of errors.

3. Test Extensively

- Thoroughly test workflows in a development environment before deploying them to production. This helps to catch and resolve issues early.

4. Regularly Review and Update Workflows

- Business processes evolve over time. Regularly review workflows to ensure they align with current business needs and practices.

5. Train Users and Stakeholders

- Ensure that all users and stakeholders understand how to interact with and manage workflows. Provide training and documentation as needed.

6. Utilize Notifications and Alerts

- Set up notifications to keep users informed about their tasks and any issues that arise. This ensures timely completion of tasks and quick resolution of problems.

7. Monitor and Analyze Performance

- Use dashboards and performance metrics to continuously monitor workflow efficiency and effectiveness. Make data-driven decisions to optimize workflows.

Detailed Steps for Managing Workflows

1. Creating a Workflow in Oracle Workflow Builder

  - Launch Oracle Workflow Builder: Access the tool from the Oracle ERP interface.

  - Define Workflow Process: Outline the steps, tasks, and transitions.

  - Add Workflow Components: Drag and drop tasks, set conditions, and define transitions between tasks.

  - Configure Task Properties: Set task parameters, such as deadlines, role assignments, and notification settings.

  - Save and Validate Workflow: Save the workflow and run validation checks to ensure there are no errors.

2. Deploying the Workflow

  - Export Workflow Definition: Export the workflow definition file from Oracle Workflow Builder.

  - Import Workflow Definition: Import the definition into the Oracle ERP system.

  - Activate Workflow: Activate the workflow to make it available for execution.

3. Monitoring Workflow Execution

  - Access Oracle Workflow Monitor: Use this tool to track workflow status.

  - View Active Workflows: Monitor active workflows, check task statuses, and view pending tasks.

  - Handle Exceptions: Identify tasks that have errors or are delayed and take corrective actions.

  - Review Audit Logs: Access audit logs to see the history of workflow executions.

4. Optimizing Workflows

  - Analyze Workflow Performance: Review performance data to identify areas for improvement.

  - Refine Workflow Design: Modify workflows to address identified issues and improve efficiency.

  - Implement Changes: Update workflows in Oracle Workflow Builder and redeploy as needed.

5. Maintaining Workflows

- Regular Reviews: Periodically review workflows to ensure they are still aligned with business processes.

- User Feedback: Collect feedback from users to identify pain points and areas for improvement.

- Update Documentation: Maintain up-to-date documentation for all workflows, including any changes made.

Conclusion

Managing workflows in Oracle ERP is a dynamic and ongoing process that requires careful planning, execution, and continuous improvement. By following best practices and leveraging the tools provided by Oracle ERP, businesses can automate complex processes, reduce manual effort, and achieve greater efficiency and accuracy in their operations. Effective workflow management not only streamlines business processes but also enhances overall organizational productivity and agility.

7.2 Integrations and Extensions

7.2.1 Third-Party Integrations

Integrating third-party applications with Oracle ERP can significantly enhance the system's functionality, allowing businesses to leverage specialized tools and services that cater to their unique needs. This section provides a comprehensive guide to understanding, planning, and implementing third-party integrations with Oracle ERP.

Understanding Third-Party Integrations

Third-party integrations involve connecting external applications or services with Oracle ERP to enable data exchange and streamline business processes. These integrations can range from simple data transfers to complex, real-time interactions. Common third-party applications integrated with Oracle ERP include Customer Relationship Management (CRM) systems, e-commerce platforms, supply chain management tools, and specialized financial software.

Benefits of third-party integrations include:

1. Enhanced Functionality: Integrations can extend Oracle ERP's capabilities by adding features not available within the core system.

2. Improved Efficiency: Automated data exchange reduces manual data entry, minimizing errors and saving time.

3. Better Data Insights: Consolidating data from various sources provides a more comprehensive view of business operations.

4. Scalability: Integrations allow businesses to scale operations by adding new tools and systems as needed.

Planning for Integration

Effective planning is crucial for successful third-party integrations. Key steps in the planning process include:

1. Identify Integration Needs: Determine which third-party applications are essential for your business processes. Consider the functionalities they offer and how they complement Oracle ERP.

2. Assess Compatibility: Ensure the third-party applications are compatible with Oracle ERP. Check for available APIs (Application Programming Interfaces) and integration tools.

3. Define Integration Scope: Outline the scope of the integration, including the specific data and processes to be integrated. Identify key stakeholders and establish their roles and responsibilities.

4. Set Objectives and KPIs: Define clear objectives for the integration project. Establish Key Performance Indicators (KPIs) to measure the success of the integration.

5. Develop a Project Plan: Create a detailed project plan that includes timelines, milestones, and resources required. Ensure you have a risk management plan to address potential challenges.

Implementing Third-Party Integrations

Once the planning phase is complete, the next step is to implement the third-party integration. This involves several key activities:

1. Select Integration Tools: Choose the appropriate tools and technologies for the integration. Common integration tools for Oracle ERP include Oracle Integration Cloud (OIC), middleware solutions, and custom APIs.

2. Configure APIs: Application Programming Interfaces (APIs) are essential for enabling communication between Oracle ERP and third-party applications. Configure the necessary APIs to facilitate data exchange.

3. Data Mapping and Transformation: Ensure that data from third-party applications is correctly mapped to the corresponding fields in Oracle ERP. Data transformation may be required to align data formats and structures.

4. Develop Integration Workflows: Create workflows that define the sequence of actions for the integration. These workflows should automate data exchange and trigger relevant processes in both systems.

5. Test the Integration: Conduct thorough testing to ensure the integration works as expected. Perform functional, performance, and security testing to identify and resolve any issues.

6. Deploy the Integration: Once testing is complete, deploy the integration to the production environment. Monitor the integration closely during the initial phase to address any issues that arise.

Best Practices for Third-Party Integrations

To ensure successful third-party integrations, follow these best practices:

1. Use Standardized APIs: Wherever possible, use standardized APIs provided by Oracle and third-party vendors. Standardized APIs are more reliable and easier to maintain.

2. Maintain Data Security: Ensure that data exchanged between systems is secure. Use encryption and secure communication protocols to protect sensitive information.

3. Monitor Performance: Continuously monitor the performance of the integration to identify and address any issues. Use monitoring tools to track data flow and system performance.

4. Document the Integration: Maintain detailed documentation of the integration process, including configuration settings, data mappings, and workflows. Documentation is essential for troubleshooting and future maintenance.

5. Regularly Update Systems: Keep both Oracle ERP and third-party applications updated to ensure compatibility and take advantage of new features and security enhancements.

6. Establish a Support Plan: Have a support plan in place to address any issues that arise after deployment. Ensure that both internal teams and third-party vendors are available to provide support.

Example Use Cases

Here are a few example use cases that illustrate the value of third-party integrations with Oracle ERP:

1. CRM Integration: Integrating a CRM system, such as Salesforce, with Oracle ERP allows for seamless data exchange between sales and finance departments. This integration enables sales teams to access real-time inventory data and financial teams to view customer transaction histories, improving customer service and financial reporting.

2. E-commerce Integration: Integrating an e-commerce platform, like Shopify, with Oracle ERP automates the order-to-cash process. Orders placed on the e-commerce site are automatically transferred to Oracle ERP for processing, inventory updates, and financial reconciliation, reducing manual data entry and errors.

3. Supply Chain Integration: Integrating supply chain management tools, such as a Transportation Management System (TMS), with Oracle ERP enhances visibility and control over logistics operations. This integration enables real-time tracking of shipments, optimizing route planning and reducing transportation costs.

4. Financial Software Integration: Integrating specialized financial software, such as a tax calculation tool, with Oracle ERP ensures accurate tax calculations and compliance. This integration automates the transfer of financial data, streamlining tax reporting and reducing the risk of errors.

Challenges and Solutions

While third-party integrations offer many benefits, they can also present challenges. Common challenges and their solutions include:

1. Data Inconsistency: Data inconsistencies can occur when integrating systems with different data formats and structures. Solution: Implement robust data mapping and transformation processes to ensure data consistency.

2. Performance Issues: Integrations can impact system performance if not properly managed. Solution: Optimize integration workflows and use performance monitoring tools to identify and address bottlenecks.

3. Security Risks: Integrating with third-party applications can introduce security vulnerabilities. Solution: Use secure APIs, encryption, and regular security audits to mitigate risks.

4. Complexity of Integration: Some integrations can be complex and require specialized expertise. Solution: Leverage integration platforms and middleware solutions that simplify the integration process and provide pre-built connectors.

Conclusion

Integrating third-party applications with Oracle ERP is a powerful way to enhance system functionality and streamline business processes. By following a structured approach to planning and implementing integrations, businesses can unlock significant value and improve overall efficiency. Whether integrating CRM systems, e-commerce platforms, supply chain tools, or specialized financial software, careful planning, robust execution, and adherence to best practices are key to successful third-party integrations.

7.2.2 Using Oracle API

Oracle ERP provides a comprehensive suite of APIs that allow developers to extend the functionality of the ERP system, integrate it with other applications, and automate business processes. Utilizing Oracle API effectively requires an understanding of its structure, capabilities, and best practices. This section will provide a detailed guide on using Oracle API, including an overview of the API architecture, types of APIs available, steps to create and manage API connections, and examples of common use cases.

Overview of Oracle API Architecture

Oracle APIs are designed to facilitate communication between different software applications, enabling them to share data and functionality. The architecture of Oracle API is based on the following key components:

1. API Gateway: Acts as an entry point for API requests, handling tasks such as authentication, rate limiting, and logging.

2. API Services: Backend services that process the requests and return responses. These services can include data retrieval, business logic execution, and transaction processing.

3. Security Layer: Ensures that only authorized users and applications can access the APIs, typically involving OAuth 2.0, JWT tokens, and API keys.

4. Documentation and Tools: Comprehensive documentation and development tools provided by Oracle to help developers understand and use the APIs effectively.

Types of Oracle APIs

Oracle ERP offers several types of APIs, each suited for different integration and customization needs:

1. REST APIs: Representational State Transfer (REST) APIs are widely used for web-based integrations. They use standard HTTP methods (GET, POST, PUT, DELETE) and are known for their simplicity and ease of use.

2. SOAP APIs: Simple Object Access Protocol (SOAP) APIs are more structured and protocol-heavy compared to REST APIs. They are often used in enterprise environments where security and transactional integrity are critical.

3. BPEL APIs: Business Process Execution Language (BPEL) APIs are used for orchestrating complex business processes, allowing for the integration of multiple web services into a cohesive workflow.

4. Java APIs: Oracle provides Java APIs for more in-depth customization and integration within Java-based applications. These APIs offer direct access to Oracle ERP's functionalities.

5. PL/SQL APIs: Procedural Language/Structured Query Language (PL/SQL) APIs are used for database-level operations, enabling developers to execute stored procedures and manage database transactions.

Steps to Create and Manage API Connections

Creating and managing API connections in Oracle ERP involves several steps, from setting up the environment to testing and deploying the APIs. Below are detailed steps to guide you through the process:

1. Setting Up the Environment:

   - Ensure that you have the necessary access rights and permissions to create and manage APIs.

   - Set up a development environment with tools like Oracle API Gateway, Oracle Integration Cloud, and a REST/SOAP client (e.g., Postman).

2. Creating API Endpoints:

   - Define the purpose and scope of the API. Identify the data and operations that the API will expose.

   - Use Oracle's API design tools to create and configure API endpoints. For REST APIs, you will define URL paths, HTTP methods, request/response formats, and parameters.

   - For SOAP APIs, you will define WSDL (Web Services Description Language) files that describe the operations and messages.

3. Configuring Security:

   - Implement authentication and authorization mechanisms to secure the API. Common methods include OAuth 2.0, API keys, and JWT tokens.

   - Configure role-based access control (RBAC) to ensure that only authorized users can access specific API endpoints.

4. Developing API Logic:

   - Write the necessary business logic to process API requests. This may involve querying databases, invoking other APIs, or executing business rules.

   - Use Oracle's development frameworks and libraries to simplify the implementation. For example, Oracle JDeveloper can be used for Java-based APIs, and SQL Developer for PL/SQL APIs.

5. Testing and Debugging:

- Use tools like Postman or SoapUI to test the API endpoints. Verify that the API correctly handles different request scenarios, including valid and invalid inputs.

- Debug any issues by reviewing logs and monitoring the API Gateway.

6. Deploying and Managing APIs:

- Once the API is thoroughly tested, deploy it to the production environment. Use Oracle's deployment tools to automate the process.

- Monitor the API's performance and usage using Oracle API Gateway's analytics and logging features. This helps in identifying and resolving any issues promptly.

Common Use Cases

Oracle APIs can be used in various scenarios to enhance and extend the capabilities of Oracle ERP. Below are some common use cases:

1. Integration with Third-Party Applications:

- CRM Integration: Integrate Oracle ERP with Customer Relationship Management (CRM) systems like Salesforce to synchronize customer data, sales orders, and invoices.

- E-Commerce Integration: Connect Oracle ERP with e-commerce platforms like Shopify or Magento to automate order processing, inventory management, and financial transactions.

2. Automating Business Processes:

- Order to Cash: Use APIs to automate the entire order-to-cash process, from receiving orders to invoicing and payment collection.

- Procure to Pay: Streamline the procure-to-pay process by integrating Oracle ERP with procurement systems, automating purchase orders, supplier management, and payment processing.

3. Custom Application Development:

- Mobile Applications: Develop custom mobile applications that interact with Oracle ERP using REST APIs, providing employees with access to ERP data and functions on the go.

- Custom Dashboards: Build custom dashboards and reporting tools that fetch data from Oracle ERP using APIs, providing real-time insights into business performance.

4. Data Integration and Migration:

- Data Synchronization: Use APIs to synchronize data between Oracle ERP and other enterprise systems, ensuring consistency and accuracy across the organization.

- Data Migration: Facilitate data migration during ERP implementation or upgrades by using APIs to extract, transform, and load data between systems.

Best Practices for Using Oracle API

To maximize the benefits of using Oracle API, it is essential to follow best practices:

1. Design for Scalability:

- Ensure that your API design can handle increasing loads and data volumes. Use pagination, filtering, and sorting to manage large datasets efficiently.

2. Ensure Security:

- Implement robust security measures, including encryption, secure authentication, and regular security audits. Protect sensitive data by adhering to data privacy regulations.

3. Maintain Documentation:

- Provide comprehensive and up-to-date documentation for your APIs. This helps developers understand how to use the APIs and troubleshoot any issues they encounter.

4. Version Your APIs:

- Use versioning to manage changes and updates to your APIs without disrupting existing integrations. Clearly communicate any deprecations or breaking changes to API consumers.

5. Monitor and Optimize Performance:

- Continuously monitor the performance of your APIs using logging and analytics tools. Identify and address any performance bottlenecks or errors.

6. Engage with the Developer Community:

- Participate in Oracle's developer community forums and events. Sharing knowledge and collaborating with other developers can help you stay updated on best practices and new features.

By understanding and leveraging the power of Oracle API, you can significantly enhance the functionality and integration capabilities of your Oracle ERP system, driving greater efficiency and business value.

7.3 Security and User Management

7.3.1 User Roles and Permissions

In any ERP system, security and user management are crucial components to ensure that sensitive business data is protected while still allowing users to perform their required tasks efficiently. Oracle ERP provides a robust framework for managing user roles and permissions, enabling administrators to define and control access to various functionalities and data within the system. This section provides a comprehensive guide to understanding, configuring, and managing user roles and permissions in Oracle ERP.

Understanding User Roles

User roles in Oracle ERP define a set of permissions that dictate what actions a user can perform and what data they can access. Roles can be broadly categorized into:

1. Functional Roles: These roles are linked to specific business functions such as finance, procurement, or human resources. For example, a Finance Manager role would have access to financial reports, journal entries, and budgeting tools.

2. Technical Roles: These roles are related to the technical maintenance and configuration of the ERP system. For example, a System Administrator role would have permissions to configure system settings, manage integrations, and perform system backups.

3. Cross-functional Roles: These roles span multiple business functions and are usually assigned to senior management or supervisory positions. For example, a Chief Financial Officer (CFO) role might have access to both finance and procurement data for oversight purposes.

Creating User Roles

Creating user roles involves defining a set of permissions that align with the responsibilities of each role. The steps to create a user role in Oracle ERP are as follows:

1. Access the Role Management Interface:

   - Navigate to the Security Console in Oracle ERP.

   - Select the 'Roles' tab to view existing roles and create new ones.

2. Define the Role Name and Description:

   - Click on the 'Create Role' button.

   - Enter a meaningful role name (e.g., 'Accounts Payable Clerk') and a description that outlines the role's responsibilities.

3. Set Role Type:

   - Choose the role type from the available options: Job Role, Duty Role, or Abstract Role.

   - Job Role: Typically associated with a specific job within the organization.

   - Duty Role: Represents a specific duty that can be assigned to multiple job roles.

   - Abstract Role: Usually represents an organization-wide role, such as Employee or Manager.

4. Assign Permissions:

   - Use the 'Function Security Policies' section to add or remove permissions.

   - Select specific tasks, data access points, and functional areas that the role should have access to.

   - Review and confirm the assigned permissions to ensure they align with the intended responsibilities.

5. Configure Data Access:

   - Define data security policies to restrict access to specific data sets.

   - Assign data access conditions based on business units, departments, or other organizational structures.

6. Review and Save:

   - Review the role configuration summary.

- Save the role and assign it to the relevant users.

Assigning Roles to Users

Once roles are defined, they need to be assigned to users based on their job responsibilities. This can be done through the following steps:

1. Access User Management:

   - Navigate to the 'User Management' section in Oracle ERP.

   - Search for the user to whom you want to assign a role.

2. Edit User Information:

   - Select the user and click 'Edit' to modify their profile.

   - Go to the 'Roles' tab within the user profile.

3. Assign Roles:

   - Click on 'Add Role' and select the appropriate role from the list of available roles.

   - Assign multiple roles if the user performs tasks that span different functional areas.

4. Review and Confirm:

   - Review the assigned roles and their permissions.

   - Confirm the changes and save the user profile.

Managing Permissions

Permissions in Oracle ERP are granular and can be customized to fit the specific needs of the organization. Managing permissions involves several key tasks:

1. Modifying Existing Roles:

   - Periodically review roles to ensure they align with current business processes and compliance requirements.

- Modify permissions as needed by adding or removing specific functions and data access points.

2. Creating Custom Permissions:

- In some cases, standard permissions may not cover all business needs. Custom permissions can be created to address these gaps.

- Use the 'Function Security Policies' interface to define custom permissions.

3. Auditing Role Assignments:

- Regularly audit role assignments to ensure users have appropriate access levels.

- Identify and rectify instances where users have unnecessary or excessive permissions.

Best Practices for Role and Permission Management

1. Least Privilege Principle: Assign users the minimum level of access necessary to perform their job functions. This minimizes the risk of unauthorized data access and reduces the impact of potential security breaches.

2. Role-Based Access Control (RBAC): Implement RBAC to streamline the management of user permissions. By grouping permissions into roles, administrators can efficiently manage access across the organization.

3. Segregation of Duties (SoD): Ensure that critical tasks are divided among multiple users to prevent fraud and errors. For example, the person who approves purchase orders should not be the same person who processes payments.

4. Regular Reviews and Audits: Conduct regular reviews and audits of user roles and permissions. This helps in identifying and correcting any discrepancies, ensuring compliance with internal policies and external regulations.

5. Documentation and Training: Maintain comprehensive documentation of role definitions and permission configurations. Provide training to users and administrators to ensure they understand their responsibilities and how to use the ERP system securely.

6. Use of Automation: Leverage automation tools within Oracle ERP to manage user roles and permissions more efficiently. Automated workflows can help in onboarding new users, assigning roles, and conducting periodic reviews.

Example Scenario: Setting Up a New Role

Let's consider an example scenario where a new role, "Procurement Specialist," needs to be created and assigned to users responsible for managing procurement activities.

1. Define the Role:

  - Role Name: Procurement Specialist

  - Description: Manages procurement processes including creating purchase orders, managing supplier relationships, and overseeing procurement budgets.

2. Set Permissions:

  - Access to the Procurement module.

  - Permissions to create, edit, and approve purchase orders.

  - Access to supplier management functions.

  - Read-only access to procurement reports and budgets.

3. Assign the Role to Users:

  - Identify users in the procurement department who will take on this role.

  - Assign the "Procurement Specialist" role to these users through the User Management interface.

4. Review and Confirm:

  - Verify that users with the new role can access the necessary functions without encountering permissions issues.

  - Conduct a review with the procurement department to ensure the role meets their needs.

By following these steps, organizations can effectively manage user roles and permissions, ensuring secure and efficient use of Oracle ERP.

Conclusion

User roles and permissions are foundational elements of Oracle ERP security and user management. By defining clear roles, assigning appropriate permissions, and regularly reviewing access levels, organizations can protect sensitive data, comply with regulations, and empower users to perform their tasks effectively. This structured approach to role and permission management helps in maintaining a secure and well-organized ERP environment.

7.3.2 Data Security Measures

Ensuring data security is a critical component of any ERP system, and Oracle ERP is no exception. Data security measures protect sensitive information from unauthorized access, breaches, and other security threats. In this section, we will explore various strategies and best practices to implement robust data security measures in Oracle ERP.

1. Understanding Data Security in Oracle ERP

Data security in Oracle ERP encompasses a wide range of practices designed to safeguard data integrity, confidentiality, and availability. The key objectives include:

- Preventing unauthorized access to data.

- Ensuring data accuracy and integrity.

- Protecting data from corruption and loss.

- Complying with regulatory and legal requirements.

2. User Authentication and Authorization

User Authentication: This is the process of verifying the identity of a user before granting access to the system. Oracle ERP supports multiple authentication methods:

- Password-based authentication: Users must enter a valid username and password to access the system.

- Multi-factor authentication (MFA): Adds an extra layer of security by requiring additional verification methods such as a mobile app or a physical token.

- Single Sign-On (SSO): Allows users to log in once and gain access to multiple related systems without being prompted to log in again.

User Authorization: Once authenticated, authorization determines the level of access and permissions a user has within the system. This involves:

- Role-based access control (RBAC): Users are assigned roles that define their permissions and access levels. For example, an "Accounts Payable Clerk" role may have access to invoice processing but not to financial reporting.

- Least privilege principle: Users are granted the minimum access necessary to perform their job functions, reducing the risk of unauthorized data access.

3. Data Encryption

Data encryption is crucial for protecting data both at rest (stored data) and in transit (data being transmitted over networks). Oracle ERP offers several encryption options:

- Transparent Data Encryption (TDE): Encrypts database files to protect data at rest. It ensures that unauthorized users cannot read the data directly from the storage.

- Network encryption: Encrypts data transmitted over the network using protocols like SSL/TLS. This prevents data interception during transmission.

4. Data Masking and Redaction

Data masking and redaction techniques hide sensitive information from unauthorized users, reducing the risk of data exposure:

- Data Masking: Replaces sensitive data with fictitious but realistic data within the development and testing environments, ensuring that developers and testers do not have access to actual sensitive information.

- Data Redaction: Dynamically obscures sensitive data within application pages, ensuring that unauthorized users cannot view sensitive information even if they have access to the application.

5. Audit and Monitoring

Regular auditing and monitoring are essential for detecting and responding to security incidents:

- Audit Trails: Oracle ERP can generate detailed audit trails that record user activities, changes to data, and system access. These logs are crucial for investigating security incidents and ensuring compliance.

- Monitoring Tools: Implementing monitoring tools such as Oracle Audit Vault and Database Firewall can provide real-time alerts and reports on suspicious activities, enabling prompt responses to potential threats.

6. Security Patching and Updates

Keeping Oracle ERP up to date with the latest security patches and updates is vital for protecting against known vulnerabilities:

- Patch Management: Regularly apply security patches provided by Oracle to address vulnerabilities and improve system security. Oracle Critical Patch Updates (CPU) are released quarterly and should be applied promptly.

- Automated Updates: Consider using automated tools and processes to streamline the patching process and ensure timely updates.

7. Data Backup and Recovery

Implementing a robust data backup and recovery strategy ensures data availability and integrity in the event of a disaster or data loss:

- Regular Backups: Perform regular backups of all critical data, ensuring that copies are stored securely offsite. Backups should include database files, application files, and configuration files.

- Disaster Recovery Plan: Develop and test a comprehensive disaster recovery plan that outlines the procedures for restoring data and services in the event of a catastrophic failure. Regularly test the plan to ensure its effectiveness.

8. Compliance and Regulatory Requirements

Oracle ERP must comply with various regulatory and legal requirements related to data security and privacy:

- Regulations: Understand and comply with relevant regulations such as GDPR, HIPAA, and SOX. These regulations often mandate specific data security measures and audit requirements.

- Data Privacy: Implement data privacy policies and procedures that ensure the protection of personal data and compliance with privacy laws.

9. Employee Training and Awareness

Human error is a significant risk factor in data security breaches. Educating employees about data security best practices is essential:

- Training Programs: Develop and deliver regular training programs on data security awareness, covering topics such as phishing attacks, password security, and data handling procedures.

- Security Policies: Establish and enforce security policies that define acceptable use of the ERP system, data handling procedures, and consequences for non-compliance.

10. Incident Response and Management

Having a well-defined incident response plan ensures prompt and effective handling of security incidents:

- Incident Response Team: Form an incident response team responsible for managing and responding to security incidents. The team should include representatives from IT, security, legal, and communications.

- Incident Response Plan: Develop an incident response plan that outlines the procedures for identifying, reporting, and responding to security incidents. The plan should include steps for containment, eradication, recovery, and post-incident analysis.

Conclusion

Implementing robust data security measures in Oracle ERP is essential for protecting sensitive information, ensuring regulatory compliance, and maintaining business continuity. By following the best practices outlined in this section, organizations can safeguard their data from unauthorized access, breaches, and other security threats, ultimately unlocking the full potential of Oracle ERP for their business operations.

CHAPTER VIII
Key Business Processes in Oracle ERP

8.1 Financial Processes

8.1.1 Budgeting and Forecasting

Budgeting and forecasting are critical components of financial management in Oracle ERP, enabling organizations to plan and control their finances effectively. This section will delve into the detailed processes, methodologies, and best practices for budgeting and forecasting within Oracle ERP.

Introduction to Budgeting and Forecasting in Oracle ERP

In Oracle ERP, budgeting and forecasting serve as pivotal tools for financial planning and decision-making. They allow organizations to anticipate future financial outcomes based on historical data, market trends, and strategic goals. Effective budgeting ensures that resources are allocated optimally across departments and projects, while forecasting provides insights into potential financial performance.

Key Components of Budgeting in Oracle ERP

Budgeting in Oracle ERP involves several key components that facilitate comprehensive financial planning:

1. Creating a Budget Structure: Define the budget hierarchy, including budget organizations, cost centers, and accounts. This structure aligns with the organizational structure and financial reporting requirements.

2. Setting Budget Targets: Establish budget targets based on historical data, revenue projections, and operational plans. Utilize tools within Oracle ERP to set quantitative goals for revenue, expenses, and profitability.

3. Allocating Budgets: Distribute budget allocations across departments or cost centers based on strategic priorities and operational needs. Use allocation methods supported by Oracle ERP to ensure equitable distribution and effective resource utilization.

4. Monitoring Budget Performance: Track budget execution against targets in real-time using Oracle ERP's reporting and monitoring features. Identify variances, analyze causes, and take corrective actions to align actual performance with budgeted figures.

Techniques for Forecasting in Oracle ERP

Forecasting in Oracle ERP involves predictive analysis to estimate future financial outcomes based on current and historical data. It enables organizations to anticipate market trends, mitigate risks, and capitalize on opportunities. The following techniques are commonly used for forecasting:

1. Time Series Analysis: Analyze historical data patterns to identify trends, seasonality, and cyclicality. Use statistical methods within Oracle ERP to extrapolate future financial performance based on past trends.

2. Scenario Planning: Develop multiple scenarios based on different assumptions and business conditions. Use Oracle ERP's scenario planning tools to simulate various outcomes and assess their impact on financial metrics.

3. Collaborative Forecasting: Engage stakeholders across departments to gather insights and inputs for forecasting. Utilize Oracle ERP's collaboration features to incorporate diverse perspectives and enhance forecast accuracy.

Integration with Financial Reporting

Integrating budgeting and forecasting with financial reporting is essential for comprehensive financial management in Oracle ERP:

- Real-time Reporting: Generate real-time reports that combine actual financial data with budgeted and forecasted figures. Use Oracle ERP's reporting capabilities to visualize variances, trends, and performance metrics.

- Variance Analysis: Conduct variance analysis to compare actual financial results against budgeted and forecasted figures. Identify deviations, analyze root causes, and implement corrective actions to achieve financial goals.

Best Practices for Effective Budgeting and Forecasting

Implementing best practices ensures that budgeting and forecasting processes in Oracle ERP are efficient and aligned with organizational objectives:

- Continuous Monitoring and Adjustments: Regularly monitor budget performance and revise forecasts based on changing business conditions and market dynamics.

- Cross-functional Collaboration: Foster collaboration between finance, operations, and strategic departments to enhance the accuracy and relevance of budgeting and forecasting inputs.

- Data-driven Decision-making: Utilize data analytics and business intelligence tools within Oracle ERP to enhance the accuracy of forecasts and support informed decision-making.

Conclusion

Budgeting and forecasting are integral to financial management in Oracle ERP, empowering organizations to plan strategically, allocate resources effectively, and achieve sustainable growth. By leveraging Oracle ERP's robust capabilities and following best practices, businesses can optimize financial performance and navigate uncertainties in dynamic market environments.

This section provides a comprehensive guide to implementing and optimizing budgeting and forecasting processes within Oracle ERP, ensuring that organizations can harness the full potential of their financial resources for strategic advantage..

8.1.2 Financial Consolidation

Financial consolidation is a critical process in Oracle ERP that integrates and aggregates financial data from multiple entities within an organization to produce consolidated financial statements. This process ensures accuracy, consistency, and compliance with regulatory standards. Here's a structured approach to cover this topic comprehensively:

Introduction to Financial Consolidation

In this section, introduce the concept of financial consolidation within the context of Oracle ERP. Explain its importance in providing a holistic view of the organization's financial health and performance.

Key Components of Financial Consolidation

1. Data Integration and Aggregation

 - Discuss how Oracle ERP consolidates financial data from various entities, business units, or subsidiaries.

 - Explain the integration process, including data extraction, transformation, and loading (ETL) mechanisms.

2. Intercompany Eliminations

 - Detail the process of eliminating intercompany transactions to avoid double-counting and ensure accurate financial reporting.

 - Describe Oracle ERP's capabilities in identifying and eliminating intercompany balances and transactions.

Financial Consolidation Processes in Oracle ERP

1. Consolidated Reporting

 - Explain how Oracle ERP generates consolidated financial statements, including balance sheets, income statements, and cash flow statements.

- Discuss the tools and functionalities available for customized reporting and analysis.

2. Currency Translation

- Address the challenges and solutions related to currency translation in multinational organizations.

- Describe Oracle ERP's support for currency conversion and its impact on consolidated financial statements.

3. Adjustments and Eliminations

- Outline the types of adjustments made during the consolidation process, such as eliminations of intercompany profits or losses.

- Provide examples and scenarios to illustrate these adjustments in Oracle ERP.

Compliance and Regulatory Requirements

1. GAAP and IFRS Compliance

- Discuss how Oracle ERP ensures compliance with Generally Accepted Accounting Principles (GAAP) or International Financial Reporting Standards (IFRS) during the consolidation process.

- Highlight specific features or modules within Oracle ERP that support regulatory reporting requirements.

2. Audit Trails and Controls

- Explain the importance of audit trails and internal controls in the financial consolidation process.

- Describe Oracle ERP's features for maintaining audit trails and ensuring data integrity and security.

Best Practices for Financial Consolidation in Oracle ERP

1. Streamlining Processes

- Provide recommendations for optimizing the financial consolidation process using Oracle ERP.

- Discuss automation tools, workflows, and best practices for efficiency gains.

2. Data Governance and Quality

- Emphasize the importance of data governance frameworks and data quality management in achieving accurate financial consolidations.

- Suggest strategies for improving data accuracy and consistency across the organization.

Conclusion

Summarize the key points covered in the section on financial consolidation in Oracle ERP. Reinforce the importance of adopting best practices and leveraging Oracle ERP's capabilities to achieve accurate and timely consolidated financial reporting.

8.2 Procurement Processes

8.2.1 Requisition to Purchase Order

In Oracle ERP, the procurement process plays a critical role in managing the acquisition of goods and services efficiently. This section will delve into the detailed steps involved in transforming a requisition into a purchase order within Oracle ERP, highlighting best practices and considerations for optimal procurement management.

Understanding Requisition Management

The procurement cycle begins with the requisition process, where internal stakeholders identify the need for goods or services. In Oracle ERP, this phase involves:

1. Requisition Creation: Users initiate requisitions through Oracle ERP's user-friendly interface. They specify details such as quantity, required delivery date, and any special instructions.

2. Approval Workflow: Requisitions typically undergo an approval process to ensure compliance with budgetary constraints and organizational policies. Oracle ERP allows for customizable approval workflows based on predefined rules and hierarchies.

3. Budgetary Controls: Integration with Oracle ERP's financial management modules ensures that requisitions align with available budgets and financial guidelines. This integration facilitates real-time budget checks to prevent overspending.

Converting Requisitions to Purchase Orders

Once a requisition is approved, it transitions into a purchase order (PO), marking the formal commitment to procure the requested items. The conversion process involves:

1. Supplier Selection: Oracle ERP enables procurement teams to select suppliers based on criteria such as price competitiveness, supplier performance metrics, and contractual obligations. This ensures optimal supplier relationship management.

2. PO Generation: Using Oracle ERP's procurement module, approved requisitions are converted into POs automatically or manually. Key information such as item details, quantities, pricing, and delivery terms are populated from the requisition.

3. Contract Management: For recurring purchases or large-scale procurements, Oracle ERP supports contract management functionalities. Contracts define pricing, terms, and conditions, streamlining the PO creation process and ensuring adherence to negotiated agreements.

Managing Purchase Orders

Once generated, POs require effective management to ensure timely fulfillment and cost control. Oracle ERP offers robust features for:

1. Order Tracking: Real-time tracking of PO status allows stakeholders to monitor procurement progress, from order placement to delivery. Integration with supply chain management modules provides visibility into inventory availability and delivery timelines.

2. Amendment and Approval: Occasionally, POs may require modifications due to changes in requirements or supplier conditions. Oracle ERP facilitates amendment workflows, ensuring all revisions undergo proper approval channels.

3. Receipt and Inspection: Upon receipt of goods or services, Oracle ERP supports inspection processes to verify quality and quantity against PO specifications. This step is critical for maintaining product standards and supplier accountability.

Optimizing Procurement Efficiency

Oracle ERP's procurement module offers several tools and strategies to enhance efficiency and mitigate risks:

1. Supplier Performance Evaluation: Continuous assessment of supplier performance metrics allows organizations to identify top-performing suppliers and address underperforming ones. Oracle ERP's reporting capabilities provide insights into delivery reliability, quality consistency, and overall supplier satisfaction.

2. Cost Management: Integration with financial management modules ensures accurate cost allocation and tracking throughout the procurement lifecycle. Oracle ERP supports cost breakdowns by category, project, or department, facilitating informed financial decision-making.

3. Compliance and Governance: Adherence to regulatory requirements and internal policies is crucial in procurement operations. Oracle ERP's compliance features enable organizations to enforce procurement policies, maintain audit trails, and ensure transparency in purchasing practices.

Conclusion

Effectively managing the requisition-to-PO process in Oracle ERP enhances organizational agility, cost-effectiveness, and supplier relationships. By leveraging Oracle ERP's comprehensive procurement capabilities, businesses can streamline operations, optimize resource utilization, and achieve strategic procurement objectives.

This section provides a comprehensive guide to mastering the procurement processes within Oracle ERP, empowering organizations to unlock greater business potential through efficient procurement management.

8.2.2 Supplier Evaluation and Selection

Supplier evaluation and selection are critical processes in Oracle ERP that ensure organizations engage with reliable and efficient suppliers to meet their procurement needs effectively. This section provides a detailed guide on how to navigate and optimize supplier evaluation and selection processes within Oracle ERP.

Introduction to Supplier Evaluation

Supplier evaluation involves assessing the performance, capabilities, and suitability of potential suppliers based on predefined criteria. This process is crucial for mitigating risks, enhancing supply chain efficiency, and achieving cost savings through strategic sourcing.

Key Steps in Supplier Evaluation

1. Define Evaluation Criteria

Before beginning the evaluation process, it is essential to establish clear criteria against which suppliers will be assessed. These criteria typically include:

- Quality and Compliance: Assessing the supplier's adherence to quality standards and regulatory requirements.

- Performance Metrics: Evaluating delivery reliability, lead times, and service levels.

- Financial Stability: Reviewing financial health, credit ratings, and stability.

- Cost and Pricing: Comparing pricing structures, discounts, and total cost of ownership.

- Innovation and Technology: Evaluating the supplier's ability to innovate and integrate with technological advancements.

2. Data Collection and Analysis

Oracle ERP facilitates data-driven supplier evaluation by centralizing supplier information and performance metrics. Key data points include:

- Performance Metrics: Analyzing historical performance data such as delivery performance, quality incidents, and customer satisfaction ratings.

- Financial Data: Reviewing financial statements, liquidity ratios, and credit scores.

- Compliance Records: Verifying certifications, licenses, and adherence to regulatory standards.

3. Supplier Scorecards and Evaluation Tools

Utilize Oracle ERP's supplier scorecard functionality to quantify and compare supplier performance against defined metrics. Scorecards provide a structured approach to:

- Performance Measurement: Assigning weighted scores to performance metrics based on their importance.

- Benchmarking: Comparing supplier performance against industry benchmarks and internal standards.

- Continuous Improvement: Identifying areas for improvement and setting targets for supplier development.

4. Collaborative Evaluation Processes

Engage cross-functional teams, including procurement, quality assurance, and finance, to ensure comprehensive supplier evaluations. Oracle ERP supports collaborative workflows for:

- Evaluation Workflows: Defining approval processes and workflows for supplier evaluation activities.

- Document Management: Storing and accessing supplier contracts, agreements, and performance reports centrally.

Selection and Onboarding of Suppliers

1. Supplier Selection Criteria

Once evaluations are complete, select suppliers based on a combination of quantitative scores and qualitative factors such as:

- Strategic Fit: Alignment with organizational goals, values, and long-term objectives.

- Capacity and Scalability: Assessing the supplier's ability to scale operations and support future growth.

- Risk Management: Mitigating risks associated with supply chain disruptions, geopolitical factors, and regulatory changes.

2. Contract Negotiation and Compliance

Oracle ERP facilitates contract management and compliance monitoring throughout the supplier onboarding process. Key functionalities include:

- Contract Templates: Standardizing contract terms, conditions, and pricing structures.

- Legal Review: Integrating with legal teams to ensure contracts comply with regulatory requirements and mitigate legal risks.

- Performance Monitoring: Establishing Key Performance Indicators (KPIs) and monitoring supplier performance post-contract signing.

3. Supplier Relationship Management (SRM)

Implement Oracle ERP's SRM module to foster collaborative relationships with selected suppliers. SRM capabilities include:

- Performance Reviews: Conducting regular performance reviews and feedback sessions.

- Continuous Improvement: Identifying opportunities for cost savings, process improvements, and innovation initiatives.

- Dispute Resolution: Resolving conflicts and disputes promptly to maintain productive supplier relationships.

Conclusion

Effective supplier evaluation and selection are foundational to successful procurement operations in Oracle ERP. By leveraging Oracle ERP's robust functionalities and best practices outlined in this guide, organizations can optimize supplier relationships, mitigate risks, and drive strategic procurement outcomes.

8.3 Inventory Processes

8.3.1 Stock Replenishment

Stock replenishment is a critical aspect of inventory management within Oracle ERP. This process ensures that optimal stock levels are maintained to meet demand while minimizing excess inventory costs. In this section, we will explore the various methods and strategies used in Oracle ERP for stock replenishment.

Introduction to Stock Replenishment

Stock replenishment involves the timely restocking of inventory items to prevent stockouts and maintain smooth operations. Effective replenishment strategies balance the costs of carrying inventory against the risk of shortages, aiming to optimize inventory levels across different product lines and warehouses.

Understanding Inventory Levels

Before delving into replenishment strategies, it's crucial to understand the concept of inventory levels managed within Oracle ERP:

- Safety Stock: Buffer inventory held to mitigate the risk of stockouts due to variability in demand or supply.

- Reorder Point: Minimum inventory level at which replenishment orders are triggered.

- Lead Time: Time taken from placing an order to receiving the goods, influencing reorder point calculations.

Methods of Stock Replenishment

Oracle ERP supports several methods for stock replenishment, each suited to different inventory management scenarios. The choice of method depends on factors such as demand variability, lead times, and cost considerations:

1. Reorder Point (ROP) Method

The Reorder Point method calculates the inventory level at which a replenishment order should be triggered. Key steps and considerations include:

- Setting Reorder Points: Determining optimal reorder points based on demand forecasts, lead times, and safety stock levels.

- Automated Reorder Generation: Using Oracle ERP's automated replenishment functionality to generate purchase orders or production orders when inventory levels reach the reorder point.

2. Minimum-Maximum Inventory Levels

The Minimum-Maximum method sets predefined minimum and maximum inventory levels for each item:

- Setting Minimum and Maximum Levels: Defining thresholds to trigger replenishment orders or adjust reorder quantities dynamically.

- Batch Ordering: Consolidating orders to take advantage of quantity discounts or reduce order processing costs.

3. Just-In-Time (JIT) Replenishment

JIT aims to minimize inventory holding costs by synchronizing inventory levels closely with demand:

- Demand-Driven Replenishment: Using real-time demand signals to trigger replenishment orders, reducing the need for excess inventory.

- Supplier Collaboration: Integrating with suppliers to streamline delivery schedules and reduce lead times.

4. Forecast-Based Replenishment

Forecast-Based methods use demand forecasts to predict future inventory requirements:

- Demand Forecasting Models: Utilizing historical data and statistical techniques to generate accurate demand forecasts.

- Safety Stock Adjustments: Adjusting safety stock levels based on forecast accuracy and market variability.

Implementation Considerations

Implementing effective stock replenishment processes requires careful planning and configuration within Oracle ERP:

- Data Accuracy: Ensuring accurate inventory data through regular cycle counts and reconciliation.

- Integration with Demand Planning: Linking stock replenishment strategies with sales forecasts and production schedules.

- Performance Metrics: Monitoring key performance indicators (KPIs) such as inventory turnover, fill rates, and stockout rates to evaluate replenishment effectiveness.

Conclusion

Stock replenishment is pivotal for maintaining optimal inventory levels and ensuring operational efficiency within Oracle ERP. By adopting appropriate replenishment strategies and leveraging Oracle ERP's capabilities, organizations can achieve cost savings, minimize stockouts, and enhance overall supply chain performance.

8.3.2 Inventory Auditing

Inventory auditing is a critical process within Oracle ERP that ensures accuracy and accountability in inventory management. This section explores the methodologies, best practices, and implementation steps involved in conducting effective inventory audits.

1. Introduction to Inventory Auditing

Inventory auditing is the systematic examination of inventory records and physical inventory to verify accuracy and reconcile any discrepancies. In Oracle ERP, inventory auditing plays a crucial role in maintaining inventory integrity, optimizing stock levels, and supporting financial reporting.

2. Importance of Inventory Auditing

Inventory auditing serves several key purposes:

- Accuracy Verification: Confirming that the physical count matches the recorded inventory levels.

- Risk Management: Identifying potential issues such as shrinkage, theft, or data entry errors.

- Compliance: Ensuring adherence to regulatory requirements and internal controls.

- Financial Reporting: Providing reliable data for financial statements and costing calculations.

3. Types of Inventory Audits

Oracle ERP supports various types of inventory audits:

- Cycle Counting: Regular, scheduled counts of specific inventory items.

- Physical Inventory Count: Comprehensive count of all inventory items at a specific point in time.

- Transactional Audits: Reviewing inventory movements and transactions for accuracy.

4. Planning and Preparation

Before conducting an inventory audit, thorough planning is essential:

- Define Audit Objectives: Clarify the goals and scope of the audit (e.g., specific items, locations).

- Schedule Audits: Determine frequency and timing based on operational needs and inventory turnover.

- Allocate Resources: Assign personnel, equipment, and time required for the audit.

5. Conducting the Audit

Steps involved in conducting an inventory audit using Oracle ERP:

- Pre-Audit Preparation: Review system settings, freeze transactions if necessary, and communicate audit plans to stakeholders.

- Physical Count: Perform the actual counting of inventory items using approved methods (e.g., barcode scanning, manual counting).

- System Verification: Input physical count data into Oracle ERP, compare against recorded quantities, and identify discrepancies.

- Root Cause Analysis: Investigate reasons for discrepancies (e.g., data entry errors, process inefficiencies).

6. Resolving Discrepancies

Addressing discrepancies found during the audit:

- Adjustment Process: Record adjustments to inventory levels in Oracle ERP based on audit findings.

- Root Cause Correction: Implement corrective actions to prevent future discrepancies (e.g., process improvements, training).

- Approval and Documentation: Obtain necessary approvals for adjustments and maintain audit documentation for compliance and review purposes.

7. Reporting and Analysis

Utilize Oracle ERP's reporting capabilities for:

- Audit Reports: Generate detailed reports on audit findings, discrepancies, and corrective actions taken.

- Trend Analysis: Analyze audit data over time to identify patterns, improve forecasting accuracy, and enhance inventory management strategies.

8. Continuous Improvement

Implement continuous improvement practices:

- Feedback Loop: Gather feedback from stakeholders involved in the audit process to refine audit procedures.

- Training and Development: Provide training on inventory auditing techniques and Oracle ERP functionalities.

- Benchmarking: Compare audit results against industry benchmarks and best practices to drive ongoing improvements.

9. Conclusion

Inventory auditing in Oracle ERP is a cornerstone of effective inventory management, ensuring that businesses maintain accurate inventory records, comply with regulations, and optimize operational efficiencies. By following structured audit processes and leveraging Oracle ERP's capabilities, organizations can mitigate risks, enhance financial transparency, and achieve sustainable business growth.

8.4 Sales and Order Processes

8.4.1 Order to Cash

The Order to Cash (O2C) process in Oracle ERP encompasses all the steps involved in fulfilling customer orders, from the initial order placement to receiving payment. This process is crucial for maintaining smooth operations and ensuring customer satisfaction. In this section, we will explore each stage of the Order to Cash process in Oracle ERP, including best practices and tips for optimization.

1. Order Management

Order management begins with the receipt of a customer order and encompasses the entire lifecycle of the order until it is fulfilled. Oracle ERP provides robust functionalities to manage various types of orders efficiently.

- Order Entry: The process starts with order entry where sales representatives or customers input orders into the system. Oracle ERP allows for different order entry methods, including manual entry and electronic data interchange (EDI).

- Order Validation: Once entered, orders undergo validation checks to ensure accuracy and completeness. This includes checking inventory availability, credit limits, and pricing rules.

- Order Approval: Some organizations require orders to be approved before processing. Oracle ERP allows configurable approval workflows to streamline this process.

2. Order Fulfillment

After order validation and approval, the fulfillment process begins, focusing on delivering products or services to customers on time and in full.

- Picking and Packing: Orders are picked from inventory based on warehouse management rules and packed for shipment. Oracle ERP supports barcode scanning and other technologies to improve accuracy and efficiency.

- Shipping: Shipping involves preparing shipment documents, selecting carriers, and arranging transportation. Oracle ERP integrates with shipping carriers to automate this process and provide real-time tracking.

- Delivery Confirmation: Once goods are delivered, Oracle ERP updates order status and triggers invoicing. Integration with delivery confirmation systems ensures accurate order status updates.

3. Invoicing and Revenue Recognition

Invoicing and revenue recognition are critical steps in the O2C process, ensuring accurate financial reporting and compliance with accounting standards.

- Invoice Generation: Oracle ERP automates invoice generation based on order details. Invoices can be customized and delivered to customers electronically or via traditional mail.

- Revenue Recognition: Compliance with revenue recognition standards such as ASC 606 is facilitated through Oracle ERP's advanced revenue management capabilities. Revenue can be recognized at different stages of the O2C cycle based on contractual terms.

4. Payment Processing

Efficient payment processing is essential for cash flow management and customer satisfaction.

- Payment Receipt: Oracle ERP supports various payment methods, including credit cards, electronic funds transfer (EFT), and checks. Payments are recorded in the system upon receipt.

- Accounts Receivable: Payments are reconciled against invoices in Oracle ERP's accounts receivable module. Automated reconciliation processes minimize manual effort and reduce errors.

5. Customer Relationship Management (CRM)

Maintaining strong customer relationships is integral to the success of the O2C process. Oracle ERP includes CRM functionalities to manage customer interactions and enhance satisfaction.

- Customer Communication: Oracle ERP facilitates communication with customers regarding order status, delivery updates, and payment reminders through integrated CRM tools.

- Customer Analytics: Analyzing customer data helps identify trends, preferences, and opportunities for upselling or cross-selling. Oracle ERP's CRM analytics provide actionable insights to improve sales and service strategies.

6. Optimization and Continuous Improvement

Continuous improvement is key to optimizing the O2C process in Oracle ERP. Organizations can leverage the following strategies:

- Process Automation: Automating repetitive tasks such as order entry, invoicing, and payment processing improves efficiency and reduces errors.

- Performance Metrics: Monitoring key performance indicators (KPIs) such as order cycle time, order accuracy, and on-time delivery helps identify areas for improvement.

- Integration with Other Modules: Integration with inventory management, financials, and supply chain modules ensures seamless data flow and enhances overall process visibility.

Conclusion

The Order to Cash process in Oracle ERP is pivotal for ensuring timely and accurate order fulfillment, invoicing, and payment processing. By leveraging Oracle ERP's robust capabilities and best practices outlined in this section, organizations can streamline operations, improve cash flow, and enhance customer satisfaction.

In the next section, we will explore Customer Relationship Management (CRM) within Oracle ERP, focusing on strategies to build and maintain strong customer relationships.

8.4.2 Customer Relationship Management

Customer Relationship Management (CRM) is a crucial component within Oracle ERP that enables organizations to manage and nurture relationships with their customers effectively. In this section, we will explore how Oracle ERP facilitates CRM processes, including customer data management, sales pipeline management, and customer service enhancements.

Introduction to Customer Relationship Management (CRM)

Customer Relationship Management encompasses strategies and technologies used by businesses to manage and analyze customer interactions and data throughout the customer lifecycle, with the goal of improving customer service relationships and assisting in customer retention and driving sales growth.

Key Features of CRM in Oracle ERP

Oracle ERP integrates robust CRM functionalities that empower businesses to streamline sales processes, enhance customer service, and leverage customer data for strategic decision-making. Key features include:

- Customer Data Management: Centralized repository for storing comprehensive customer information, including contact details, purchase history, preferences, and interactions.

 - Sales Force Automation (SFA): Tools and automation to manage the sales process efficiently, from lead generation to opportunity management and deal closure.

- Marketing Automation: Automation of marketing tasks such as campaign management, lead nurturing, and customer segmentation based on behavior and demographics.

- Service and Support Management: Tools to manage customer support interactions, track service requests, and ensure timely resolution of issues.

- Analytics and Reporting: Insights into customer behavior, sales performance, and service metrics through built-in analytics and customizable reports.

Implementing CRM in Oracle ERP

Implementing CRM within Oracle ERP involves several key steps to ensure successful adoption and integration with existing business processes:

1. Needs Assessment: Assess current CRM practices and identify business goals to determine the scope and objectives of CRM implementation.

2. Data Migration and Integration: Ensure seamless migration of existing customer data into Oracle ERP and integration with other modules such as Sales and Marketing.

3. Customization and Configuration: Tailor Oracle CRM modules to align with specific business requirements, including workflow automation, user interface customization, and data fields customization.

4. User Training and Adoption: Provide comprehensive training programs to educate users on CRM functionalities, best practices, and utilization of CRM tools to maximize efficiency and effectiveness.

5. Continuous Improvement: Establish a feedback loop for ongoing evaluation and refinement of CRM processes to adapt to changing business needs and customer expectations.

Benefits of CRM in Oracle ERP

- Enhanced Customer Satisfaction: Improved customer service delivery and responsiveness lead to higher customer satisfaction and loyalty.

- Increased Sales Revenue: Streamlined sales processes, effective lead management, and targeted marketing campaigns contribute to revenue growth.

- Better Decision-Making: Access to real-time customer data and analytics enables informed decision-making and strategic planning.

- Operational Efficiency: Automation of repetitive tasks and streamlined workflows reduce manual effort and operational costs.

Conclusion

Customer Relationship Management in Oracle ERP plays a pivotal role in transforming how organizations interact with and serve their customers. By leveraging CRM functionalities effectively, businesses can gain a competitive edge, drive growth, and foster long-term customer loyalty.

8.5 HR Processes

8.5.1 Recruitment and Onboarding

Recruitment and onboarding are critical components of Human Resource (HR) management, as they directly impact the quality and performance of the workforce. Oracle ERP provides comprehensive tools to streamline these processes, ensuring that organizations can efficiently attract, hire, and integrate new employees.

Recruitment Process

1. Job Requisition and Posting

- The recruitment process begins with identifying the need for a new position or filling a vacancy. This is done through a job requisition, which outlines the role's requirements, responsibilities, and qualifications. In Oracle ERP, managers can create and submit job requisitions for approval. Once approved, these requisitions can be posted internally and externally to attract candidates.

- Creating Job Requisitions: Managers can use Oracle ERP to create detailed job requisitions. These can include job descriptions, required skills, experience levels, and other relevant information.

- Approval Workflow: Oracle ERP supports an approval workflow for job requisitions. This ensures that all necessary approvals are obtained before the job is posted.

- Job Posting: Once approved, job requisitions can be posted to various job boards, the company's career site, and internal job boards.

2. Candidate Sourcing

- Sourcing candidates involves attracting potential employees through various channels. Oracle ERP integrates with job boards, social media platforms, and recruitment agencies to widen the reach of job postings.

- Integration with Job Boards: Oracle ERP can automatically post job openings to popular job boards and social media platforms.

- Employee Referrals: The system can also manage employee referral programs, encouraging current employees to refer qualified candidates.

- Talent Pools: Oracle ERP allows the creation and management of talent pools for future job openings. This ensures a ready pipeline of qualified candidates.

3. Application Management

- Once candidates apply, Oracle ERP manages their applications through a centralized system. This includes tracking the status of each application, scheduling interviews, and communicating with candidates.

- Application Tracking: The system tracks each application from submission to hire or rejection.

- Automated Communications: Oracle ERP can send automated emails to candidates, acknowledging receipt of their applications and providing updates on their status.

- Interview Scheduling: The system can coordinate interview schedules between candidates and interviewers, sending calendar invites and reminders.

4. Screening and Selection

- Screening involves evaluating candidates to determine their suitability for the role. Oracle ERP offers tools for resume parsing, skills assessment, and background checks.

- Resume Parsing: The system can automatically extract relevant information from resumes, making it easier to compare candidates.

- Skills Assessment: Oracle ERP can integrate with assessment tools to evaluate candidates' skills and competencies.

- Background Checks: The system can manage the background check process, ensuring that all necessary checks are completed before an offer is made.

5. Interviewing

- Interviewing is a critical step in the selection process. Oracle ERP provides tools to streamline this process, including interview templates, evaluation forms, and feedback collection.

- Interview Templates: Managers can create standardized interview templates to ensure consistency.

- Evaluation Forms: Interviewers can use evaluation forms within Oracle ERP to rate candidates on various criteria.

- Feedback Collection: The system collects feedback from all interviewers, providing a comprehensive view of each candidate's strengths and weaknesses.

6. Job Offer and Hiring

- Once a candidate is selected, Oracle ERP facilitates the job offer process, including offer letter generation, approval workflows, and communication with the candidate.

- Offer Letter Generation: The system can generate customized offer letters based on predefined templates.

- Approval Workflows: Oracle ERP ensures that all necessary approvals are obtained before the offer is extended.

- Candidate Communication: The system manages communication with the candidate, including sending the offer letter and tracking acceptance or rejection.

Onboarding Process

1. Pre-boarding

- Pre-boarding begins once a candidate accepts a job offer. This phase includes completing necessary paperwork, provisioning equipment, and preparing the new hire for their first day.

- Documentation: Oracle ERP can send new hires electronic versions of necessary documents, such as tax forms, employment contracts, and company policies.

- Equipment Provisioning: The system can coordinate with IT and facilities to ensure that new hires have the necessary equipment and workspace.

- Welcome Information: New hires can receive welcome packets containing information about the company culture, team members, and their role.

2. Orientation

- Orientation helps new hires acclimate to the company and their role. This includes introductions to team members, training on company policies, and an overview of job responsibilities.

- Welcome Meetings: Oracle ERP can schedule welcome meetings with key team members and managers.

- Policy Training: New hires can complete mandatory training on company policies, including code of conduct, IT security, and safety procedures.

- Role Overview: Managers can provide an overview of the new hire's responsibilities, expectations, and performance metrics.

3. Training and Development

- Training is crucial for new hires to develop the skills needed for their role. Oracle ERP supports comprehensive training programs, including e-learning modules, on-the-job training, and mentoring.

- E-Learning: The system offers a library of e-learning modules that new hires can complete at their own pace.

- On-the-Job Training: Managers can assign specific tasks and projects to help new hires gain practical experience.

- Mentoring: Oracle ERP can facilitate mentorship programs, pairing new hires with experienced employees.

4. Integration and Socialization

- Integration and socialization help new hires feel like part of the team and the company. This includes team-building activities, networking opportunities, and social events.

- Team-Building Activities: Oracle ERP can organize team-building activities to help new hires build relationships with their colleagues.

- Networking Opportunities: The system can schedule networking events, such as lunch-and-learns or coffee chats, to encourage interaction with employees from different departments.

- Social Events: New hires can be invited to company social events, fostering a sense of belonging and camaraderie.

5. Performance Management

- Performance management ensures that new hires are meeting expectations and progressing in their role. Oracle ERP provides tools for setting goals, tracking performance, and providing feedback.

- Goal Setting: Managers can set SMART goals (Specific, Measurable, Achievable, Relevant, Time-bound) for new hires, aligned with company objectives.

- Performance Tracking: The system tracks progress towards goals, providing real-time updates and performance metrics.

- Feedback and Reviews: Oracle ERP facilitates regular feedback and performance reviews, helping new hires understand their strengths and areas for improvement.

6. Continuous Support and Development

- Continuous support and development ensure that new hires continue to grow and succeed in their role. Oracle ERP offers tools for ongoing training, career development, and succession planning.

- Ongoing Training: The system provides access to additional training resources, ensuring that employees can continue to develop their skills.

- Career Development: Oracle ERP supports career development plans, helping employees set long-term career goals and identify opportunities for advancement.

- Succession Planning: The system can identify high-potential employees and prepare them for future leadership roles through targeted development programs.

By leveraging Oracle ERP's recruitment and onboarding capabilities, organizations can streamline these processes, reduce time-to-hire, and improve new hire retention. This not only enhances the efficiency of HR operations but also ensures that the organization attracts and retains top talent.

8.5.2 Performance Management

Performance Management within Oracle ERP is a crucial process that ensures employees' activities and outputs align with the organization's strategic goals. This process involves setting performance expectations, monitoring and evaluating employee performance, and providing feedback and development opportunities to enhance productivity and achieve business objectives.

Overview of Performance Management

Performance Management in Oracle ERP encompasses a series of systematic and integrated processes that help organizations maximize the performance of their workforce. The primary components include:

1. Goal Setting: Establishing clear, measurable objectives for employees that align with the company's strategic goals.

2. Performance Monitoring: Continuously tracking employee performance against set goals using various tools and metrics.

3. Performance Appraisal: Conducting regular reviews to evaluate employee performance, identify strengths and weaknesses, and provide constructive feedback.

4. Development and Training: Offering training programs and development opportunities to address skill gaps and enhance employee capabilities.

5. Rewards and Recognition: Implementing a system to reward high-performing employees and recognize their contributions to the organization.

Setting Up Performance Management in Oracle ERP

1. Configuring Performance Management Framework

   - Define Performance Plans: Create performance plans that outline the key objectives, metrics, and timelines for different roles within the organization.

   - Establish Competencies: Identify the core competencies required for each role and incorporate them into the performance evaluation criteria.

   - Set Up Performance Rating Scales: Configure rating scales to assess employee performance against predefined competencies and objectives.

   - Create Performance Templates: Develop standardized performance review templates that can be used across different departments and roles.

2. Goal Setting and Alignment

   - Goal Creation: Managers and employees collaboratively set SMART (Specific, Measurable, Achievable, Relevant, Time-bound) goals that align with the organization's strategic objectives.

- Goal Alignment: Ensure that individual goals are aligned with team and organizational goals to foster a cohesive and unified approach to achieving business targets.

- Goal Visibility: Utilize Oracle ERP's dashboard and reporting tools to provide visibility into goal progress and alignment at various organizational levels.

3. Performance Monitoring and Feedback

- Continuous Monitoring: Leverage Oracle ERP's performance tracking tools to monitor employee progress in real-time. This includes tracking key performance indicators (KPIs) and milestones.

- Regular Check-ins: Implement regular check-in meetings between managers and employees to discuss progress, address challenges, and provide ongoing feedback.

- Feedback Mechanisms: Use Oracle ERP's feedback tools to gather input from multiple sources, including peers, subordinates, and clients, to provide a comprehensive view of employee performance.

4. Performance Appraisal

- Appraisal Cycles: Define and configure the frequency and timing of performance appraisals, such as annual, bi-annual, or quarterly reviews.

- Evaluation Process: Utilize the performance templates and rating scales to conduct thorough evaluations of employee performance. This includes assessing goal achievement, competencies, and overall contribution to the organization.

- Appraisal Meetings: Schedule formal appraisal meetings where managers and employees discuss performance evaluations, provide feedback, and set new goals for the upcoming period.

5. Development and Training

- Identify Skill Gaps: Use performance appraisal data to identify areas where employees need improvement or additional training.

- Training Programs: Develop and implement training programs that address identified skill gaps and support employee development.

- Development Plans: Create individualized development plans for employees, outlining specific actions, training, and support needed to achieve career growth and performance improvement.

6. Rewards and Recognition

- Performance-Based Rewards: Design and implement a reward system that recognizes and rewards high-performing employees. This can include monetary bonuses, promotions, and other incentives.

- Recognition Programs: Establish recognition programs that highlight and celebrate employee achievements, fostering a positive and motivating work environment.

- Career Advancement: Provide career advancement opportunities for top performers, aligning their career paths with the organization's strategic needs.

Detailed Steps for Implementing Performance Management in Oracle ERP

Step 1: Initial Setup and Configuration

- Access the Performance Management Module: Log in to Oracle ERP and navigate to the Human Capital Management (HCM) suite. Access the Performance Management module to begin the configuration process.

- Define Performance Management Framework: Set up the foundational elements, including performance plans, competencies, rating scales, and templates, as previously outlined.

- User Roles and Permissions: Assign appropriate roles and permissions to managers, employees, and HR administrators to ensure they have access to the necessary tools and information.

Step 2: Goal Setting

- Create and Assign Goals: Managers create and assign goals to employees through the Performance Management module. Employees can also propose their goals for manager approval.

- Align Goals: Ensure that individual goals are aligned with departmental and organizational objectives. Use Oracle ERP's alignment tools to visualize goal relationships and dependencies.

Step 3: Performance Monitoring

- Track Progress: Utilize the system's tracking tools to monitor progress against set goals. Managers and employees can update progress, add comments, and attach relevant documents.

- Schedule Check-ins: Set up regular check-in meetings through Oracle ERP's calendar and scheduling tools. Document discussions and action items from these meetings in the system.

Step 4: Performance Appraisal

- Initiate Appraisal Cycles: HR administrators initiate the performance appraisal cycles as per the configured schedule. Notifications are sent to managers and employees to complete their respective evaluations.

- Conduct Evaluations: Managers use the appraisal templates to evaluate employee performance. Employees can also perform self-assessments and provide additional feedback.

- Review and Finalize Appraisals: Managers and employees discuss the appraisal results during formal meetings. Final evaluations are documented in the system, and new goals are set for the next period.

Step 5: Development and Training

- Analyze Appraisal Data: HR and managers analyze appraisal data to identify common skill gaps and development needs across the organization.

- Design Training Programs: Develop targeted training programs to address identified needs. Use Oracle ERP's Learning Management System (LMS) to deliver and track training.

- Implement Development Plans: Create and assign development plans to employees, detailing specific actions and training required. Monitor progress and adjust plans as needed.

Step 6: Rewards and Recognition

- Performance-Based Rewards: Based on appraisal results, determine eligibility for performance-based rewards. Configure the reward system to ensure timely and accurate disbursement of incentives.

- Recognition Initiatives: Launch recognition programs, such as Employee of the Month, to highlight and celebrate outstanding performance. Document and track recognition within the system.

- Career Advancement: Identify high-potential employees and provide opportunities for career advancement. Use Oracle ERP's talent management tools to map out career paths and succession planning.

Best Practices for Effective Performance Management

1. Clear Communication: Ensure that performance expectations and goals are clearly communicated to employees. Use Oracle ERP's communication tools to keep everyone informed and engaged.

2. Regular Feedback: Provide continuous feedback to employees, not just during formal appraisals. Regular check-ins and real-time feedback help address issues promptly and keep employees motivated.

3. Data-Driven Decisions: Leverage performance data to make informed decisions about training, development, rewards, and career advancement. Oracle ERP's analytics tools provide valuable insights to support decision-making.

4. Employee Involvement: Involve employees in the goal-setting and appraisal process. Encourage self-assessments and open dialogue to foster a culture of transparency and collaboration.

5. Alignment with Business Goals: Ensure that individual performance goals are aligned with the organization's strategic objectives. This alignment drives overall business success and enhances employee engagement.

By implementing a robust Performance Management process in Oracle ERP, organizations can effectively manage and enhance employee performance, drive business success, and create a culture of continuous improvement.

Appendices

Glossary of Terms

Accounts Payable (AP):

A financial management process involving the management and processing of outgoing payments owed by a company to its suppliers or vendors. This includes activities such as invoice processing, payment disbursement, and maintaining supplier records.

Accounts Receivable (AR):

A financial management process involving the management and collection of money owed to a company by its customers. This includes activities such as issuing invoices, managing customer accounts, and collecting payments.

Asset Management:

The process of managing a company's tangible and intangible assets. This includes tracking asset acquisition, depreciation, maintenance, and disposal to optimize their use and ensure accurate financial reporting.

BI Publisher:

Oracle's Business Intelligence Publisher, a reporting and publishing application that enables users to create, manage, and deliver various types of reports and documents.

Budgeting:

The process of creating a plan to allocate resources, set financial goals, and predict future financial performance. Budgeting involves estimating revenues, expenses, and other financial figures over a specific period.

Chart of Accounts (COA):

A structured list of an organization's general ledger accounts, used to classify financial transactions in the general ledger. The COA provides a framework for recording and reporting financial information.

Cost Allocation:

The process of assigning indirect costs to various cost objects, such as departments, products, or projects. This helps in accurately reflecting the cost of each cost object and supporting cost management and pricing decisions.

Customer Relationship Management (CRM):

A strategy and technology used to manage interactions with current and potential customers. CRM systems help organizations improve customer service, enhance customer relationships, and drive sales growth.

Data Visualization:

The graphical representation of data and information. Data visualization tools in Oracle ERP help users understand complex data sets by presenting data in visual formats such as charts, graphs, and dashboards.

Depreciation:

The process of allocating the cost of a tangible asset over its useful life. Depreciation reflects the wear and tear, aging, or obsolescence of the asset and is used for accounting and tax purposes.

Enterprise Resource Planning (ERP):

A type of software that organizations use to manage and integrate the important parts of their businesses. An ERP software system can integrate planning, purchasing inventory, sales, marketing, finance, human resources, and more.

Execution Phase:

The phase in an ERP implementation project where the planned activities and tasks are executed. This phase involves configuring the ERP system, migrating data, training users, and testing the system before it goes live.

Fixed Assets:

Long-term tangible assets owned by a company that are used in its operations to generate income. Fixed assets include property, plant, and equipment, and they are subject to depreciation over time.

Forecasting:

The process of predicting future financial performance based on historical data, trends, and assumptions. Forecasting helps organizations plan for future revenues, expenses, and resource needs.

General Ledger (GL):

The central repository for a company's financial data, where all financial transactions are recorded. The GL is used to produce financial statements and reports, providing a comprehensive view of the company's financial position.

Go-Live:

The point in an ERP implementation project when the ERP system is officially launched and becomes operational. During the go-live phase, the system is fully deployed, and users begin using it for daily operations.

Human Capital Management (HCM):

The comprehensive set of practices and tools used to manage an organization's workforce. HCM includes recruiting, onboarding, training, performance management, payroll, and other HR functions.

Inventory Auditing:

The process of verifying the accuracy and completeness of inventory records. Inventory auditing involves physical counts, reconciliation with system records, and ensuring that inventory levels are accurately reflected.

Inventory Management:

The process of overseeing the ordering, storing, and using a company's inventory. This includes managing raw materials, components, and finished products, as well as ensuring optimal inventory levels.

Invoice Processing:

The process of handling incoming invoices from suppliers, including verification, approval, and recording in the accounts payable system. Invoice processing ensures that invoices are accurately paid on time.

Journal Entries:

The records of financial transactions in the accounting system. Journal entries include debits and credits to various accounts and are used to maintain the accuracy of the general ledger.

Labor Costing:

The process of tracking and allocating labor costs to various projects, departments, or activities. Labor costing helps organizations understand the true cost of labor and manage their workforce expenses effectively.

Order to Cash (O2C):

The end-to-end process of receiving and processing customer sales orders and collecting payment. The O2C process includes order management, order fulfillment, invoicing, and cash collection.

Payroll Management:

The process of managing employee compensation, including calculating wages, withholding taxes and deductions, and distributing paychecks. Payroll management ensures that employees are paid accurately and on time.

Performance Management:

The process of evaluating and improving employee performance through goal setting, feedback, and performance reviews. Performance management helps organizations align employee performance with business objectives.

Procurement Management:

The process of acquiring goods and services from suppliers. Procurement management includes activities such as sourcing, purchasing, and supplier management to ensure that the organization obtains quality products at the best prices.

Project Planning:

The process of defining the scope, objectives, and steps required to complete a project. Project planning involves creating a project plan, allocating resources, and setting timelines to ensure successful project execution.

Requisition:

A formal request to purchase goods or services, typically initiated by an employee or department. Requisitions are reviewed and approved before being converted into purchase orders.

Resource Allocation:

The process of assigning available resources, such as personnel, equipment, and budget, to various projects or activities. Effective resource allocation ensures that resources are used efficiently to achieve organizational goals.

Sales Order Processing:

The process of handling customer orders from the time they are received until the products are delivered. Sales order processing involves order entry, order confirmation, and fulfillment activities.

Security Measures:

The practices and technologies used to protect ERP systems and data from unauthorized access, breaches, and other security threats. Security measures include user authentication, access controls, and data encryption.

Standard Costing:

A cost accounting method that assigns a predetermined cost to each unit of production or service. Standard costing helps organizations budget and control costs by comparing actual costs to standard costs.

Supplier Evaluation:

The process of assessing and selecting suppliers based on criteria such as quality, reliability, price, and delivery performance. Supplier evaluation helps organizations choose the best suppliers and maintain strong supplier relationships.

System Audits:

The process of reviewing and assessing the performance and security of an ERP system. System audits ensure that the ERP system is functioning correctly, data integrity is maintained, and security measures are effective.

Tax Management:

The process of managing and complying with tax regulations, including calculating, collecting, and remitting taxes. Tax management ensures that an organization meets its tax obligations and avoids penalties.

Time Tracking:

The process of recording the amount of time employees spend on various tasks and activities. Time tracking helps organizations monitor productivity, manage labor costs, and ensure accurate payroll processing.

User Roles and Permissions:

The assignment of specific access rights and privileges to users based on their roles within the organization. User roles and permissions help ensure that users have the appropriate access to perform their job functions while maintaining data security.

Workflow Automation:

The use of technology to automate and streamline business processes. Workflow automation in Oracle ERP helps reduce manual effort, improve efficiency, and ensure consistency in process execution.

This glossary provides detailed explanations of key terms and concepts used in Oracle ERP, helping readers understand the terminology and functionality of the system.

Conclusion

As we reach the end of "Oracle ERP Essentials: Unlocking Business Potential," it's clear that Oracle ERP is a powerful tool that can transform the way organizations operate. This book has guided you through the various modules and functionalities, offering a comprehensive understanding of how to leverage Oracle ERP to enhance efficiency, accuracy, and overall business performance.

Implementing an ERP system is no small feat. It requires careful planning, robust execution, and continuous improvement. By following the best practices, strategies, and detailed processes outlined in this book, you are well-equipped to successfully implement and utilize Oracle ERP in your organization.

Remember, the journey doesn't end here. As technology evolves, so too will Oracle ERP. Staying informed about updates, new features, and industry trends is crucial for maintaining the competitive edge that Oracle ERP offers. Continue to explore, learn, and adapt, ensuring that your ERP system remains a cornerstone of your business strategy.

We hope this book has provided valuable insights and practical guidance, empowering you to unlock the full potential of Oracle ERP. The road to mastering ERP systems is ongoing, but with the knowledge gained from this book, you are well on your way to achieving operational excellence.

Acknowledgments

First and foremost, we would like to extend our heartfelt gratitude to you, our readers, for choosing this book. Your decision to invest in "Oracle ERP Essentials: Unlocking Business Potential" is greatly appreciated. We hope that the knowledge and insights shared within these pages will prove invaluable in your ERP journey.

A special thank you to the team of experts and contributors who provided their insights, experiences, and knowledge. Their dedication and hard work have made this book a comprehensive resource for Oracle ERP users.

We also wish to acknowledge the countless professionals who have shared their real-world experiences and challenges. Their stories and feedback have been instrumental in shaping the content of this book, ensuring it is both practical and relevant.

To our families and friends, your unwavering support and encouragement have been a source of strength throughout this writing process. Thank you for believing in us and for your patience during the countless hours spent bringing this book to life.

Lastly, we would like to thank the broader Oracle ERP community. Your commitment to innovation, collaboration, and excellence is truly inspiring. It is our hope that this book will contribute to the ongoing success and growth of this dynamic community.

Thank you once again for your support. We wish you every success in your ERP endeavors and hope that "Oracle ERP Essentials: Unlocking Business Potential" becomes a valuable companion on your journey to operational excellence.

www.ingramcontent.com/pod-product-compliance
Lightning Source LLC
LaVergne TN
LVHW081333050326
832903LV00024B/1140